Gift.
7/94
UA

ENTREPRENEURSHIP EDUCATION

ENTREPRENEURSHIP EDUCATION

Current Developments, Future Directions

EDITED BY
Calvin A. Kent

QUORUM BOOKS

New York · Westport, Connecticut · London

Library of Congress Cataloging-in-Publication Data

Entrepreneurship education : current developments, future directions /
   edited by Calvin A. Kent.
       p. cm.
   Includes bibliographical references.
   ISBN 0–89930–523–7 (lib. bdg. : alk. paper)
   1. Business education—United States.   2. Economics—Study and
teaching—United States.   3. Entrepreneurship—Study and teaching—
United States.   4. Entrepreneurship—Study and teaching
(Secondary)—United States.   5. Entrepreneurship—Study and teaching
(Elementary)—United States.   I. Kent, Calvin A.
   HF1131.E54   1990
   658.4'21'071073—dc20   90-30007

British Library Cataloguing in Publication Data is available.

Library of Congress Catalog Card Number: 90–30007
ISBN: 0–89930–523–7

First published in 1990

Quorum Books
88 Post Road West, Westport, CT 06881
An imprint of Greenwood Publishing Group, Inc.

Printed in the United States of America

∞

The paper used in this book complies with the
Permanent Paper Standard issued by the National
Information Standards Organization (Z39.48-1984).

10 9 8 7 6 5 4 3 2 1

Contents

Illustrations

Preface

This book has a modest objective of setting forth what we do and do not know about how to educate entrepreneurs. It collects the best thoughts of many of the nation's experts in the area of economics and entrepreneurship education. Those who wrote these chapters share a common commitment to increased understanding of the American economy and the essential role the entrepreneur performs in that economy.

Many of the chapters in this book began as papers presented at the "Entrepreneurship/Economics/Education (E^3)" conference at Widener University in March 1988. This conference was sponsored by the Joint Council on Economic Education under a grant from the J. Howard Pew Freedom Trust of Philadelphia, Pennsylvania. The purpose of that conference was to gather the ideas of those individuals who had worked for years providing entrepreneurship and economics education to the elementary and secondary school students of this nation. It was a preparatory step in the development of the E^3 project for the Philadelphia public schools. That project, which is described later in this book, was an attempt to use entrepreneurship as a method of reaching economically disadvantaged students by providing them with the skills, attitudes, and insights they need to succeed not only as entrepreneurs but as productive citizens as well.

To that core, other chapters were added to fill the gaps. Several chapters began as papers presented at the Towbes Foundation conference in Santa Barbara, California, in August 1988. Entitled "Economic Education in the

Pre-College Setting," it was conducted by the Reason Foundation. Still other papers were specifically commissioned for this volume. All papers were extensively updated and rewritten for inclusion here.

The editor extends his thanks not only to the authors, but also to Eric Valentine of Quorum Books for his guidance and advice. Special thanks go to Patricia Cornett of the Center for Private Enterprise at Baylor University, who was responsible for typing the manuscript, and to Janice Losak and Diane Fariss, also of the center, for their assistance in the preparation of the final manuscript. Nita Sue Kent did yeoman service in editing the various chapters.

ENTREPRENEURSHIP
EDUCATION

mental forces that cause entrepreneurship to come about, such as the
s of a job. The third approach, labeled the *venture school,* recognizes
t entrepreneurial efforts are part of an ongoing process and are not
lated or random events. Unlike the other two approaches, which are
tic, this approach stresses the dynamic aspect of the entrepreneurial
ent.

Gunderson is critical of what he calls the *Schumpeterial approach* to
plaining entrepreneurship. This approach, named after the Austrian
onomist Joseph Schumpeter, equates entrepreneurship with innovation.
owever, Schumpeterian innovation takes place on a very grand scale. To
humpeter, innovation consists of new ideas whose impacts are so great
at they destroy competing industries and remake whole segments of so-
ety. According to Gunderson, this view makes entrepreneurs seem larger
an life and more impressive than they really are. There is a certain ap-
eal to the Schumpeterian model because it seems to correspond to the
ublic's preconception of how entrepreneurs operate by taking risks and
reatively destroying old industries. However, it is Gunderson's contention
hat this view is distorted.

According to Gunderson, this view preconditions the way in which en-
repreneurs are portrayed in history. Since Schumpeter's entrepreneurs are
giants destroying their competitors and almost single-handedly remaking
ociety, it is easy for historians and others to depict entrepreneurs as individuals acquiring power arbitrarily and exercising it in a capricious and
destructive manner. Such has been the usual historical treatment of the so-
called robber barons, Rockefeller, Morgan, and Gould.

What is wrong with the Schumpeterian model? Gunderson contends that
entrepreneurship is really a process of small incremental innovations rather
then giant leaps forward. While there are some notable examples of the
latter, most entrepreneurial effort is involved in making small modifications or changes in products or services that better meet consumer needs
or improve productivity through better technology. Innovation is, then, a
slow process that requires many decades to come to fruition, and not
something that happens overnight and instantly transforms the way business has been conducted.

Gunderson provides us with a better explanation of the entrepreneurial
process. He still sees entrepreneurship as being linked directly to innovation, but he sees the innovative process resulting from becoming proficient in the use of established bodies of knowledge. Gunderson's entrepreneur is focused, seeing what others have overlooked. Gunderson supplies
us with a new and insightful definition of entrepreneurship as

drawing from a wide range of skills capable of enhancement to add value to a
target niche of human activity. The effort expanded in finding and implementing
such opportunities is rewarded by income and independence as well as pride in
creation.

1

Introduction: Educating the Heffalump

Calvin A. Kent

Entrepreneurs have been equated with heffalumps (Kilby, 1971). While
heffalumps were introduced in the *Winnie-the-Pooh* stories decades ago
(Milne, 1926) and *The House at Pooh Corner* (Milne, 1928), no one has
been able to precisely describe them or state with certainty what they are.
However, heffalumps are known by what they do, for they are both large
and important. So it is with the entrepreneur. No one has precisely defined
what the entrepreneur is, but even so, the contributions of entrepreneurs
to the material well-being of humankind are both great and important.

This book is concerned with how we educate both existing entrepreneurs and those who will be entrepreneurs in the future. The authors of
these chapters do not find it necessary to reestablish the importance of
the entrepreneurial process. That has been done elsewhere (Gilder, 1984;
Drucker, 1985). It is now well accepted that entrepreneurs are those individuals who bring about an improvement in the human condition. Without them, there simply would not be any material progress.

Nonetheless, a nagging question remains. Are entrepreneurs born or can
they be created? While none of these authors would deny that there may
be some genetic and environmental proclivities that tend to destine some
people toward entrepreneurial careers, the preponderance of evidence
suggests that many more people have entrepreneurial potential than ever
become entrepreneurs. Education, then, has a central responsibility in
identifying and nurturing those who can be the change agents in the de-

cades to come, and can make a profound difference in the future supply of entrepreneurs. How that can be done is what this book is all about.

The volume is divided into four parts. In the first part, there are some introductory essays concerning the scope and theory of entrepreneurship and the relationship between entrepreneurship and education. The second part deals with entrepreneurship at the collegiate level, where the last ten years have seen a significant growth in entrepreneurial studies. Part three deals with the efforts made to identify early and create the educational environments for elementary students that will cause them in later life to consider the entrepreneurial path. The final part is concerned with the various aspects of entrepreneurship education at the secondary level.

The articles in all four parts raise substantial issues, not just about entrepreneurship education, but about education in general. In many instances, they call for a complete rethinking of our approaches to education. If the suggestions in these chapters are followed, we will have even greater successes and our education system will perform better, not only for those who will be entrepreneurs, but for all students wherever their lives may take them. What follows is a brief synopsis of the major findings in each chapter:

ENTREPRENEURSHIP AND EDUCATION

Bill Rushing correctly notes in Chapter 2 that the 1980s have brought about a renewed emphasis on the entrepreneur. Traditionally, economics has seen individuals as producers, consumers, and voters, but economics has failed to see the vital role of the entrepreneur in the process of economic growth and development. Rushing sees understanding of the role of entrepreneurship and economic progress as critical to the understanding of the dynamics of an economic society and to insuring its future well-being.

Rushing's chapter begins with a summary of the various ways that the entrepreneur has been defined by economists. His historical investigation produces many overlapping and contradictory definitions of the entrepreneur and the entrepreneurial process. Some observers have seen entrepreneurs as people who assume risks under conditions of uncertainty. Others have seen entrepreneurs as innovators, decision makers, suppliers of financial capital, superintendents, organizers, coordinators, and industrial leaders, while another group has limited the definition of an entrepreneur to those who are proprietors, arbitrageurs, and resource allocators.

Rushing does not choose among these competing definitions, but rather indicates that studying entrepreneurship cannot be done from a static perspective because entrepreneurship is a dynamic process. Above all, Rushing feels that the entrepreneur has to deal with uncertainty by innovating in a competitive environment with less than perfect information. In a dy-

namic economic system, innovation is a cause of chang chaos are the consequence, and economic progress is t

Since it is impossible to correctly identify those ve possessing entrepreneurial potential, entrepreneurship be extended as broadly as possible throughout the total ulum to catch in its net all those who might later fulfill preneur. Any society can benefit from the enhancement talent, as the development of entrepreneurship impacts nomic growth and well-being. It is Rushing's contentio programs can directly affect the extent of entrepreneuria society. As a result, the progress of that society will depe tiveness of its entrepreneurship education programs.

He suggests that one approach for teaching entrepreneu on historical context and to describe the role of entrepren nomic history. Contending that economics cannot be fu without comprehending the role of the entrepreneur, the i must understand the role and importance of the entrepre done, what will be created is the political base for policie courage rather than discourage additional entrepreneurial a

The second and parallel approach to entrepreneurship edu on the assumption that teaching entrepreneurship can enł velop the traits that are associated with entrepreneurial suc vide the skills that entrepreneurs will need to function witł omy. No one approach or method can be delineated that wi perform this function. Entrepreneurship education needs to veloping innovation, risk taking, imagination, problem solvii sion-making skills.

The two approaches mentioned by Rushing are not mutuall The first approach develops within the population a broader and appreciation of the entrepreneur's role, while the secoı develop and expand the pool of entrepreneurial talent within omy. Entrepreneurship education is not, according to Rushing, situation. Instead, it should be integrated and continued thro formal education, from programs in the earliest grades to coι mature adults.

MODELS OF ENTREPRENEURSHIP

Gerry Gunderson in Chapter 3 redirects the focus of entrepr educators away from the traditional view of entrepreneurship developed over the years. Gunderson says that there are three proaches that are used to explain entrepreneurship. The first att explain entrepreneurship by reference to certain personal traits t duce success. The second approach, called *event studies,* focuses

1

Introduction:
Educating the Heffalump

Calvin A. Kent

Entrepreneurs have been equated with heffalumps (Kilby, 1971). While heffalumps were introduced in the *Winnie-the-Pooh* stories decades ago (Milne, 1926) and *The House at Pooh Corner* (Milne, 1928), no one has been able to precisely describe them or state with certainty what they are. However, heffalumps are known by what they do, for they are both large and important. So it is with the entrepreneur. No one has precisely defined what the entrepreneur is, but even so, the contributions of entrepreneurs to the material well-being of humankind are both great and important.

This book is concerned with how we educate both existing entrepreneurs and those who will be entrepreneurs in the future. The authors of these chapters do not find it necessary to reestablish the importance of the entrepreneurial process. That has been done elsewhere (Gilder, 1984; Drucker, 1985). It is now well accepted that entrepreneurs are those individuals who bring about an improvement in the human condition. Without them, there simply would not be any material progress.

Nonetheless, a nagging question remains. Are entrepreneurs born or can they be created? While none of these authors would deny that there may be some genetic and environmental proclivities that tend to destine some people toward entrepreneurial careers, the preponderance of evidence suggests that many more people have entrepreneurial potential than ever become entrepreneurs. Education, then, has a central responsibility in identifying and nurturing those who can be the change agents in the decades to come, and can make a profound difference in the future supply of entrepreneurs. How that can be done is what this book is all about.

The volume is divided into four parts. In the first part, there are some introductory essays concerning the scope and theory of entrepreneurship and the relationship between entrepreneurship and education. The second part deals with entrepreneurship at the collegiate level, where the last ten years have seen a significant growth in entrepreneurial studies. Part three deals with the efforts made to identify early and create the educational environments for elementary students that will cause them in later life to consider the entrepreneurial path. The final part is concerned with the various aspects of entrepreneurship education at the secondary level.

The articles in all four parts raise substantial issues, not just about entrepreneurship education, but about education in general. In many instances, they call for a complete rethinking of our approaches to education. If the suggestions in these chapters are followed, we will have even greater successes and our education system will perform better, not only for those who will be entrepreneurs, but for all students wherever their lives may take them. What follows is a brief synopsis of the major findings in each chapter:

ENTREPRENEURSHIP AND EDUCATION

Bill Rushing correctly notes in Chapter 2 that the 1980s have brought about a renewed emphasis on the entrepreneur. Traditionally, economics has seen individuals as producers, consumers, and voters, but economics has failed to see the vital role of the entrepreneur in the process of economic growth and development. Rushing sees understanding of the role of entrepreneurship and economic progress as critical to the understanding of the dynamics of an economic society and to insuring its future well-being.

Rushing's chapter begins with a summary of the various ways that the entrepreneur has been defined by economists. His historical investigation produces many overlapping and contradictory definitions of the entrepreneur and the entrepreneurial process. Some observers have seen entrepreneurs as people who assume risks under conditions of uncertainty. Others have seen entrepreneurs as innovators, decision makers, suppliers of financial capital, superintendents, organizers, coordinators, and industrial leaders, while another group has limited the definition of an entrepreneur to those who are proprietors, arbitrageurs, and resource allocators.

Rushing does not choose among these competing definitions, but rather indicates that studying entrepreneurship cannot be done from a static perspective because entrepreneurship is a dynamic process. Above all, Rushing feels that the entrepreneur has to deal with uncertainty by innovating in a competitive environment with less than perfect information. In a dynamic economic system, innovation is a cause of change. Uncertainty and chaos are the consequence, and economic progress is the reward.

Since it is impossible to correctly identify those very young students possessing entrepreneurial potential, entrepreneurship education should be extended as broadly as possible throughout the total education curriculum to catch in its net all those who might later fulfill the role of entrepreneur. Any society can benefit from the enhancement of entrepreneurial talent, as the development of entrepreneurship impacts positively on economic growth and well-being. It is Rushing's contention that education programs can directly affect the extent of entrepreneurial talent within a society. As a result, the progress of that society will depend on the effectiveness of its entrepreneurship education programs.

He suggests that one approach for teaching entrepreneurship is to focus on historical context and to describe the role of entrepreneurship in economic history. Contending that economics cannot be fully understood without comprehending the role of the entrepreneur, the intelligent voter must understand the role and importance of the entrepreneur. If this is done, what will be created is the political base for policies that will encourage rather than discourage additional entrepreneurial activity.

The second and parallel approach to entrepreneurship education is based on the assumption that teaching entrepreneurship can enhance and develop the traits that are associated with entrepreneurial success and provide the skills that entrepreneurs will need to function within the economy. No one approach or method can be delineated that will completely perform this function. Entrepreneurship education needs to focus on developing innovation, risk taking, imagination, problem solving and decision-making skills.

The two approaches mentioned by Rushing are not mutually exclusive. The first approach develops within the population a broader knowledge and appreciation of the entrepreneur's role, while the second seeks to develop and expand the pool of entrepreneurial talent within the economy. Entrepreneurship education is not, according to Rushing, a one-shot situation. Instead, it should be integrated and continued throughout all formal education, from programs in the earliest grades to counseling for mature adults.

MODELS OF ENTREPRENEURSHIP

Gerry Gunderson in Chapter 3 redirects the focus of entrepreneurship educators away from the traditional view of entrepreneurship as it has developed over the years. Gunderson says that there are three basic approaches that are used to explain entrepreneurship. The first attempts to explain entrepreneurship by reference to certain personal traits that produce success. The second approach, called *event studies,* focuses on environmental forces that cause entrepreneurship to come about, such as the loss of a job. The third approach, labeled the *venture school,* recognizes that entrepreneurial efforts are part of an ongoing process and are not isolated or random events. Unlike the other two approaches, which are static, this approach stresses the dynamic aspect of the entrepreneurial event.

Gunderson is critical of what he calls the *Schumpeterial approach* to explaining entrepreneurship. This approach, named after the Austrian economist Joseph Schumpeter, equates entrepreneurship with innovation. However, Schumpeterian innovation takes place on a very grand scale. To Schumpeter, innovation consists of new ideas whose impacts are so great that they destroy competing industries and remake whole segments of society. According to Gunderson, this view makes entrepreneurs seem larger than life and more impressive than they really are. There is a certain appeal to the Schumpeterian model because it seems to correspond to the public's preconception of how entrepreneurs operate by taking risks and creatively destroying old industries. However, it is Gunderson's contention that this view is distorted.

According to Gunderson, this view preconditions the way in which entrepreneurs are portrayed in history. Since Schumpeter's entrepreneurs are giants destroying their competitors and almost single-handedly remaking society, it is easy for historians and others to depict entrepreneurs as individuals acquiring power arbitrarily and exercising it in a capricious and destructive manner. Such has been the usual historical treatment of the so-called robber barons, Rockefeller, Morgan, and Gould.

What is wrong with the Schumpeterian model? Gunderson contends that entrepreneurship is really a process of small incremental innovations rather then giant leaps forward. While there are some notable examples of the latter, most entrepreneurial effort is involved in making small modifications or changes in products or services that better meet consumer needs or improve productivity through better technology. Innovation is, then, a slow process that requires many decades to come to fruition, and not something that happens overnight and instantly transforms the way business has been conducted.

Gunderson provides us with a better explanation of the entrepreneurial process. He still sees entrepreneurship as being linked directly to innovation, but he sees the innovative process resulting from becoming proficient in the use of established bodies of knowledge. Gunderson's entrepreneur is focused, seeing what others have overlooked. Gunderson supplies us with a new and insightful definition of entrepreneurship as

drawing from a wide range of skills capable of enhancement to add value to a target niche of human activity. The effort expanded in finding and implementing such opportunities is rewarded by income and independence as well as pride in creation.

Entrepreneurs expend an enormous amount of effort in working out the logic of their endeavors As a result, they simply know more than others do, and since they know more, they are likely to see what others have overlooked. Entrepreneurship, then, is the acquiring of knowledge and the specialized skills necessary to implement that knowledge. This means that entrepreneurs do not accept what others know. They reexamine the logic of relationships that others ignore in the mistaken belief that the relationships could not be any different.

The risks and rewards of entrepreneurship are also discussed by Gunderson in this path-breaking chapter. The public's perception that entrepreneurial success requires the assumption of exceptional amounts of risks, he rejects. Entrepreneurs control risk by acquiring superior knowledge and having access to information that others do not have. Because others do not have it, they perceive the risk as being greater than what it really is. Entrepreneurs are different than other people, not only because they possess knowledge and insights that others lack, but also because they thrive on the prospect of change, which others find discomforting.

While the public widely assumes that the principal motivation of the entrepreneur is the accumulation of wealth, Gunderson sees other rewards as more important. Entrepreneurship is a lifestyle choice that is made not principally because it offers high income. Gunderson estimates that 80 percent of today's entrepreneurs could make more money working for someone else. What entrepreneurs really do is buy independence and the opportunity to shape their own ventures. Money is not unimportant because it does allow the entrepreneur more freedom to operate, but an exclusive focus on financial rewards leads to the wrong conclusions about what drives the entrepreneur.

Gunderson concludes his chapter by introducing us to his innovation model of entrepreneurship. This model sees entrepreneurship as a continuous stream of innovations which, over a long period of time, reshape technology and the economy. Innovation happens when the rewards to entrepreneurs, both monetary and otherwise, are appropriate for the effort they must expend. In this model, competitors are not ruthlessly dispatched through the process of creative destruction. Rather, innovation is a slow process that allows competitors to adapt and change if they will. If they choose not to change, then their demise is clearly justified. This theory is better supported by the historical evidence of how entrepreneurs actually operate than is the Schumpeterian model.

ELEMENTS OF A SUCCESSFUL ENTREPRENEURSHIP EDUCATION PROGRAM

Canada's Gary Rabbior in Chapter 4 provides a practical blueprint for successful entrepreneurship education programs. This blueprint, if followed at all levels of education, would produce not only more students eager to become venture initiators, but also more students who, while they may never start their own businesses, will possess those characteristics and traits that are necessary for success in any endeavors. Entrepreneurship education should not be focused on providing something new for young people, but rather in removing the barriers that have eroded the self-confidence and self-esteem of today's students. The process of education has dissipated students' spirit of adventure and their willingness to take initiative and risk, factors that are the soul of entrepreneurship.

Entrepreneurship should be defined in the broadest possible context, as a process of creative change. It may result in the formation of a new business, but then again it may not. The purpose of entrepreneurship education should be to foster creative activity and independent action wherever it is needed.

What is traditionally viewed as entrepreneurial activity (starting a business) should not be the only goal or outcome of an entrepreneurship education program. There are tremendous benefits to be gained from entrepreneurship education in addition to that of spawning the next generation of business initiators. A population that is more creative, innovative, risk-taking, and acclimated to change is a population that is more likely to be successful in all its endeavors. Narrowing the limits of an entrepreneurship education program to just a single goal of producing more new business start-ups would be folly.

Prescription is not to be the heart of entrepreneurship education. The entrepreneur is a searcher, an explorer, and an adventurer, and the education program should be geared to inspiring and assisting individuals who possess those characteristics. It will therefore be impossible to prescribe a rigid program of entrepreneurship education, since an effective entrepreneurship program will depend on the ingenuity, innovation, and inspiration of an effective educator who is willing to tailor the classroom setting to the needs of the student and the particular circumstances and opportunities of the day. The need for clearly established objectives at the start of an entrepreneurship education program is vital. Without this, the program can not be effectively evaluated.

Rabbior concludes his chapter by laying out the twenty-five criteria that he feels need to be encompassed in all entrepreneurship education programs, whether at the elementary, secondary, or collegiate level. All twenty-five of these criteria require flexibility and innovativeness. They decry structure and predetermined outcomes, and they stress fun and excitement within flexible learning environments. Entrepreneurship cannot be taught by non-entrepreneurial teachers in non-entrepreneurial settings. Consequently, we must rethink our approach not only to entrepreneurship education but to education in general.

THE EVOLVING NATURE OF COLLEGIATE ENTREPRENEURSHIP EDUCATION

At the collegiate level, entrepreneurship education has not only grown but has also changed over the last two decades. In Chapter 5, Robert Ronstadt details those changes and forecasts the future of collegiate entrepreneurship education as it moves into the next decade.

There exist two schools of entrepreneurship education. The old school, which was founded and flounders on the practices of the past, embraces myths about entrepreneurs that were never right or relevant. The old school grew out of a mentality of small business management, which stressed action above analysis and assumed that most people would wait until late in their careers before beginning their first ventures, and would put an inordinate amount of stress on developing a business plan. Instructional content during the class often focused on having practicing entrepreneurs tell their own "war stories," which were often substituted for a rigorous curriculum.

The new school of entrepreneurship sees entrepreneurs as critical thinkers as well as doers. While experience is not irrelevant, the new school sees that any age is the right age to begin an entrepreneurial career. The new school does not stress the need for students to prepare a lengthy and detailed business plan, but focuses instead on a venture feasibility study which will hopefully avoid prematurely locking potential entrepreneurs into their initial concept. The new school also sees entrepreneurship as a career, not just as a single event. Entrepreneurship is viewed as a series of multiple ventures in which the entrepreneur starts many new projects, not just one. While classroom speakers can add both interest and flavor to the course, they are not the principal means of conveying knowledge to the students. There is no substitute for a rigorous curriculum.

The new school also sees entrepreneurship as a multidisciplinary study, not as an adjunct to a department of management. Psychology, sociology, and political science all provide important insights that the entrepreneur needs to have communicated during the educational process.

Ronstadt thinks that all college students should be required to take a course in entrepreneurship. Since entrepreneurs are increasingly likely to come with collegiate backgrounds not obtained in a traditional school of business, designing entrepreneurship programs to meet these students' needs is on his agenda for the 1990s.

ENTREPRENEURSHIP EDUCATION FOR POTENTIAL PRACTICING ENTREPRENEURS

One of the most productive areas of entrepreneurship education concerns potential and practicing entrepreneurs who are not enrolled in traditional college and university programs. Fred Kiesner reports in Chapter 6 on research that he has conducted on entrepreneurs and educators. It is his purpose to clarify the special situations of potential and practicing entrepreneurs as consumers of formal and informal education training programs. His studies, while preliminary, indicate what works and what does not, and thus provide guidance for collegiate entrepreneurship educators who wish to work with potential and practicing venture initiators.

There is a disparity in perception between college professors who provide entrepreneurship training to nontraditional students and the students themselves. The faculty rate their own offerings as more valuable than does the small business community. Kiesner notes that the faculty must take into account the entrepreneurs' negative reactions as they design and develop programs.

Surprisingly, though, the studies do indicate that most of the nontraditional students held some positive feelings about the college and university programs. As a general rule, the owners do have an appreciation of the potential value of college and universities as a resource.

When the faculty and the business owners were asked to identify what they considered to be the most ideal methods of conducting effective programs for the practicing business venturer, their views again differed. The nontraditional students simply did not accept college and university faculty as experts, they saw them as lacking experience, and their offerings as being largely irrelevant to the "real world." Entrepreneurship courses produced by trade groups and professional organizations are more favorably received than courses produced on college campuses. Training programs that are industry-specific and focus on specific problems are better received than more generalized offerings.

Kiesner concludes that nontraditional students who are small business owners want programs at off-work times, which often conflicts with the desires of faculty. Early in the year seems to be the most popular time among small business owners to take training programs, and courses offered near holidays, during the vacation months, or near tax deadlines will fail to draw big enrollments. The providers of the courses do not need to be concerned with academic credit. The nontraditional students are seeking the training for knowledge and not for credentials.

Kiesner notes the paradox that while in these courses college professors often teach their students to study their markets to determine the needs of the consumers and to provide goods and services specifically tailored to meet those needs, academicians never seem to practice what they preach when devising offerings for nontraditional students.

ENTREPRENEURSHIP EDUCATION IN COLLEGES AND UNIVERSITIES

Certainly one of the most significant trends in higher education over the last decade has been the growth of entrepreneurship programs. From very humble beginnings as courses in small business management, entrepreneurship education has moved to the forefront on many university campuses. These programs serve many different audiences, including the traditional undergraduate and graduate students. Colleges and universities also provide programs for practicing and potential entrepreneurs who are not regularly enrolled students. Many universities provide training to teachers at all education levels so they can effectively teach entrepreneurship in their classrooms. A few schools have even developed programs to teach those who will work with entrepreneurs, such as bankers, lawyers, consultants, government officials and CPAs (Certified Public Accountants). Colleges are also involved in sponsoring student entrepreneur clubs, in conducting seminars for secondary students, and in recognizing outstanding entrepreneurial achievements.

In Chapter 7, this author has reviewed these programs and the completed research that attempts to measure their effectiveness. Principal emphasis was on the courses for traditional undergraduate and graduate students. These programs have grown tremendously on college campuses both because of student demand and because administrators have been able to raise funds to establish programs, chairs, and endowments in entrepreneurial studies.

It is important to understand the fundamental difference between small business management courses and entrepreneurship courses. Small business management is a very narrow field that provides instruction on how to run a small business. Entrepreneurship education may include small business management, but goes well beyond to cover the steps necessary to innovate, start a business, and carry it forward.

The content of entrepreneurship courses is fairly standard among the college campuses. Usually these consist of readings from texts and magazines, and lectures by guest speakers in addition to the classes' regular instructors. The primary teaching device is often the case study, and most of these courses involve some sort of business plan as a culminating activity. However, there is evidence that too much emphasis is placed on the business plan. There is further evidence that entrepreneurship courses need to be less structured and better designed to fit the needs and unique personalities of entrepreneurial students. The stress in the entrepreneurship courses should be on students doing independent projects with a high level of hands-on work.

While most instructors are satisfied with the texts currently available in entrepreneurship education, college texts need to be more practical and less theoretical, and should use a higher-level approach that would be more challenging to the students. Practicing entrepreneurs are very critical of the materials that have been developed for their use. What is emphasized in the texts does not correspond to the problems that the entrepreneurs face in the outside world. Too little attention is given to marketing and selling, and too much to finance and accounting. Likewise, there is too little coverage of manager-employee relationships, and too much coverage of accounting and tax topics.

The content of collegiate programs in entrepreneurship has also come under criticism. These programs are usually found in schools of business, and tend to be located in management or strategic planning departments. These courses, then, reflect the bias of those departments. As a result, the curriculums are incomplete, often failing to include any entrepreneurial history or economics. While there is unanimous agreement that entrepreneurship is an interdisciplinary field, very little progress has been made in integrating psychological and sociological insights into the course offerings and programs.

Most colleges and universities that have entrepreneurship programs also provide opportunities for students to consult with small businesses, usually through the Small Business Institute (SBI) program. Surprisingly, there has been little research done on the effectiveness of such programs, and what has been reported is largely anecdotal. The more successful programs are those in which a faculty member, who serves as the supervisor, is directly and continuously involved with the students while they do their project. SBI projects tend to be very narrowly focused, dealing with very specific problems of firms. Entrepreneurship students would gain more from being involved in planning start-ups and in dealing with the total operation of a business. SBI projects need to be rigorously graded, and students should not be assigned projects for which they do not have adequate academic background.

There are two models of entrepreneurship education programs currently being followed on college campuses. The *composite model* consists of a series of courses taught out of traditional academic departments. These include courses in small business management, venture taxation, venture finance, and computers for small business. The second model is the *integrated model,* which is delivered through a separate department or center for entrepreneurship studies. Courses here are independent of the traditional departments. While entrepreneurship students should take the usual introductory business school courses, the integrated model provides special courses for them beyond the introductory stage.

The integrated model is more effective than the composite approach. Since the teachers are part of the same department, they are usually more motivated and committed to entrepreneurship. Under the composite model, the courses in entrepreneurship are usually adjuncts assigned to a teacher whose principal interests lie elsewhere. A separate entrepreneurship studies program gives the program more visibility and administrative support. Finally, the integrated model makes it less likely that gaps and overlaps will develop in the curriculums.

In evaluating courses for nontraditional students, there are two basic types of programs. The first of these is the *networking model,* which brings together potential or practicing entrepreneurs to hear inspirational speeches from successful businesspeople. The networking model allows maximum time for speakers to interact with seminar attendees. Their principal value is in motivating potential and practicing entrepreneurs, allowing them to establish contacts that may be of value to them later.

The second model is the *skills seminar,* which focuses on particular topics in which the potential or practicing entrepreneur may need additional instruction. These may include finance, accounting, marketing, insurance, or business planning. There has been very little research done to evaluate the effectiveness of such programs.

Despite the growth of entrepreneurship programs at the college and university level, many of these remain tradition-bound. Too often they fail to consider the fact that potential entrepreneurs possess different characteristics and attitudes than does the general student population as a whole. Courses need to be designed with that recognition in mind. The underlying assumption of many collegiate courses in entrepreneurship is that entrepreneurs are born and not made; therefore, training is provided only for those who have already demonstrated entrepreneurial characteristics.

ENTREPRENEURSHIP EDUCATION FOR FAMILY BUSINESS

As entrepreneurship education in colleges and universities has matured, it has begun to develop subdisciplines. One of these is family business. Craig Aronoff and Mary Cawley discuss in Chapter 8 what they feel will be a dramatic development in entrepreneurship education in the years to come. The two most potent institutions in America are family and business. When they combine, they produce an endlessly fascinating study.

While academicians may be attracted to family business by the dramatic elements, family business is also of vast economic social and cultural importance to America. Between 90 and 95 percent of all businesses in America are family-controlled, and 80 percent of all America's millionaires own a family business. Despite the significance of family business, there are still less than twenty universities that offer curriculum in the area, but this number is likely to grow quickly in the years to come. More and more, the popular press as well as academic journals are carrying articles on family business.

The authors find it difficult to define just what is a family business. Traditional definitions that deal with the percentage of ownership and control in a family's hands are not completely adequate because they ignore considerations of values and attitudes. What the authors propose is a systems model that consists of three intersecting circles representing the family, management, and ownership dimensions of the family business. The interaction in the overlap between these three spheres constitutes the fertile ground for further academic activity.

Academicians may respond to family business through the traditional methods of teaching, research, and service. The service component is currently running ahead of both research and teaching. A market has emerged for seminars and consulting with family businesses to which academic institutions have responded primarily by conducting seminars. Participants in these seminars are unique since they often encompass several generations, several management levels, and different types of businesses. In fact, the only common denominator is that participants are all from family businesses. The core of these seminars consists of management development, interpersonal communications, strategic planning, conflict resolution, financial planning, retirement, and transitional planning.

The teaching of family business is now becoming integrated into collegiate business curriculum. Most often it is found under the umbrella of entrepreneurship studies or in courses dealing with organizational behavior and management. Perhaps the biggest teaching impediment is that few professors have had actual hands-on experience with family business. Being narrowly trained in their specific disciplines, they are unable to deal with the *overlap issues*.

The authors review the research that has been done in the area, and find that, by and large, it has been inadequate and unsophisticated. Despite these failures, the time is ripe for additional research. However, there is a major research problem since family business research requires the interaction of disciplines that have not cooperated in the past. Psychology, accounting, economics, sociology, and law must all combine if family business research is to be successful. Family business studies will continue to grow on campuses not only because the subject is important, but because funding is becoming available as successful families recognize the need for a more systematic response to the issues that family business presents. Often they are willing to supply the funds to support programs.

RESTRUCTURING ELEMENTARY EDUCATION TO MAKE IT ENTREPRENEURIAL

In Chapter 9, Marilyn Kourilsky deals with an unhappy phenomenon. A significant percentage of students in kindergarten demonstrate entrepreneurial characteristics, but by the time high school approaches, only a minute percentage of high school students still possess the traits. Dealing with the question of why that is so provides an important blueprint for how entrepreneurship education should be restructured, not only at the elementary level, but at all levels.

Society must find ways to encourage and enlarge the entrepreneurial spirit, and the schools are a principal vehicle by which this can be done. Kourilsky sees the schools as failing principally because the classroom can be compared to a planned or a command economy, where the teacher serves the function of producer and the student is the consumer. The essential economic decisions of "what, how, and for whom" are totally centralized and decided by the teacher, who performs the same role as the planner in a command economy. Unlike a market economy, in the classroom there is almost no autonomy given to consumers. Students are forced into molds where the principle motivation is to avoid failure rather than to achieve success.

There is a strong tendency in the schools to reward *convergent academic performance*. This performance is linked to the restrictive notions of what qualifies as intelligence. In today's classroom only one type of intelligence is recognized, the analytical. There are at least two other types of intelligence, the innovative and the practical, which are largely ignored in the classroom today yet are essential characteristics of successful entrepreneurs.

Today's elementary students have been socialized through their school experience, and this has diminished their proclivity toward entrepreneurial thinking and behavior. The total classroom environment needs to be reformed if entrepreneurship is to be encouraged. This can be done by creating a new educational environment in which the creative divergent traits of the entrepreneurial spirit are fostered and enhanced, and by insuring that at strategic points in the schooling process there are programs that will enable the students to experience entrepreneurial thinking and behavior.

This can be accomplished by establishing entrepreneurial practices that transfer ownership of the classroom from the planner (teacher) to the consumer (student) as is characteristic of a market economy. Emphasis should be placed on the process of explanation and inquisitiveness, not on producing correct answers on a quiz. The most widely cited characteristic of the entrepreneur is the need for achievement, but few classroom practices are consistent with that need.

Basically, Kourilsky is saying that elementary students need to be taught in a way that minimizes their fear of failure and rewards behavior that is both innovative and persistent even if it does not necessarily produce the correct answers. Kourilsky's thoughts must be considered radical since she suggests that the first step in a successful program of entrepreneurship education is not the providing of courses or materials that deal with the topic but in a total restructuring of the educational process beginning in the elementary grades.

ENTREPRENEURSHIP EDUCATION IN THE ELEMENTARY GRADES

In Chapter 10 Bill Rushing selects studies from the literature on the psychology of entrepreneurs and evaluates them in light of what they reveal about the proper methods of entrepreneurship delivery in the elementary grades. The four studies all reach a similar conclusion: The need for achievement is the most important characteristic possessed by entrepreneurs. As a result, entrepreneurs have low dependency needs and are principally motivated by themselves rather than by others.

The studies also agree that there are great difficulties in measuring entrepreneurial potential. Therefore, we are limited in our capacity to identify potential entrepreneurs early on and to channel them into appropriate programs. The research reviewed by Rushing suggests that successful entrepreneurship education programs at the elementary grades will focus on goal setting, achievement motivation, and persistence.

The studies reviewed do not always agree with each other. While some find that risk taking is an important characteristic and should be enhanced through an educational program, others find that it is not a good indicator of future entrepreneurial behavior. However, all agree that the potential supply of entrepreneurs is greater than what is actually produced by the education system.

Rushing then turns his attention to a review of the existing programs for students in the elementary grades. The programs that have been successful foster learning by doing and present entrepreneurs as positive role models for elementary students.

Rushing does not feel that entrepreneurship and economics education should be integrated rather than divorced from each other in the elementary curriculum. The challenge for economics educators is to introduce entrepreneurship into the elementary grades while continuing to emphasize the more traditional economic concepts. In the elementary grades, the focus of the entrepreneurship program should be on the fundamentals of economics and also on the development and enhancement of the entrepreneurial attitudes and characteristics identified in the studies previously reviewed. During the later elementary grades, students should be made aware of entrepreneurial opportunities throughout the economy.

ENTREPRENEURSHIP EDUCATION FOR YOUNG ADOLESCENTS

Understanding how the economy functions and the role of the entrepreneur in that economy is not going to be casually acquired by merely being part of the economy. This is the contention of Ronald Banaszak, who sees a need for a requirement that formal instruction in both economics and entrepreneurship should be given to all students. In Chapter 11, his focus is on economics and entrepreneurship education for young adolescents, those between the ages of twelve and sixteen, who otherwise do not receive adequate formal instruction about our economy and entrepreneurs.

The lack of understanding about our economy simply means that our young people are incapable of functioning as economic decision makers. This is not only unfortunate but also dangerous because Americans are being asked to make critical decisions on a vast array of sophisticated issues both in their individual lives and collectively. Banaszak sees that economics and entrepreneurship are well suited for studies in the middle grades (six through nine). Economics/entrepreneurship/education allows students to examine their own personal development by studying role models and to explore the larger society they are about to enter. Economics is the science of decision making, and young adolescents face an enormous range of alternatives, requiring that they not only make choices but also be willing to live with the consequences. Learning about entrepreneurs who have creatively responded to their environment and who have seized control of the situations in which they find themselves can be a positive factor in helping young adolescents take charge of their own lives.

Banaszak feels there are certain values that should be included as the goals of a successful entrepreneurship/economics/education program for young adolescents. Among these are developing a commitment to the basic values of the American economic system and understanding what distinguishes it from competing economic systems found in the world. At the same time, however, the student should develop a healthy skepticism for answers that are stated too simply or defined too narrowly. Specifically, Banaszak sees two desired outcomes from an entrepreneurship/economics/education program in the middle grades. First is the knowledge of the role and function of entrepreneurs in a market-driven economy, and second is the understanding and practice of entrepreneurial characteristics such as self-esteem, willingness to take risks, innovativeness, and the acceptance of responsibility for personal actions and persistence.

Traditional economics and entrepreneurship education is inappropriate for adolescent learners as it is too abstract and mathematical. Entrepreneurship and economics education needs to focus on a few key concepts and make them relevant to the lives of the student learners. Principal stress must be laid on the process of decision making and the acceptance of consequences for those decisions. The appropriate approach for entrepreneurship and economics education is to employ the concept of the economic landscape with which the student is already familiar. Building on the familiar, economic and entrepreneurship educators can link new knowledge to the students' existing education base and provide additional insights to familiar institutions and events.

Banaszak provides suggestions for the appropriate presentation of economic and entrepreneurship consent to young adolescents. These programs should be concrete; the student should be actively involved in the learning process, with the new knowledge related to the knowledge that the students have already gained from their environment.

ENTREPRENEURSHIP IN THE SECONDARY CURRICULUM

Entrepreneurship is a topic that can and should be integrated into the secondary curriculum in a variety of courses. In Chapter 12, this author explores ways in which this should be accomplished.

Entrepreneurship can better be defined by its results than by its characteristics. Entrepreneurs introduce new products or services into the market, develop and implement new technologies, open new markets, discover new sources of supply, or reorganize existing enterprises. Consequently, entrepreneurship is more than starting a new business. It is any innovative activity in large corporations, nonprofit organizations, or even in government agencies or socialist enterprises.

Integrating entrepreneurship into the secondary curriculum begins with awareness. Students need to be aware of the importance of entrepreneurship in the economy and of the possibility of entrepreneuring as a career choice for themselves. Without both types of awareness, it is extremely unlikely that the student will even consider entrepreneurship or have a favorable attitude toward the role of entrepreneurs in society.

The second step in integrating entrepreneurship into the curriculum at the secondary level is to convey the skills that entrepreneurs need. There are two types of skills, the first of which are technical insights. Students must be knowledgeable about the field in which they entrepreneur. However, in addition to these technical skills, entrepreneurs also need certain other managerial skills which can be taught to them. These skills, such as management, finance, and personnel, are included in most entrepreneurship curriculums at the secondary level.

Where should entrepreneurship be integrated into the specific courses at the high school level? The most obvious, of course, is economics. The entrepreneur is often overlooked in high school economics texts and courses. There are certain places in the study of microeconomics where the concept of entrepreneurship should be introduced. Students should learn that entrepreneurship is a distinct factor of production along with land, labor, and capital. Second, students should know that entrepreneurs create disequilibrium by destroying old markets and perceiving new ones before they even exist. Entrepreneurs do not fit easily into the static models of most microeconomics analysis. Students should recognize that an entrepreneur does not just respond to existing forces in the market but creates entire new markets that never existed before.

Students also need to understand the role of profits. Profits are not the principal motivating force behind the entrepreneur, but they are important. High profits do not necessarily mean successful entrepreneurial activity, as these profits may be due to monopolistic conditions in the market. Also, microeconomics should include the role of the entrepreneur in innovation because it is this innovative activity that distinguishes the entrepreneur from other players in the marketplace.

On the macroeconomic side, students need to recognize the position of entrepreneurs in promoting economic growth both in the developed and the undeveloped world. Without entrepreneurial activity, nations stagnate. It has been assumed by most economists that entrepreneurship is an automatic process that will be forthcoming if aggregate demand is simply high enough. This is not the case. As far as investment is concerned, too much emphasis is placed on the role of interest rates and the supply of money. Too little emphasis is placed on how the entrepreneur decides whether to invest. The inclusion of entrepreneurs in high school economics courses will make the real world not only more understandable, but more exciting as well.

Entrepreneurship should be also be a central feature in courses dealing with business education. Business education students as well as economics students need to comprehend how entrepreneurs work, function, and create jobs. Certainly courses in government should have an entrepreneurial focus. When regulation and taxation are discussed, these should be viewed as impacting the entrepreneurial environment and thereby directly influencing the behavior of the economy.

Courses in psychology could also focus on the entrepreneur asking the questions: What makes entrepreneurs perform as they do? What are the unique characteristics of entrepreneurs that distinguish them from others? How can those characteristics be identified and enhanced? Sociology is also a fertile field for integrating entrepreneurship. Questions can be asked such as: Why are some ethnic groups more entrepreneurial than others? How do factors in the environment, such as family and friends, influence the decision to entrepreneur? How can outsiders be integrated into the economy through entrepreneurial activity?

The only course at the high school level in which there is now an extensive discussion of entrepreneurship is American history. Unfortunately, the entrepreneur in U.S. history is often inaccurately portrayed as the "robber baron" whose goal was to line his own pocket by bilking an unsuspecting public. As recent historical analysis has shown, this view of the entrepreneur was never accurate, yet it is still the one generally portrayed in high school texts. It is small wonder, then, that most high school students do not see entrepreneurship as an attractive vocation. Correctly portraying the role of the entrepreneur should become a top priority for history courses.

Science courses are also an area in which entrepreneurship could be

included. Scientific inventions by themselves are barren unless those innovations are developed and brought to the marketplace. This nation is
definitely in the high tech age. The role of the entrepreneur not only in
coming up with new ideas but also in introducing those ideas into the
marketplace should at least be mentioned in science courses.

ECONOMICS IN THE ENTREPRENEURSHIP CURRICULUM

John Clow in Chapter 13 recognizes that economics has often been divorced from entrepreneurship courses and curriculums as they have developed at the secondary level. As is noted in his chapter and several others in this book, entrepreneurship education at the secondary level is often
narrowly focused on the skills needed by managers of small businesses. It
is Clow's contention that economics must be integrated into any entrepreneurship program at the secondary level if that entrepreneurship program
is to convey the necessary insights and understanding to the next generation of entrepreneurs. There are four primary objectives of economics in
an entrepreneurship program. First, the students should develop a general
understanding of the economic principles that operate in our economic
system. Second, students should develop an understanding of how businesses of all sizes operate in that system. Third, students should develop
an understanding of the role of the entrepreneur or intrapreneur within
the economic system. Fourth, they should develop a general understanding of what is necessary for a budding entrepreneur to participate in the
system.

In order for those goals to be accomplished, Clow delineates specific
economic generalizations that form the nexis for the understanding of economics that entrepreneurship students should have. Among these are the
facts that the American economic and political system encourages private
enterprise and that entrepreneurs are the idea people within the economy,
the ones who organize the other factors of production. In addition, students should understand that entrepreneurs create the jobs that are available in our economy. Also, students need to know that every decision
made by an entrepreneur involves an opportunity cost; that something
must be given up if something else is to be obtained. Perhaps the most
difficult economic understanding for entrepreneurship students is to realize and understand that most decisions involve small or marginal changes.
Houses are built one brick at a time, and most entrepreneurial and economic activity consists of small steps rather than giant leaps.

In addition, entrepreneurship students need to understand the role of
prices and how they pass signals to buyers and sellers. Failing to respond
to those signals will spell doom for any venture. Understanding the role of
profits in the economy is also essential. Profits are the motivating force
behind economic behavior. Self-interested entrepreneurs will respond to

the profit incentive. Since innovation and entrepreneurship often create new ways of doing things and new technologies, entrepreneurship students need to understand that there are a variety of ways in which productivity can be increased in the economy and that part of the entrepreneurial function is to search for those ways.

Entrepreneurs also need to know that they will be competing in a market economy with other producers and sellers, and that there are many ways in which entrepreneurs compete against each other in addition to price. Entrepreneurship students need to understand that government regulations and intervention affect the marketplace and set the perimeters within which entrepreneurs must function. A positive political environment is an essential element in their success as entrepreneurs. While entrepreneurs are often independent people, they need to understand that the nature of an economy is interdependency. It is through the market that these interrelationships are worked out in practice.

ENTREPRENEURSHIP IN VOCATIONAL EDUCATION

Vocational educators were the first to recognize the importance of entrepreneurship and to begin to include it in their curriculums. The role of entrepreneurship in vocational education is reviewed by Catherine Ashmore in Chapter 14. Ashmore presents a lifelong entrepreneurship education model to explain what entrepreneurship education means to different audiences at different stages of their educational development.

Stage one is basic understanding. The student can early on learn the fundamentals of economics. In stage two the student begins to understand business organizations. The student should learn the language of business and begin to see problems from the perspective of the entrepreneur. Moreover, the student's awareness of the potential of entrepreneurship as a career for them should be increased. Creative applications takes place in stage three. Ashmore contends that at this level the student is ready to develop a unique business idea and carry the decision-making process through the preparation of a business plan. It is recognized that these plans will be neither as detailed or complete as plans that may be constructed later. What is important is that the student learn the steps that need to be followed and the process of rational thinking that underlies business planning.

At this point there is a break in the lifetime learning model because it is anticipated that students will need to acquire other education and real world experiences that will contribute to their later success as entrepreneurs. Many entrepreneurs upon leaving school will work for others, gathering knowledge in the industry and insights about the market that will serve them well in the future.

Stage four in the lifetime model is the actual business start-up. At this point entrepreneurs have an idea to which they are committed and are going forward to establish their venture. The potential entrepreneur will need short courses and other special assistance designed to deal with the unique problems of launching a venture. Stage five refers to business growth. The business has been established but now must be managed and hopefully taken through a phase of rapid growth.

Ashmore recognizes that not all small business owners are entrepreneurs. A true entrepreneur not only establishes a business but also makes the business grow and carries it through a period of constant change. All others are merely small business managers. However, most true entrepreneurs start out as small business persons, usually founding their first businesses at a young age. The majority of these business initiators begin their business in an area in which they have already had job experience, financing their ventures from their own personal savings and the investment of family and friends.

Vocational education programs across the United States are funded by the U.S. Department of Education with the funds going to the state departments of education. These local school programs can be grouped into six major areas: agriculture, business education, health care, home economics, marketing education, and trade and industrial education.

Each state has elected a different route to infusing entrepreneurship education into their vocational programs. There is no single national model; it is recognized that what is effective in one setting may not work in others.

Ashmore makes a key point: The choice to infuse entrepreneurship education into the vocational curriculum still rests with the individual teachers. For most teachers this will not be easy because they are not familiar with the area of entrepreneurship and have little training in the area and little time to learn about it on their own. Unless the individual teacher believes that entrepreneurship is important, it is not likely to become part of his or her teaching plan.

A major strategy to encourage infusion is to conduct teacher in-service workshops, but since in-service workshops are expensive to either the state or the local systems, this will require significant commitment from administrative leaders. Each state should develop its own entrepreneurship curriculum materials for use in the vocational programs.

Students also learn about entrepreneurship outside their regular vocational classes. Entrepreneurship is often a topic included in summer leadership camps sponsored by various community organization or civic clubs. Vocational student organizations also provide an avenue for entrepreneurship education. Distributive Education Clubs of America (DECA) has an entrepreneurship contest that culminates at the national level.

Entrepreneurship can also be taught at both secondary technical schools and community colleges. To a degree this is already being done under the

provisions of the Job Training Partnership Act. The purpose of these programs is to help existing entrepreneurs solve their problems and thereby
encourage growth and success in their enterprises.

EXPERIENCE-BASED PROGRAMS IN ENTREPRENEURSHIP EDUCATION

A recurrent theme in this volume is that the most successful entrepreneurship education programs are those that are student-based and nontraditional in their approach. This theme is further developed by Judy Brenneke in Chapter 15. Hands-on entrepreneurship education experiences are
the most likely to produce successful results.

Participation in simulations, gaming, and role playing are the best opportunities to allow students to formulate responses that are truly entrepreneurial. These simulations need to be structured so that mistakes will
not be crucial to students' academic futures, thus encouraging them to
take risks. Experience-based programs are more likely to be successful when
children participate in real as opposed to vicarious experiences, are active
rather than passive learners, and actually make decisions, the consequences of which they will bear.

How should experience-based economic education be done? Entrepreneurship education should not be akin to science fiction, which takes place
outside the students' realm of experience. Experience-based programs should
be used as supplements to the standard textbook and lecture teaching
methods, and should encourage the students in the use of both inductive
and deductive thinking. This consists of placing them in the middle of real
world situations and providing them with the opportunity to reason their
way to solutions. Not only do students gain by going through experience-
based activities, but reinforcement is provided when students review with
the class what learning took place, focusing on the outcomes of the simulations.

Case studies are one important way of providing an experience-based
entrepreneurship education program. Before doing a case study, students
need to be familiar with the criteria for making decisions and to use those
steps in working through the case study. While cases can be simple or
detailed, depending on the abilities of the students, all should be clearly
rooted in sound economic principles.

However, case studies are not the only method of experience-based entrepreneurship education. Games and simulations, such as the highly successful Mini-Society developed by Marilyn Kourilsky, are equally, and often
more, effective. The major problem with games and simulations is that
they can be fun without being educational. Debriefing to highlight what
was learned is essential. During this debriefing, what transpired in the simulation needs to be directly related to parallel situations in the real world.

Yet another approach to experience-based entrepreneurship education is role playing. This technique describes a situation and allows the student to spontaneously respond without any previous scripting.

Field trips are also an excellent experience-based teaching method. Even though these are becoming increasingly difficult as school expenses and liability rise, a properly constructed field trip is a tremendous learning experience. Field trips provide the opportunity for students to see entrepreneurs in action on their own grounds. The entrepreneurial event no longer appears so remote.

Using these experience-based teaching techniques will produce students who not only know more about entrepreneurship but who also will be excited about the prospect of entrepreneurship and will recognize the relevance of entrepreneurship to their own lives.

INTERNSHIPS IN ENTREPRENEURSHIP EDUCATION

In Chapter 16 Margaret Murphy details one model for experience-based learning in economics and entrepreneurship education. This model is an internship/mentorship program that brings together students and mentors in an on-the-job learning situation. Such an internship provides invaluable opportunities for the student to experience the world of work in a safe environment. By that Murphy means that the student does not stand to lose by an actual job and the mentor is not expected to commit to the student as an employee. In a mentorship the adversarial employee-employer relationship is eliminated.

The internship program should provide the experiential component in a total entrepreneurship economics curriculum. Before the internship is conducted, the students need to have received conceptual instruction in both economics and entrepreneurship. It is important that during the internship the students be required to relate their experiences as interns to the material that has been previously communicated to them. It is equally essential that following the internship an extensive period of debriefing take place in which the students relate what they have learned in the classroom.

Murphy describes an ideal internship program. There should be two sequential placements at different work sites that should give the students different perspectives on the world of work. Both students and their mentors must complete a contract. The student agrees to maintain a log, develop a profile on the company, participate in regular evaluation sessions with the mentor and follow a disciplined life-style. Mentors agree to orient the student to the firm, to work with the student on a continuing basis, and to provide regular feedback to the program director.

It is important to stress the difference between an internship and a summer job. An intern should actually function side by side with the entrepreneur, fully participating in all activities and decisions that the entrepreneur makes. The intern should not be treated like additional summer help and assigned some job to do on a regular basis. If this approach is taken, then the purpose of the internship is defeated. *Elbow rubbing* means exactly that. Interns should be fully included so that they can experience the real world of entrepreneurial decision making and learn firsthand the relevance of economics.

ENTREPRENEURSHIP EDUCATION FOR AT-RISK STUDENTS

There is mounting evidence that a crisis is looming in America's future. Our economy is producing jobs, but our education system is not producing students whose skills and attitudes meet the requirements of those jobs. There has been a crescendo of criticism levied against the school systems in general and high schools in particular for having failed to produce either the quantity or quality of workers that the economy now demands. It is Mike MacDowell's contention in Chapter 17 that this situation must be addressed immediately and that entrepreneurship education has a role to play in the solution.

The failures of American high schools are well documented, particularly in inner city schools. In inner city schools over half the students drop out before they are eighteen, and many of those who do graduate have extremely limited reading, writing, and reasoning skills. However, what is equally distressing is that these students understand nothing about labor markets or the rudiments of the economy in which they will be expected to live and operate. Failure to understand the workplace and the economy that generates it often means that students also fail to see the relevance of education or why they need to develop the appropriate attitudes and skills to participate in that economy.

MacDowell debunks the myth that at-risk students will make the best entrepreneurs. While there are examples of dropouts who have become successful entrepreneurs, these are few. Most high school dropouts simply do not have the skills or understanding to succeed as entrepreneurs or anything else. What is equally distressing is that these students are not likely to be hired by entrepreneurs because they simply do not have the job skills those entrepreneurs are seeking. This is an even more critical problem for smaller businesses than for larger ones since smaller businesses are more labor-intensive and are usually the providers of entry-level jobs for most people.

It is difficult for the general public to understand that there are two types of inadequacies that at-risk students possess. First, they simply have not had the skills taught to them, and second, they lack sufficient economic knowledge to participate in the marketplace. The important qualities for success are good language skills, positive work habits, the ability to solve problems, and the desire to continue to learn. These should be imparted by both the visible and the invisible school curriculum. Often it is the invisible school curriculum that defeats at-risk students. That invisible curriculum is made up of the values and the attitudes communicated to the students by the school environment in which they find themselves.

How is entrepreneurship education part of the solution to the problem? Good programs that teach about entrepreneurship are entrepreneurial in themselves. They rely on adequately prepared teachers and meaningful experiences for students. It is important that neither the materials nor the structure of the schools stifle the teacher or the student by reducing flexibility. MacDowell points to two programs being developed by the Joint Council on Economic Education as examples of a curriculum that could benefit at-risk students.

ENTREPRENEURSHIP EDUCATION IN THE URBAN SCHOOLS

With falling test scores and dropping student performances, the consensus has been reached that American education is no longer delivering the quality product the nation needs, leaving the country vulnerable to its industrial, commercial, and military competitors. The decline in educational quality has tended to be concentrated in the urban schools of the nation. This author finds in Chapter 18 that the urban school creates a unique challenge to entrepreneurship educators. Students in the inner city are molded by the environment of crime, poverty, and hopelessness in which they find themselves. These students and their families have become virtually dependent on government handouts for their existence.

Unfortunately, an idea began to develop a few years ago that the problems of youth in the inner city could all be solved if we could somehow make entrepreneurs out of them. This expectation is unrealistic. Nonetheless, entrepreneurship education certainly could be a positive part of a program designed to deal with the problems of the inner city.

The environment in which formal education takes place is constrained by three factors: the students, the schools, and the teachers. Inner city students are generally poor academic achievers, coming from nontraditional families that produce a high dropout rate and severe problems of absenteeism. In addition, urban students have generally had no experience with the market economy and therefore understand little about how it functions or the roles of entrepreneurs within it. Generally, many urban students also lack entrepreneurial role models that can serve to inspire and guide them in the workplace.

The inner city schools themselves fail to provide the appropriate environment for learning to take place. Often the urban schools simply lack resources to provide the necessary materials or release time for teachers from other duties to work with students. The urban schools tend to be highly bureaucratic and, as a result, inflexible. This is, of course, the antithesis of the environment necessary for entrepreneurship education to take place. The inner city high schools have also tended to become custodial rather than educational. The first concern is safety, with education taking second place.

The third part of the urban educational environment concerns the teachers. Urban teachers themselves tend to be inflexible, often operating under union contracts that would not allow them to be flexible even if they wanted to. Urban teachers have heavy teaching loads and therefore resist new courses or infusing new ideas. Urban teachers, like their counterparts elsewhere, tend to be poorly trained in either economics or entrepreneurship. Perhaps the greatest criticism of the urban teachers is they tend to have negative attitudes toward, and low expectation of, their students. Given these constraints, it will be difficult for any education program, much less one in entrepreneurship, to be successful.

The Entrepreneurship/Economics/Education (E^3) project was designed to use entrepreneurship as a vehicle for changing students' attitudes about themselves and the world in which they will work. It consists of infusion courses in both world and American history to make students aware of entrepreneurship and the contributions of entrepreneurs to economic growth and rising living standards. An eleventh grade course focuses on both economics and entrepreneurship with particular emphasis being placed on developing among the students the personal attributes and attitudes to allow them to succeed as entrepreneurs or in any other occupation. Following the eleventh grade course, a mentorship program allows students to rub elbows with successful entrepreneurs who have come from backgrounds similar to their own. The E^3 program then concludes with a twelfth grade course that ties together the economic concepts learned in the previous course and observed in the mentorship. More advanced economic theory is also included, and the students are allowed to plan their own ventures and conceive and carry out a class project for the improvement of their schools.

In the years to come the E^3 project will be expanded to other school systems throughout the nation. It is not a panacea, but it is one way in which the urban school environment can be changed for the better.

REFERENCES

Drucker, Peter F. 1985. *Innovation and Entrepreneurship*. New York: Harper and Row.

Gilder, George. 1984. *The Spirit of Enterprise*. New York: Simon and Schuster.

Kilby, Peter. 1971. *Entrepreneurship and Economic Development*. New York: The
    Free Press.
Milne, A. A. 1926. *Winnie-the-Pooh*. London: Macmillan.
————. 1928. *The House at Pooh Corner*. London: Macmillan.

PART ONE

Scope and Theory

2

Entrepreneurship and Education

Francis W. Rushing

The 1980s may be known as the decade in which entrepreneurship has emerged as an important element in the dynamics of modern economies. New small businesses have become the major source of new job creation. Individuals and small businesses have made major contributions to the discovery of new technologies and to their commercial application. In short, the 1980s have brought about a renewed emphasis on the individual as entrepreneur, as producer and consumer, and as voter.

Entrepreneurship is now being taught in collegiate courses and, in some cases, academic majors in entrepreneurship have been initiated. The study of entrepreneurship and entrepreneurs has proven itself worthy of scholarly pursuit in research and instruction. The focus has been primarily at the college and university level. However, the more entrepreneurship is investigated, the greater the case that emerges for entrepreneurship instruction in grades K–12 as well as at the collegiate level. The relevant questions are not concerned with whether entrepreneurship should be taught in precollege programs but, rather, what should be taught, and when and how to teach the materials.

The study and promotion of entrepreneurship should be based on some rationale as to why entrepreneurship is important to the economic well-being of society. One hypothesis is that entrepreneurship "is a creative process, that entrepreneurial activity stimulates innovation, and that economic growth depends upon the existence of an innovative environment.

If these premises hold, then there should be a high degree of correlation between entrepreneurship and economic growth" (Williams, 1981, p. 517). Therefore, understanding the role of entrepreneurship in economic progress (as measured by increases in per capita income and the quality of life) is critical to our understanding of the dynamics of our society and its future well-being. The first question to be considered in achieving this understanding of the linkages between innovation and economic growth is, "What is entrepreneurship?" Once answered, this question suggests additional questions, such as:

- If entrepreneurship is critical to economic progress, can a society enhance the number of entrepreneurs and its level of entrepreneurial activity?
- Can our educational institutions play an important role in the enhancement process?
- What educational programs have the greatest probability of achieving this objective?
- How do educators implement such programs?

This chapter focuses on the first question, yet the remaining issues are addressed as well.

The chapter is divided into three additional parts. The second part summarizes the role of the entrepreneur in economics and describes where current research places the entrepreneur in the economic literature and what characteristics entrepreneurs possess. This section also struggles with the question of whether entrepreneurship can be taught in a way that will increase the number of active entrepreneurs.

The third part identifies two approaches to teaching entrepreneurship. Each approach is different, yet, if utilized together, they should not only provide an individual with an understanding of entrepreneurship but also develop his or her talents to be an entrepreneur. This section of the paper will attempt to discuss what directions entrepreneurial education might take at the precollege and college levels. The final part is a brief conclusion.

ENTREPRENEURSHIP AND ECONOMICS

The entrepreneur's role within economic activities has been a part of economic literature for centuries, yet the description of the entrepreneurial function has been different among the various economists who have addressed the topic. For instance, economic literature (attributed to the specific economists in parentheses) has described the nature and role of the entrepreneur in the following manner:

1. A person who assumes the risk associated with uncertainty (Cantillon, Thunen, Mangoldt, Mill, Hawley, Knight, Mises, Cole, Shackle)

2. A supplier of financial capital (Smith, Turgot, Ricardo, Bohm-Bawerk, Edgeworth, Pigou, Mises)

3. An innovator (Bandeau, Bentham, Thunen, Schmoller, Sombart, Weber, Schumpeter)

4. A decision maker (Cantillon, Menger, Marshall, Wieser, Walker, Deynes, Mises, Shackle, Cole, Kirzner, Schultz)

5. An industrial leader (Say, Walker, Marshall, Wieser, Sombart, Weber, Schumpeter)

6. A manager or superintendent (Say, Mill, Marshall, Menger)

7. An organizer or coordinator of economic resources (Wieser, Schmoller, Sombart, Weber, Clark, Schumpeter)

8. A proprietor of an enterprise (Wieser, Pigou)

9. An employer of factors of production (Walker, Keynes, Wieser)

10. A contractor (Bentham)

11. An arbitrageur (Cantillon, Kirzner)

12. A person who allocates resources to alternative uses (Kirzner, Schultz) (Hebert and Link, 1982, pp. 107–108)

Various theories have placed the entrepreneur in both static and dynamic environments. Upon review of these authors one finds support for either approach, but the weight of the evidence is that the entrepreneur is an important causative agent of economic dynamics. If the entrepreneur is set within a static economic model, then the role assigned to him or her is one of repeating procedures and techniques already learned and implemented (Hebert and Link, 1982). Under these conditions, the entrepreneur is actually a passive entity who might be better described as a manager. However, the case for the entrepreneur as a dynamic figure seems stronger.

Entrepreneurs must deal with uncertainty and innovation and do so in a competitive environment with imperfect information. In this dynamic environment, entrepreneurs are an important destabilizing force in the economy, while their other characteristic of utilizing perception for adjusting to change may help to provide stability. These two characteristics are not contradictory because different entrepreneurs utilize them at the same time across the different industries or sectors of the economy. Innovation is the cause of change, uncertainty is its consequence, and progress is its reward.

One consensus that seems to have formed concerning entrepreneurs is that their productive activity is individualistic rather than social (Hebert and Link, 1982). This has led some economists to believe that entrepreneurship can only be developed to its fullest extent in an economic system that permits individuals the freedom to pursue productive activities and receive personally the benefits, whether monetary or nonmonetary, of their achievements. Historically, the scholars who have explored the role of entrepreneurship have assumed the system and the entrepreneur to be capitalist. The entrepreneur fits within the neoclassical theories of economic growth and income distribution as an innovator and a risk taker. The characteristics of the entrepreneur emphasized within these theories may differ, but he or she clearly plays a role in each.

Neoclassical economists have never adequately dealt with the entrepreneur within microeconomic theory. As William J. Baumol has said,

Look for him [the entrepreneur] in the index of some of the most noted of recent writings on value theory and in neoclassical or activity analysis models of the firm. The references are scanty and more often they are totally absent. The theoretical firm is entrepreneurless—the Prince of Denmark has been expunged from the discussion of Hamlet. (Baumol, 1968, p. 66)

The role of entrepreneurs within economic theory is important, but this intellectual struggle must be left to the economic theorist. For our purposes as educators we must proceed to explore the characteristics entrepreneurs possess that can be taught, enhanced, or developed in the educational environment.

Mark Casson in his book *The Entrepreneurs: An Economic Theory,* says that the theory of entrepreneurship rests upon the following definition: "An entrepreneur is someone who specializes in making judgmental decisions about the coordination of scarce resources" (Casson, 1982, p. 23). Baumol describes the entrepreneur as one whose job is "to locate new ideas and put them into effect . . . [H]e cannot allow things to get into a rut and for him today's practice is never good enough for tomorrow" (Baumol, 1968, p. 65). Entrepreneurship is considered as an ongoing function in which opportunities exist for the gathering and coordination of resources. Opportunities will exist as long as new information is becoming available that could alter the efficient allocation of resources. New information may be either totally new knowledge such as scientific breakthroughs or the updating of knowledge in the light of a recent event (Casson, 1982).

Casson has developed a list of "qualities" that one must possess in order to fulfill the functional definition of an entrepreneur. These are

- self-knowledge
- imagination
- practical knowledge
- analytical ability

- search skill
- foresight
- computational skill
- communication skill
- organizational skill (Casson, 1982)

These attributes correspond to Casson's view that entrepreneurship is closely related to decision making. The above qualities, when possessed by an individual, facilitate the processing of new information and the necessary translation of such into economic outcomes beneficial to the entrepreneur through profits and the attainment of other personal objectives.

All the entrepreneurial qualities listed are to some extent innate, yet there are those that seem to lend themselves to enhancement through education, training, and practical experience. For instance, analytical and computational skills can be taught, while practical knowledge and search skills, as well as delegation and organizational skills, can be gained by experience. In addition, imagination and foresight are two indispensable qualities of the entrepreneur; imagination is almost entirely innate, while foresight, although innate, can to some extent be enhanced by experience.

It is difficult to screen for the qualities of an entrepreneur in the population. How are educators to recognize entrepreneurial potential in time to enhance the requisite talents or characteristics? Entrepreneurs are frequently identified only by their actions; that is, entrepreneurs self-identify themselves through their entrepreneurial behavior. This leaves educators in a dilemma. If we cannot identify the entrepreneur early, then by what means do we attempt to insure that the entrepreneurs that do exist will emerge in the future to fulfill their economic role? How important is education to the development of the entrepreneur?

Clearly, some entrepreneurial qualities can be enhanced through formal education. The entrepreneur is probably more of a generalist than a specialist. Therefore, general training may be more beneficial than advanced training. Higher education, particularly graduate education, imposes a trade-off between time in the classroom and business experience, the other important element in the enhancement of entrepreneurial skills (Casson, 1982). The rigidities of formal education may inculcate uniform attitudes among potential entrepreneurs and thus destroy their individuality and diversity. As Casson observes, there is a tendency in formal education to raise only the questions for which there are precise answers, while entrepreneurs characteristically are concerned with situations for which there are no precedents (Casson, 1982).

Another segment of the literature on entrepreneurship focuses on cataloging the attributes of successful entrepreneurs. Research studies on the personal characteristics of entrepreneurs seem to indicate a relative consensus (Welsh and White, 1981). These attributes include risk taking, imagination, self-confidence, desire to control one's economic destiny, willingness to work long and hard, and the ability to cope with failure as well as manage success. Research has also shown that the confidence to start a business is often developed in situations where there are role models within the family and among peers. Previous work experience in the marketplace often helps determine for an entrepreneur the type or types of business to form and the products and services to produce. These experiences, together with education, help prepare an entrepreneur to take on the great number of tasks involved in establishing and operating a new business (Cooper, 1983).

Progress in entrepreneurial research over the last ten years has provided a useful profile of entrepreneurs, describing both their personal characteristics and their functions and roles within society. The challenge to educators is to use this knowledge effectively to design and implement entrepreneurship programs.

APPROACHES TO TEACHING ENTREPRENEURSHIP

The first premise of this chapter is that any society would benefit from the enhancement of entrepreneurial talent, since it impacts positively on economic growth and well-being. The second premise is that educational programs can directly affect the extent to which entrepreneurial talent is developed within the population. Therefore, it is important to determine the content as well as how and when to teach entrepreneurship within our academic and nonacademic programs. One approach to teaching entrepreneurship would be to focus on entrepreneurs in a historical context and describe the development of the world's economies.

Economic growth is highly correlated with increases in productivity resulting from technical change. Many economists have attempted to break down overall growth into its causal components; particularly, growth in labor and capital inputs and any change in their quality. However, regardless of which empirical study one reads, each has a large percentage of growth that cannot be attributed to increase in capital and labor. This residual is frequently labeled *technical change*. The significance of this residual can be better appreciated when it is pointed out that some studies show the percentage of growth associated with technical change to be as high as 87.5 percent (Baumol, 1968). Whatever the numerical value of the residual, one might conclude that entrepreneurship is one part, although the exact proportion is not known (Baumol, 1968). In fact, some would argue that humankind's technical progress relies heavily on the individual entrepreneur/inventor/adaptor/innovator rather than the large research and development efforts of corporations or institutions. The latter seem to make only marginal changes, while the former is most often the source of dramatic shifts in technology, sometimes resulting in the rise of new industries (Brenner, 1987).

If as educators we can accept these conclusions, economics cannot be fully understood without comprehending the role of the entrepreneur in economic history. History and economics courses in K–12 classrooms as well as university undergraduate and graduate education seem the appropriate context within which entrepreneurship can be taught. One approach is by examining the role of individual entrepreneurs within a number of different economies over historical time periods. Wyatt, Cartright, Ford, Edison, Whitney, Land, and Jobs all played critical roles in economic and technical progress, and a look at their contributions can help explain the nature of the dynamics not only of economics, but of society as well.

There is a second reason to teach entrepreneurship in a historical context. If entrepreneurs are prime promoters of change, economic policies at the national, state, and local levels should be designed to stimulate entrepreneurial behavior as well as derive the largest possible benefits for society from entrepreneurs fulfilling their role. Since economic policies are influenced by the voters, the greater the extent to which voters understand the importance of the entrepreneur, the greater the political base for policies that encourage rather than thwart their activities. Current economic policies reflect, in part, the failure of economists to incorporate the role of entrepreneurship in their models. Thus, we presently formulate economic policy by focusing on a variety of fiscal and monetary instruments, while changes in tax incentives or property rights may well be a better approach to economic objectives such as employment growth than, for instance, lowering the interest rate by 1 percent or increasing the federal deficit by another twenty-five billion dollars. The public should be enabled to take sides in the debate over whether to abolish the Small Business Administration or reduce the federal budget on research and development.

A second approach to teaching entrepreneurship is predicated on the assumption that educators can enhance or even develop the traits associated with entrepreneurship and then teach the skills necessary to perform those entrepreneurial functions within the economic processes extant in the society. While the first approach teaches the importance and context of entrepreneurship and may be infused with social studies, business history, or economics courses, the second approach is a long-term, broad-based process designed to develop or enhance individual entrepreneurial attributes and provide knowledge regarding business survival skills. This approach dictates that the educational programs be spiral in nature: They must start in the early grades and continue through collegiate courses; then, they should go on to special seminars and programs in continuing education.

In the discussion above, the entrepreneur has been described as an innovator, risk taker, and insightful decision maker. Birth provides the innate qualities of the individual, but their development is achieved through education and life's experiences. The individual's intelligence and imagination may be given, but the likelihood of their being used is influenced by the environment.

Effectively designed programs to develop entrepreneurship would increase the number of entrepreneurs who become active players in the economic environment. One might call these individuals *realized* as opposed to *potential* entrepreneurs. All the identified attributes of entrepreneurs can be positively affected in some manner by education. The question is not "whether" but "how?"

First, we must assume that we as educators cannot screen for entrepreneurial talent with sufficient degrees of accuracy to separate these individuals from the population in general. Thus, for the immediate future, programs should be general enough to encompass the greatest possible proportion of American youth. Second, we would argue that entrepreneurship is an important and integral part of economics. Thus, entrepreneurial education is a subset of economics education. Third, the development of entrepreneurial talent should not be limited only to economics courses, classrooms, and professional teachers, and, fourth, the enhancement of entrepreneurial talent can be achieved through a multitude of methods and materials in a variety of settings and among all ages.

Entrepreneurial education or training should focus on developing innovation, risk taking, imagination, and problem solving; in other words, the decision-making skills. These skills can best be developed through active programs. Students should be presented with open-ended situations that require them to work through problems and situations with changing conditions. Through the process, students will develop the skills of adapting to new information and making decisions with imperfect knowledge.

A great danger of "formal" education, even entrepreneurial education, is that it fosters doing the correct thing: getting *the* right answer. Education needs to teach critical thinking, seeking solutions to problems not previously encountered. Scientific and technical progress depends on individuals who can see relationships not previously seen, or use new, as well as old, information to make discoveries. Other situations should be designed to promote risk taking. Students should be confronted with the reality of trading off risks and rewards. Success should be positively reinforced, while failure should be presented as a temporary condition from which to learn in order to achieve future successes. Internship and mentor programs should provide models for students. These experiences should reinforce classroom instruction and activities.

Another entrepreneurial characteristic that can be developed within the general curriculum is self-reliance, the ability not only to face new situations but also to survive in a competitive environment. Although focusing on the individual is important, people must learn to cooperate because entrepreneurs, although individualistic, must foster teamwork if their businesses are to be profitable.

Entrepreneurial programming should be incorporated into the K–12 curriculum. Programs like Kinder-Economy and Mini-Society are valuable early programs. Supplements to the general economic education instruction should be case studies, which present role models for the children while, at the same time, identify and reinforce economic concepts and business skills. Activities associated with the cases should require the use of problem-solving skills, and students should be confronted with open-ended situations. Printed cases and video films on entrepreneurs can be used almost interchangeably, although both should be accompanied by instructional materials. Students should have exposure to forming and operating a business under conditions of risk. The early years are important in beginning to inculcate the business management skills that reflect analytical abilities and computational, communication, and organizational skills. Forming a business is only the first entrepreneurial act; getting it to survive is the prime objective of an entrepreneur. Business failures generally reflect the decisions and judgment of people. Thus, management skills are necessary for a successful business, whether they are possessed by the entrepreneur or someone he or she hires.

Entrepreneurial training has a natural home within economics courses in most curricula. The students of the 1980s should have the opportunities to do a number of different computer-oriented activities. Perhaps the most relevant are business simulations that incorporate increasing sophistication with respect to organization and decision-making variables and scenarios. The Stock Market Game has proven popular among high school students, and the risk-taking aspects should be emphasized.

Students should write case studies based on local entrepreneurs. The research should be done by the students, and each case analyzed by them in order to identify the factors contributing to the success of the entrepreneur. Some unsuccessful entrepreneurs should be studied as well, since more new businesses fail than succeed, and determining the reasons for failure might help others avoid the same pitfalls.

Some programs should be focused on special groups such as minority or female students. Minorities, particularly blacks, are underrepresented among the ranks of successful entrepreneurs. Special programming should attempt to overcome obstacles blacks encounter, such as the lack of role models, low self-esteem, and the frustration of failure. Finally, skills that are necessary for entrepreneurial success should be taught in the K–12 programs since higher education is less available to minorities than the rest of the population.

This comprehensive approach to entrepreneurship education may seem overwhelming to educators because it spans many grade levels and disciplines. With planning and coordination, it is feasible. However, there are other alternatives that would be variations on the programs discussed above; for instance, infusing entrepreneurship into existing economics courses at the secondary level or designing new courses pertaining exclusively to entrepreneurship. Each educational organization will have to consider the alternatives, subject to its particular constraints. Hopefully, entrepreneurship education will be considered and implemented at all educational levels.

CONCLUSION

The entrepreneur is an individual who deals with uncertainty and generates innovation. He or she has acquired, through birth, education, and/or experience, the decision-making skills to take advantage of his or her unique insight into new information generated in the system. The entrepreneur possesses a willingness to assume risk and work hard, and has the confidence in his or her abilities to venture down new paths. The family and environment play an important role in forming the attitudes of the entrepreneur. Role models are important. The entrepreneur emerges from the interplay of genetic transferral, environmental influences, individual learning, and life's experiences to become a force for change through entrepreneurship.

In this chapter two approaches are proposed that are not mutually exclusive. The first approach attempts to develop for the population a broader knowledge of and appreciation for the entrepreneur's role in economic progress. One consequence of this broader understanding may be more effective public policies to stimulate entrepreneurial activities. The second approach is more comprehensive and certainly more ambitious. This approach attempts to increase the pool and successful application of entrepreneurial talent within the economy. It begins with the young student and continues through formal education to specialized programs and counseling for mature adults. Enhancing the instruction in entrepreneurial education is an important challenge for economics educators. As a group, we have much experience in designing curriculums, developing materials, training teachers, and measuring the effectiveness of all these activities. Now we need to turn our attention to infusing entrepreneurial education and training into our schools and colleges.

There are already some good materials available. We should become familiar with them while we design and produce new programs. We should investigate the entrepreneurial content of economics textbooks at the secondary and collegiate levels. We should encourage and support further research on the entrepreneur and the entrepreneurial functions, assessing what works and what fails. Although we should proceed with deliberate speed, we should not be hasty. For educators, broadening and deepening the entrepreneurial component of our programs should be based on an understanding of the role of entrepreneurship in economics and on good pedagogy in education.

REFERENCES

Baumol, William J. 1968. "Entrepreneurship on Economic Theory." *American Economic Review* 58, no. 2 (May): 64–71.

Brenner, Reuven. 1987. *Rivalry: In Business, Science, Among Nations.* New York: Cambridge University Press, Chapter 5, pp. 97–123.

Casson, Mark. 1982. *The Entrepreneurs: An Economic Theory.* Totowa, N. J.: Barnes and Noble, pp. 23, 25, 36, 357.

Cooper, Arnold C. 1983. "Entrepreneurship: Starting a New Business." Pamphlet. National Federation of Independent Business, p. 7.

Hebert, Robert F., and Albert N. Link. 1982. *The Entrepreneur: Mainstream Views and Radical Critiques.* New York: Praeger, pp. 107–108, 110.

Welsh, John A., and Jerry F. White. 1981. "Converging on the Characteristics of Entrepreneurs." In *Frontiers of Entrepreneurship Research,* edited by K. H. Vesper. Wellesley, Mass.: Babson College, Center for Entrepreneurial Studies, pp. 504–515.

Williams, Edward. (1981). "Innovation, Entrepreneurship and Brain Functioning:" In *Frontiers of Entrepreneurship Research,* edited by K. H. Vesper. Wellesley, Mass.: Babson College, Center for Entrepreneurial Studies, pp. 516–536.

3

Thinking About Entrepreneurs: Models, Assumptions, and Evidence

Gerald Gunderson

The 1980s heightened Americans' appreciation of the function that entrepreneurs perform in society. Entrepreneurs are credited with creating jobs, introducing valuable new products, and keeping the economy competitive in world markets. Numerous articles, books, and television programs have portrayed successful entrepreneurs, in no small part because many individuals would like to replicate the qualities responsible for their success.

APPROACHES TO EXPLAINING ENTREPRENEURSHIP

While the concerns of the general public dominated media coverage of entrepreneurship in the 1980s, scholars actually stepped up their investigations into its fundamental nature. Much of their effort was directed within three explanatory approaches. The first was to explain entrepreneurs by reference to personal traits that produced success. Personal characteristics, such as initiative or analytic skills, however, have yet to prove of much value in predicting achievement. Besides being difficult to measure, these characteristics are reshaped by entrepreneurs as part of their striving to become successful.

The second category, called event studies, focuses on environmental forces. Rather than emphasizing personal, self-starting qualities—the "entrepreneurs are born" approach—this framework assumes that they are shaped by forces beyond their control. The loss of a job or the encouragement of acquaintances' successes in starting their own enterprises are believed to be critical in compelling entrepreneurs to get underway.

The third approach, the venture school, understood the shortcoming of the static, cross-section method that the first two approaches employed. It recognized that entrepreneurial efforts typically are an ongoing process. Discoveries in the course of such efforts require major realignments in the initial premises on the enterprise itself. These three approaches are detailed in Robert C. Ronstadt's *Entrepreneurship: Text, Cases and Notes* (1984), which provides an encyclopedic survey of recent work on entrepreneurship.

Our understanding of entrepreneurs has also been advanced by some less classifiable, but very insightful, work. Mark Casson's *The Entrepreneur* (1982) developed the economic basis for entrepreneurs; Peter Drucker's *Innovation and Entrepreneurship* (1985) spelled out the practice of entrepreneurship in detail; Paul Hawkin's *Growing a Business* (1987) offered insightful comments on patterns in successful businesses; and Howard H. Stevenson, Michael J. Roberts, and H. Irving Grousbeck's *New Business Ventures and the Entrepreneur* (1989) analyzed entrepreneurial tactics. Despite substantial, thoughtful effort, however, we are not yet able to specify the basic properties of entrepreneurship to a degree that they can explain the success of particular entrepreneurs. While some rules of thumb appear to be generally applicable, models that enhance our understanding in ways such as predicting components of the activity do not yet exist. It will require a better understanding of basic forces before we can offer aspiring entrepreneurs much specific advice.

THE SCHUMPETERIAL APPROACH

I recently verified this lack of operational guidance in the process of writing *The Wealth Creators: An Entrepreneurial History of the United States* (1989). The work examined more than forty entrepreneurs over almost four centuries, an unusually large and diverse sample for such a study. While the viewpoints of Casson, Drucker, Hawkins, and Stevenson et al. were most helpful, no source provides a comprehensive approach yet. I also discovered that most individuals other than scholars who are actively pursuing the topic use another, more traditional approach, which has also been employed by most people who have written biographies of entrepreneurs and general historical accounts. I have dubbed it *Schumpeterial* because even though Joseph Schumpeter would have dissented with some of its tenets, its general approach and spirit follow his path-breaking work. His ideas, capped by the publication of his landmark book *Capitalism, Socialism, and Democracy* (1942), bolstered the general appreciation of entrepreneurs. No doubt it was valuable elevating public awareness of their social function toward a level more appropriate to the entrepreneurs' sizeable contribution, but in the process Schumpeter also articulated a particular model of how he supposed entrepreneurs perform their function. His description comprises much of the common explanation, which has proven remarkably durable because it captured the way most people instinctively expect entrepreneurs to behave. The explanatory framework is so deeply embedded that even scholars who have studied individual entrepreneurs in detail—thereby often encountering examples that contradict the Schumpeterial approach—tend to pigeonhole them into that preconceived framework.

The central premises of the Schumpeterian model are that entrepreneurs assume an exceptionally large level of risk, assemble large amounts of capital, and implement innovations powerful enough to restructure major industries. When successful, the enterprises become very powerful by destroying competing industries and remaking large sections of the social milieu. On the other hand, such efforts will leverage shortcomings into spectacular failures. Accordingly, entrepreneurs are expected to take on roles larger than life, becoming heroic leaders who are bound to attract widespread attention.

The attractiveness of the Schumpeterian model appears to derive from the appeal of its logical underpinnings. Its conclusions follow directly from the assumptions people naturally make about the way innovation is achieved. For example, both riskiness and "creative destruction" result from assuming that innovation occurs in steps that are so large—breakthroughs, really— that they immediately dictate entire new industries and make existing ones obsolete. Such a change demands that an entrepreneur be fearless, implementing an opportunity quickly before others can seize it. A corollary of this is that once an opportunity has been discovered, it becomes widely appropriable; there are no proprietary barriers to profitable ideas. Thus, the critical skill for success is the dispatch and daring to exploit an opportunity before others can preempt it.

Models such as the Schumpeterian view of entrepreneurship are important—indeed, they are necessary for most individuals to make sense of their world. However, the function of guiding simplification that a model performs also slants the way in which we interpret situations. Consider the way it preconditions the portrayal of history from which we draw so much implicit guidance and so many justifications for contemporary policies. History is not simply a listing of events and conditions, but rather is the order that the chronicler imposes upon them. Most history has been assembled by scholars adhering to the Schumpeterian model.

The choice of models can be critical because each implies different distributions of social rewards. For example, innovations that develop suddenly appear to result more from the luck of time and place than from the developer's effort. The entrepreneur in the Schumpeterian model, therefore, seems to be receiving a reward that could well have gone to others.

Moreover, the apparent arbitrariness of the return to innovation suggests it may not be socially necessary. The reward plays little social function other than a windfall for recipients. Finally, the sudden destruction of competitors seems a heavy price to pay. Seemingly productive enterprises and livelihoods are lost, again through a process that seems arbitrary and without compelling benefits.

A vivid example of the impact this interpretation can make appears in portrayals of late-nineteenth-century American history, the period in which the role of entrepreneurs is given most emphasis. The standard treatment of entrepreneurs in that period is the Schumpeterian model, which is evident in the characterization of prominent entrepreneurs as "robber barons." Entrepreneurs have been depicted as acquiring power arbitrarily and exercising it in a capricious, destructive manner against hapless competitors. While the combination of qualities of innovation we have termed Schumpeterian lead logically to such results, Schumpeter would have disagreed that these are the actual results. Individuals such as John D. Rockefeller and J. P. Morgan have received considerable derision relative to the recognition accorded their positive roles. Some entrepreneurs, such as Jay Gould, have been almost universally lambasted as an influence America would have been much better without. For example, consider the treatment by the best-known college American history textbook. Gould is cited as a "notorious New York stock gambler and is accused of "looting the Erie Railroad by stock watering." He, John D. Rockefeller, and other national entrepreneurs are characterized by "a riot of individual naturalism . . . for the strong to wrong the weak" (Morison, 1965, pp. 729, 732, 764).

PROBLEMS WITH THE SCHUMPETERIAN MODEL

Despite the intrinsic appeal of the Schumpeterian model, there is now a predominance of evidence indicating that it misleads in critical dimensions. First, the number of practicing entrepreneurs is much larger than a model depicting them in heroic roles would predict. Also, they operate throughout all sectors of the economy rather than being confined to high tech or growth sectors where changes seem most dramatic. Furthermore, most of their efforts appear to be incremental rather than large, dramatic contributions.

Components of the typical process of innovation such as those mentioned above contradict the Schumpeterian view. It is truly exceptional for a new sector to be created ready-made in a form of "Eureka" discovery. Major innovations require decades to reach fruition. Not only is the enabling technology likely to be much more complex than outsiders presume, but the interactions with consumers and suppliers multiply the complexity, necessitating numerous iterations to fine-tune institutions to deliver services appropriately. No wonder it has always required a minimum of fifty years to complete the development of any major growth industry.

This extended development explains qualities that experienced entrepreneurs stress to be central but that are puzzling in the Schumpeterian context. Practitioners almost universally express the necessity for persistence. Other variations on this theme include the following: problems are seldom solved as much as whittled down, failure is not so much defeat as an opportunity for suggestions of beneficial changes, every problem is an opportunity in disguise, and so on. Rather than Schumpeterian breakthroughs, this is the language of patient, sustained effort.

The persistence required to develop entrepreneurial knowledge suggests another important dimension whereby the Schumpeterian approach goes astray. Because the relevant information is developed gradually, it is difficult for nonpractitioners to copy it without themselves going through a comparable, drawn-out process of discovery. Innovations are less appropriable than is generally assumed. Scholars have recently reinforced this conclusion in several ways. Both Paul Hawkin, and Thomas Peters and Robert Waterman in their bestselling book *In Search of Excellence* recognize that entrepreneurs often have a deep, personal identification with their product (Peters and Waterman, 1982). This helps them recognize desirable qualities in the product that are difficult to articulate and convey to others. In effect, the entrepreneur's personal taste for appealing product characteristics is a very efficient alternative to eliciting the subtle, complex information as to precisely what succeeds in the marketplace. Ben and Jerry's passionate feelings about ice cream, for example, have proved a much better guide to how customers will react to a new offering than extensive reports by chemists on texture, acridity, and fat content. (This Vermont manufacturer of premium ice cream takes its name from its founders, Ben Cohen and Jerry Greenfield. The company is often used in business schools as a model to explore participatory management.) Of course, this heavy reliance on experiential, intuitive judgment about a product or service makes duplication by competitors all the more difficult.

Entrepreneurs commonly employ several other tactics that promote learning about their particular product or service. One is to specialize in a particular product or type of technology. In contradiction to a widely held presumption, entrepreneurs are not promoters who move among disparate projects where little of the learning in one can be transferred to the next. Rather, they stay with an approach long enough to implement a good share of possible incremental learning. Even when one venture fails, they often try a related effort employing the same technology. Robert Ronstadt has labeled this the *corridor principle*. It recognizes that the tactic of learning from mistakes within a venture can be generalized to learning among ventures.

Such tactics for acquiring information about entrepreneurial opportunities makes appropriation by nonparticipants more difficult. Outsiders can duplicate the process only through the extended effort of "paying their dues." In other words, critical parts of the necessary knowledge become useful only when they are embodied in specific organizations and locations. This accords with much of what is now commonly understood about the economics of information: Each location, organization, and time often alters the applicable information. To apply modern parlance associated with another issue, much of the information used by entrepreneurs is *insider information*.

TOWARD A BETTER EXPLANATION

The thrust of the above discussion suggests an alternative framework with better explanatory promise. Not only is it consistent with the patterns cited above, but it also incorporates other generalizations about entrepreneurs that previously were explained ad hoc.

Entrepreneurship seems best described as the practice of innovation. This should be understood to extend well beyond the development of engineering or technical knowledge to include institutional and social arrangements, and to also take advantage of the skills and preferences of individuals. While this definition agrees with the ultimate result employed by the Schumpeterians, it builds upon very different—and evidently improved—premises about innovation.

The innovative nature of entrepreneurship distinguishes it from the functions of becoming proficient in established bodies of knowledge. The latter must be acquired in a relatively short time. The former, by its very nature, must build in an incremental fashion, shaping each trial by insights gleaned from previous efforts. This also establishes the division between entrepreneurship and management, as the latter is commonly defined. Management is in no sense a mechanical function, but it is generally considered the activity of making the most of a given, static environment. Entrepreneurship is improving the environment within which management operates. Most businesses necessarily pursue both functions, although of course in differing proportions.

The distinction between innovation and learning suggests why we observe firms maintaining a competitive advantage over rivals for decades. Such an edge is unlikely to rest on keeping an important piece of information secret indefinitely. Rather, leading firms produce a stream of improvements that competitors may follow with equivalents but find difficult to transcend. Thus, the ultimate task for competitors is not to develop or duplicate particular inventions, but to foster an environment that permits a continuing flow of competitive innovations.

ENTREPRENEURSHIP DEFINED

We are now ready to offer a more detailed definition of entrepreneurship:

Entrepreneurship is drawing from a wide range of skills capable of enhancement to add value to a targeted niche of human activity. The effort expended in finding and implementing such opportunities is rewarded by income and independence as well as pride in creation.

It is worthwhile to examine these specifications further. For example, begin with "a wide range of skills." Entrepreneurs are often characterized as "doers" rather than "thinkers." Certainly, entrepreneurs have a bias for initiating action compared to much of the general population, but they also devote enormous effort to working out the logic of their endeavors. This mixture is to be expected because that research—even well outside scientific areas—that works out the basic linkages of an activity greatly reduces the labor-intensive trials necessary to identify and implement a process. Entrepreneurs instinctively order their efforts according to these implications, but casual observers are likely to characterize the entrepreneur's tactics by observing the final, public stages of introducing the product instead.

In their understandable focus on final results, the average person is also likely to conclude that "entrepreneurs are born, not made." Of course, this overlooks the sustained effort necessary to reach a rewarding level of mastery. As one old saying put it, "It only takes twenty years of hard work to become an overnight success." In addition to uncovering the specific information necessary to create a new product, entrepreneurs also require skills tied to the activity. Peter Drucker captured this quality in his statement that entrepreneurship is a practice, and not just a body of knowledge. Like doctors and lawyers, entrepreneurs benefit only to the degree that they can apply their insights. Thus, whatever his or her innate abilities, much of the success of an entrepreneur depends on the effort he or she puts into developing the skills.

It seems fair to conclude that successful entrepreneurs not only increase new areas of applied knowledge, they also recreate themselves. Acquiring new personal skills and vantages proves to be a central component of their mission. Many undertake this task in an ad hoc, incremental fashion, developing specific abilities as evolving conditions dictate. On the other hand, some clearly pursue a deliberate strategy. Andrew Carnegie, for example, followed a textbook-perfect model of career planning. His first positions developed a solid reputation of dependability which he used, in turn, to acquire skills in communications, accounting, management, marketing, and financial markets. He also accumulated his own capital and cultivated contacts for additional quantities. Thus, when opportunities for large operations in steel began to coalesce about 1870, he was the best prepared. Of course, he continued to develop his skills, particularly those of higher-order management and leadership, as his steel operations expanded.

As the example of Carnegie suggests, entrepreneurs also can benefit from a wide array of skills. Entrepreneurs employ analytical as well as intuitive skills. They can use both technical and managerial abilities. Moreover, they can vary greatly in personality, ranging from the exuberant extroversion of Samuel Colt to the studied introspection of Jay Gould. What is also evident is that entrepreneurs can shape their management teams and operating styles to complement their strengths and compensate for their shortcomings. This helps explain why the pool of potential entrepreneurs is so much larger than commonly pictured.

ENTREPRENEURIAL LEARNING

Because the prime function of entrepreneurs is eliciting and implementing knowledge, we would expect that their major activities would be shaped to encourage that end. Research requires a willingness to be surprised, or, as Paul Hawkin reports of successful entrepreneurs, they do not presume to know. They must be very open to potential solutions because a goodly portion of leads are suggested through seemingly remote, unrelated uses. Scholars of entrepreneurship have begun identifying this important quality as being *veridical,* by which they mean that entrepreneurs reexamine the logic of relations that most people ignore because they assume that things could not be any other way. It seems likely that future study will identify this open-minded, idiosyncratic inquisitiveness as a central property of entrepreneurs.

While entrepreneurs must be inquisitive, they must also somehow focus their energy on feasible pursuits. The paradox of the dispersed nature of information is that while useful combinations are often pieced together from disparate sources, the vast majority of information is irrelevant—indeed, it is a hindrance for any given entrepreneurial effort. Entrepreneurs almost invariably control this dichotomy by developing a clear vision of the precise service they are attempting to create. The goal allows them to cut through the clutter of life's impressions, extracting the promising ones while discarding the vast, irrelevant majority. Lillian Vernon Katz of Mt. Vernon, New York, who has been so successful in catalogue sales for mid-priced household and gift items, illustrates that trait superbly. She scans large numbers of publications, seeking products that her well-honed instincts tell her will appeal to her clientele. Her excellent track record in such choices exemplifies the entrepreneurs' advantage. A focused, and indeed passionate, vision to interpret impressions can be very productive, alerting entrepreneurs to suggestive observations from much more disparate sources than typical individuals would notice. At the same time, carefully formulated goals allow entrepreneurs to apply their innovative energy to the most promising sources.

Successful growing ventures add another dimension to entrepreneurial learning. They expand beyond the founder's hands-on control, compelling him or her to learn to transmit influence indirectly through the structure of the organization. The difficulty of shifting to this mode is indicated by its status as one of the largest sources in entrepreneurial failure. It requires conscious restraint to allow others to attempt, with the concomitant share of failure, what one can do faster oneself. It is also more difficult to articulate and encourage abstract goals such as building an innovative organization rather than personally attacking concrete problems. However, there is an underlying continuity between the two roles. Both are aimed toward stimulating product-directed research, in earlier stages by the entrepreneur alone, and then later only through influence in nudging the entire organization in that direction.

As the organization expands, the founding entrepreneur moves toward becoming a full-time manager. There has been a long-standing quandary as to the proper manner for distinguishing between the two functions. Recently, scholars have sought to further distinguish between management, which in this context has been defined as supervising a static or non-learning organization, and leadership. Authorities such as Warren Bennis (Bennis and Namus, 1985) consider the latter to consist of the guidance a manager provides his organization in learning to serve new demands. In other words, leadership is really the practice of innovation within a large institution. If that link had been recognized earlier, the separate study of leadership might not have developed, but might rather have developed as part of—and might have sped up—studies in entrepreneurship.

RISKS AND REWARDS OF ENTREPRENEURSHIP

Note that our definition of entrepreneurs says nothing about risk. Probably the assumption most widely held by the general public is that entrepreneurial success necessarily requires assuming exceptional amounts of risk. This is frequently a surprise to practicing entrepreneurs because their standard operating procedure is to attack problems, which is to say, to make things work by learning how to control them. At least in their own domains entrepreneurs actually reduce risks. The proverb that applies in this case is: "The person who shapes the future is less likely to be surprised by it."

Casual observers probably misjudge this orientation for several reasons. First, as previously discussed, they see major innovations as single, once-and-for-all endeavors. If that were correct, a project would be very risky, indeed, most likely prohibitively so, as the number of permutations of elements likely to misfire became immense. However, solving problems sequentially allows the entrepreneur to sell a product and pay its costs even while using the market as a laboratory to improve it.

The second reason is the difference in the access to information between an entrepreneur and a casual observer. While the latter can only see the task in its global enormity, the entrepreneur knows much more about possible avenues of improvement. The general populace would not recognize many of the latter, let alone the detailed information about each that entrepreneurs collect in the process of grappling with them. Thus, what entrepreneurs see as solvable tasks appear overwhelmingly intimidating to outsiders. The difference, again, is explained by the specificity of information—to the participating entrepreneur, but not to virtually everyone else.

One quality that may well prove to be good for distinguishing entrepreneurs from other individuals is that the former initiate action. Many people are uncomfortable with change, fearing both the process and the results. Entrepreneurs, however, seem to thrive on the prospects of change, even recognizing that a large fraction of trials will prove to misfire. Risk and the discomfort of the unknown appear to be often intertwined in many observers' minds. Thus, the unpleasant role of risk bearer attributed to entrepreneurs may reflect much of the public's dislike of initiating action.

Another widespread presumption that the definition does not acknowledge is that a critical skill for entrepreneurs is raising capital. This probably grows out of the assumption that innovations must be implemented rapidly in large doses in order to both implement economies of scale and head off the competition. Hence, raising capital from external sources would be a critical skill. If, however, as our foregoing discussion suggests, innovation is more gradual, retained earnings and an established record of growing assets make financing much easier. Moreover, entrepreneurial firms usually make above-average returns on their invested capital, which gives them all the more leverage in financing expansion. John D. Rockefeller often told how "he wore out the knees of his trousers begging bankers for loans" in his early years in refining, but for most of his career investors lined up waiting to get a chance at Standard Oil's profits.

Paul Hawkin has recently taken this line of reasoning further, arguing that too much capital—rather than too little—is the greater danger to entrepreneurs. Capital can serve as a crutch by paying for more inputs instead of completing the harder task of squeezing more from the inputs already in hand. Being on a short leash of capital focuses the entrepreneur's attention on the central task of creating knowledge.

The last sentence of the expanded definition of entrepreneurship explores the rewards that drive the activity. While the popular view associates entrepreneurs with making money—particularly very large amounts made by certain well-publicized examples such as Donald Trump—surveys of successful practitioners consistently rank the opportunities for creativity and independence above income. Reported anonymously, the responses are unlikely to be slanted for public consumption. Besides, they track closely with entrepreneurs' behavior. The predominance of new businesses—at least 80 percent—are life-style choices in that in all likelihood the income will be less than what a comparable effort working for someone else would return. Thus, these entrepreneurs are, in effect, buying independence and the opportunity to shape their own ventures.

It is not unreasonable to argue that the small retail and service enterprises that make up most of the life-style businesses are not really entrepreneurial anyway. They establish a business in a new location, but most of its practices duplicate those proven elsewhere. Clearly, however, the remaining minority of entrepreneurs qualify in that they fashion new products and technologies and the institutions to mobilize them. Because they add more value, these enterprises grow much larger and reward their initiators accordingly. Earlier such entrepreneurs obviously spent a great deal in their personal consumption, such as the tangible artifacts of large mansions which later become public museums. However, a much larger portion of their wealth went toward promoting their personal interests, which were quite diverse and often required an entrepreneurial component to implement. John D. Rockefeller pioneered historic and scenic preservation. William Gillette promoted utopian and socialist communities. Andrew Carnegie and Henry Ford tried to promote world peace by financing peace ships—which were failures. The point is that when the entrepreneurs created degrees of freedom—the opportunities to do things because of their success in earlier ventures—they chose to pursue additional creative projects. This does not disprove the theory that entrepreneurs might be primarily driven by money or even something else like personal power because more income enables more of other opportunities. However, the general pattern of behavior suggests entrepreneurs are most interested in creation, which, after all, is the defining product of the activity they have elected to pursue.

THE INNOVATIVE MODEL OF ENTREPRENEURSHIP

In contrast to the Schumpeterian model, our innovative approach implies a markedly different interpretation of historical events. The long gestation of innovations makes them much less a chance occurrence as well as insuring that the rewards to entrepreneurs are appropriate for their efforts and creative contributions. The rewards also play an important social role of enlisting the dedication necessary to develop the contributions. Finally, competitors have considerable time to adjust to the new innovations; if they choose not to do so, their demise is justified by an obvious neglect of consumer interests.

Careful examinations of the lives of the individual entrepreneurs cited above also leads to a much more positive assessment, one more in line with the innovation model. Allan Nevins's *Study in Power: John D. Rock-efeller, Industrialist and Philanthropist* (1953) and Vincent Carusso's *The Morgans: Private International Bankers, 1854–1913* (1987) depict extended contributions. Of particular import is Maury Klein's *The Life and Legend of Jay Gould* (1986) which not only demonstrated a lifetime of productive creativity, but also showed how a systematic distortion of Gould's record by the press began even while he was comparatively young. When Gould died in 1892, the press turned on Rockefeller as the stereotypical villain of the day. This suggests how deeply felt are the instincts underlying the Schumpeterian model. At the turn of the century they were so compelling that they swamped substantial, contradictory evidence of positive contributions. Obviously, the prevailing Schumpeterian model is attractive but the stakes in developing a better explanation of economic behavior make a commensurate effort at revision worthwhile.

NOTE

This chapter has benefitted from suggestions of John Baden, Tom DiLorenzo, Paul Heyne, Robert Higgs, P. J. Hill, Calvin A. Kent, Dwight Lee, and Roger Meiners.

REFERENCES

Bennis, Warren, and Burt Namus. 1985. *Leaders: The Strategies for Taking Charge.* New York: Harper and Row.

Carusso, Vincent. 1987. *The Morgans: Private International Bankers, 1854–1913.* Cambridge, Mass.: Harvard University Press.

Casson, Mark. 1982. *The Entrepreneur.* Totowa, N. J.: Barnes and Noble.

Drucker, Peter. 1985. *Innovation and Entrepreneurship.* New York: Harper and Row.

Gunderson, Gerald. 1989. *The Wealth Creators: An Entrepreneurial History of the United States.* New York: Truman Talley Books, E. P. Dutton.

Hawkin, Paul. 1987. *Growing a Business.* New York: Simon and Schuster.

Klein, Maury. 1986. *The Life and Legend of Jay Gould.* Baltimore, Md.: Johns Hopkins University Press.

Morison, Samuel E. 1965. *The Oxford History of the American People.* New York: Oxford University Press.

Nevins, Allen. 1953. *Study in Power: John D. Rockefeller, Industrialist and Philanthropist.* New York: Scribner.

Peters, Thomas, and Robert Waterman. 1982. *In Search of Excellence; Lessons from America's Best-Run Companies.* New York: Harper and Row.

Ronstadt, Robert. 1984. *Entrepreneurship: Text, Cases and Notes.* Dover, Mass.: Lord Publishing.

Schumpeter, Joseph. 1942. *Capitalism, Socialism and Democracy.* New York: Harper and Row.

Stevenson, Howard H., Michael J. Roberts, and H. Irving Grousbeck. 1989. *New Business Ventures and the Entrepreneur.* 3d ed. Homewood, Ill.: Irwin.

4

Elements of a Successful Entrepreneurship/Economics/ Education Program

Gary Rabbior

Much of the discussion in entrepreneurship education has focused on how to motivate, interest and inspire our young people as though these were motivations that they have never possessed.

Current research shows that in many instances people are indeed born with ambition, motivation, and a willingness to take risks, but encounter barriers that erode this spirit of adventure. Rather than providing something new for young people, entrepreneurship education needs to remove some of the barriers that have eroded self-confidence and self-esteem and, along with them, the spirit of adventure and the willingness to take initiative and risk—the spirit of entrepreneurship. These findings should be considered when we plan and develop programs for young people in the area of entrepreneurship education.

The focus should be placed on the potential outcomes from entrepreneurial activity and the identity of the potential entrepreneurs. Spending time searching for an appropriate definition of entrepreneurship is not constructive. We should not put blinders on ourselves regarding who may or may not be an entrepreneur according to some definition arrived at by consensus or we will look at many young people and judge that they do not fit. Historical biases regarding who can and cannot be an entrepreneur will persist. It is time to broaden the scope for entrepreneurship, not narrow it to some limiting definition. If instead we look at what we hope will be the outcome of entrepreneurship education and entrepreneurial activity, then we can focus on the necessary skills and training and assign the potential for entrepreneurship to every young person—not just those few we judge to be likely candidates. Hopefully, one of the greatest benefits of a program such as this will be the surprises we will find regarding which youth catch the entrepreneurial spirit and bring it into effective practice.

Furthermore, there is "the dark side" of entrepreneurship. As desirable as entrepreneurship may be in practice, there are certain side effects that people must accept. This is especially true for intrapreneurship, or creative change within a corporation. Some of the needs of entrepreneurs in the corporate structure may run counter to the norm and pose managerial problems and challenges. Entrepreneurs are change agents; they disrupt the status quo. Many people do not welcome this, and an entrepreneurial environment can be frustrating for those who like order, tradition, and regularity.

Furthermore, it is important to be clear that entrepreneurial activity is not a compulsory outcome of an entrepreneurship education program. There are many benefits to be gained from entrepreneurship education in addition to the hopes that new entrepreneurs will be spawned. Some entrepreneurial spirit is better than none. Programs can enhance self-confidence and self-esteem, and they may encourage students to stay in school longer. It is also important for youth simply to understand entrepreneurship and the role it plays in our society. Entrepreneurship education programs should not be assessed based on the number of entrepreneurs that they create. After all, after planting the seeds via education, it will be some years before most students will ever launch an entrepreneurial venture anyway. For meaningful evaluation, then, it is vital that from the outset any entrepreneurship education program be planned, designed, and implemented with very clear objectives. Furthermore, the objectives should be prioritized. These predetermined objectives will serve as the criteria for program evaluation. Far too many entrepreneurship education initiatives have been established without clear objectives. Evaluation efforts have been frustrated because it was not clearly determined at the outset what the program was attempting to achieve.

In keeping with the true spirit of entrepreneurship, we should never be satisfied with any program in entrepreneurship education. We should always aspire to do better by challenging what is being done and looking for ways to improve. Even if efforts to improve a program are frustrated, the ambition will always ensure that the entrepreneurial spirit is embodied within the program and the entrepreneurial edge is ever-present.

Prescription is not at the heart of entrepreneurship. The entrepreneur is a searcher, an explorer, an adventurer. True to this, an education program that is guaranteed effective in inspiring and assisting entrepreneurship is impossible to prescribe. The effective entrepreneurship education program lies in the ingenuity, innovation, and inspiration of the effective educator—a program tailored to needs, circumstances, and opportunities.

The contents of this chapter present what I believe are important criteria for the educational designer to keep in mind while seeking to find the keys to unlock the spirit of entrepreneurship in the youth of the nation.

Entrepreneurship itself is an essential component of effective entrepreneurship education. The way I teach entrepreneurship will be different from the way that you teach it and, ideally, you will always be attempting to teach it better than I. The goal of the entrepreneurship educator should always be to look for new opportunities, generate new ideas, and keep as much spirit embodied in the educator as one is hoping to impart to youth.

First, in designing any program in this area, it is vitally important that the designer clearly establish the objectives of the program. Is the aim to create entrepreneurs or to inspire entrepreneurial initiative? Is it intended to increase awareness of entrepreneurship or to plant the seeds for the future? Is it to create jobs, or is it designed to affect behavior and alter feelings of self-confidence and self-esteem? Any of these, some of these, or a number of other objectives may be established for an entrepreneurship education program. Regardless, the design of the program should be predicated on a set of clearly established objectives.

Similarly, it is vitally important to establish clear criteria for evaluation linked to the program objectives. However, it is startling how frequently a program in entrepreneurship is designed without objectives, and if objectives are established, evaluation efforts often lack correlation. People will say that a certain entrepreneurship education program was unsuccessful because no new ventures were generated even though the design of the program may not have been created for that purpose. The program designer must be very specific about the program's objectives and the criteria by which the success of the program, and the program participants, will be judged.

Never be satisfied with your program: This represents the true spirit of entrepreneurship. The effective entrepreneurship educator and the effective program will never be partners of complacency. Even if the efforts to find new and better ways are frustrated, the ongoing search will keep the entrepreneurial spirit alive. The successful entrepreneurship educator and the successful program will always ride the crest of the wave of high and positive expectations. The program should personify the spirit of the "little engine that could" and the exemplary educator will lead students up that hill—perhaps puffing and panting—but always with the expectation that it can be done and they can achieve. I am a firm believer that young people will live up—or down—to our expectations of them. Nowhere in education will it be more important to have faith and confidence in ourselves and our students than in a program of entrepreneurship education.

The problem for many students is that no one has ever expected very much from them, and as a result they have come to expect little of themselves. In the end, nothing is expected and, in return, nothing is accomplished. It is unfair to expect youth to readily alter their expectations of themselves. Such a responsibility must lie with another generation—one that takes the initiative to raise its expectations and, in the process, raises the sights, hopes, dreams, and self-confidence of our young people. No effort is more certain of failure than one that is expected to fail. Similarly, we can hope that there is no better fuel for the inspiration of successful entrepreneurship than expecting students to be their best.

I believe the following criteria represent important elements in the design of an effective entrepreneurship education program. They are not prioritized.

Criteria #1: *Do not focus on "right answers"—a single right answer should not be sought or expected.*

The entrepreneur does not accept the fact that there is *a* right answer, but seeks out new and better answers. A program in entrepreneurship education should engender this attitude in its students. Students should challenge everything and put everything to the test. Does it stand up, is there a better way? This process affects class discussion, evaluation, teacher presentation, and components of education.

As it is, most students are highly oriented to "right-answer" learning. They have learned the system in school: Find out what the teacher says, or wants to have said, and give that information back on tests. Modern school programs concentrate on left-brain, linear thinking, whereas the unstructured, creative energy lies over on the right hemisphere. Many students who might do well in studying entrepreneurship—and in applying it—have already been assessed in regular programs as underachievers and possessing lower educational standing than their counterparts who are left-brain–dominant, can handle linear thinking, and score better grades as a result.

This has several significant implications. First, there are the lowered expectations on the part of teachers of the students who have not done well in regular school programs. Success and accomplishment are not expected. Second, the student's own sense of self-confidence may have been eroded and personal expectations of success may be low. One can argue that in such a situation, irreparable damage may be done by the time the student reaches high school and that altering attitudes is unlikely. I disagree. All one has to do is examine the transition of many students once they leave the school system and "find their niche" to see changes in self-confidence. What has to change is the learning environment within which they judge themselves. That environment must be clearly shifted from one in which there is linear instruction focused on right-answer learning, which many students find elusive and reserved for those peers whom they already believe are smarter and more able.

It is crucial to establish a program that shifts away from the linear and from a focus on right answers. Not only is it appropriate to promote an attitude of looking for "new" right answers, but it also creates a new learning arena in which all students may come to feel that they stand on a level playing field—or at least not on an educational Mount Everest.

Criteria #2: *The program should be designed so that it is highly participatory with a "hands on" focus. It should be activity-based.*

Entrepreneurs are action-oriented. They are doers. They are movers and shakers who stir things up. As Schumpeter said, they are "creative destructors," destroying the old as they create the new. In keeping with the nature of the entrepreneur, the program should not place the student in the role of passive learner. The student should be involved in activities, research, investigation, planning, and the hunt for opportunities and new ideas. The students should use, exercise, and develop their entrepreneurial muscles, not let those muscles stay flabby. Learning by doing is not only a good way to learn about entrepreneurship, it also demonstrates clearly that entrepreneurship is not for the lazy. Entrepreneurship involves energy and hard work. There is no better place to find that out than in the program of learning.

Criteria #3: *The program should be goal- and achievement-oriented.*

Entrepreneurs are goal-oriented. They are motivated by accomplishment. They are also affected by accomplishment. Accomplishment refuels the tank and enables them to continue the drive to new and better initiatives. A program in entrepreneurship should establish clearly defined goals and expect the students to do the same. It is important to have both short-term and long-term goals. Students, and entrepreneurs, can become frustrated if the only hopes for accomplishment lie far down the road. This is particularly true when working with students who have little experience with the world of achievement and accomplishment. Many students do not believe that they have accomplished a single thing in their lives. This is a conclusion largely established by an exclusive focus on broad, far-reaching goals.

Criteria #4: *The program should encourage short-term accomplishments.*

The effective program should allow the student to have frequent and clearly identifiable experiences with accomplishment. There should be short-term goals that vary from student to student, focused on accomplishment in the student's area of strength, where success has a high probability. Goals may be anything from writing a new song or creating a new recipe to designing a new dress or throwing ten consecutive foul shots. Students must develop a sense that they are able people who have the potential to accomplish things. They must be attuned to the importance of goal setting and perceive how goal setting can help focus their efforts, help their planning, and contribute toward the likelihood of success. In addition, they must be allowed to experience a sense of accomplishment and to reexperience that sensation as frequently as possible. Accomplishment and goal setting must become a motivator for students as much as they are for the entrepreneur.

Criteria #5: *The program should focus on challenges to the status quo.*

The first criteria stressed the importance of shifting the focus away from right-answer learning. Past right answers to problems should be challenged and better ways should be sought. Students should learn that everything can be improved and all old answers should be challenged. The status quo should be regarded as a passing phase, a stage in the evolution to a better world full of new and better ideas.

Criteria #6: *The program should have a community integration focus.*

No area of educational activity has more of a need—or a more positive potential—for community integration than entrepreneurship education. Entrepreneurs are hunters in their environments. They learn about their environment: They study it, examine it, turn it upside down, and look for what is wrong, what is needed, and what can be done. In short, they are constantly on the hunt for opportunities. Students in entrepreneurship programs can learn from entrepreneurs in their community. They can see what has been done well, and can identify community needs, problems, and solutions. Students can observe changes and identify opportunities. Bridges of all sorts can be built between the school and the community. Not only can the community be a fertile learning ground, students can also make a contribution to the community through their research, discoveries, and activities.

Criteria #7: *The program should utilize a variety of approaches and teaching styles.*

The primary objective of a program in entrepreneurship education is to reach out to different types of students, encourage them to view their world differently, and alter their behavior. We are looking to motivate and inspire them, to turn on their creative powers and channel their energies. This is no meager task, and will not be accomplished via a narrow band of teaching strategies. As educators, we will have to shake up the way students view the world and, in many cases, shake them up in the process. At the same time, creativity and inspiration flow from variety, from something a little different. An effective program in entrepreneurship education will have to employ a variety of teaching styles and techniques in order to reach students who learn differently, to expose them to variety and change, to lead them by creative example, and to keep their minds from encountering a rut.

Criteria #8: *The program should have elements that surprise the student and present the unexpected.*

In keeping with the previous point, the program should surprise students and reinforce the fact that the world is not always as they expect it to be. In fact, students can also learn that they do not have to accept the world as they see it or expect it to be. Things can be different. In addition, surprise is effective in varying their line of thinking. It bumps linear thinking off its course, and can lead the learner to a new road, a new thought, a new discovery. Surprise keeps the spark alive and the mind sharp.

Now, by surprise, I do not mean that the sneaky instructor looms behind the door to blow a trumpet in the ear of the unsuspecting student. Rather, I mean that students should be surprised by the teaching method, by the point of view expressed, by who is in class, by what they are asked to do or are able to achieve, and so on. The program should live—and it should live as a variety of characters exposing students continually to new thoughts and new ways of thinking.

Criteria #9: *The program should present familiar information in unfamiliar contexts.*

It is obvious that comfort and complacency are not key elements of the successful entrepreneurship program. Instead, the program should help students on their journey into a world of new perspectives, new thoughts, new imaginings, and new visions. Students should be introduced to the ways in which existing information can be turned on its head. Frequently entrepreneurs are distinguished from others not because they are looking at different things or have access to different information but rather because they use the same information differently. Entrepreneurs distort the picture they see while looking for new images and new possibilities. To encourage this in students, teachers should help by taking existing information, established beliefs, and long-accepted methods and presenting that information in new and innovative ways that help students look for new possibilities.

Criteria #10: *The program should be easily amended and augmented by each individual teacher.*

The methods and strategies I have discussed obviously cannot be accomplished if the teacher has to operate from prescribed resources and methodologies. Teachers, particularly teachers new to entrepreneurship education, should certainly be given assistance and guidance, but, more important, they should be given freedom. Their students, the community, and the resources will vary. Nothing could be closer to impossibility than attempting to design a "teacher-proof" or highly prescribed entrepreneurship education program.

Criteria #11: *The program should provide focus for entrepreneurial ventures and initiatives—not only small business start-ups.*

Entrepreneurship encompasses more than starting a new small business. Conversely, many new small business start-ups are not entrepreneurial. They may involve risk and they may take initiative, but unless they offer something that is in some way new and improved, they represent self-employment, not entrepreneurship.

At the same time, an entrepreneur, as an individual who mobilizes resources into new and more productive uses, can as easily work within an established corporation, community service, school, or government as in a small business venture. Most students who participate in entrepreneurship education programs will probably not start up their own small businesses. Many, however, will apply their skills, attitudes, and knowledge to entrepreneurial endeavors in other forms of initiative. This broad application should be encouraged through the design of the program, the activities, the research, the case studies, and the examples of entrepreneurship in the community that are examined.

Criteria #12: *The program should be fun and exciting.*

Entrepreneurship is fun and exciting and the program should be as well. Research has shown the correlation between what they call the *aha* experience and the *ha ha* experience. Fun, excitement, and humor encourage innovative thinking. It leads the mind down new and often wacky paths, down which frequently lie insight and new perspective. Fun, humor and excitement are powerful learning tools and motivators and should be an integral part of any program in entrepreneurship education.

Criteria #13: *The program should enable frequent and unanticipated feedback.*

Entrepreneurs require ongoing assessment of their progress and accomplishment. They are motivated by a sense of accomplishment—however small the progress may be. Furthermore, they need feedback—an indication of whether they are on track or need to alter their course. Students in an entrepreneurship education program should receive ongoing and regular feedback. They should learn how to undertake personal assessment and evaluation. In addition, feedback should not occur only when it is expected and anticipated. Motivation and impact can also come from the unexpected. If it is unexpected, feedback may be even more meaningful to the student and taken to heart. The most important element, however, is for the feedback to be frequent and to provide a persistent source of directive information to the entrepreneurial student.

Criteria #14: *The program should entail approaches and activities that seek to build self-confidence in the student.*

There is no more important attribute of entrepreneurship than a sense of self-confidence, the belief in oneself and one's own ideas. Entrepreneurs are agents of change, and change is usually resisted. Entrepreneurs will continually confront roadblocks and resistance from individuals who do not support or believe in their ideas. They will have to convince others of the soundness of their thinking to muster support. To confront and overcome the resistance they will encounter, it is imperative that entrepreneurs have a sense of self-confidence. Unfortunately, activities in our school system today work against the instilling of self-confidence in youth. Many young people come to believe that they do not measure up or have "what it takes." These are not the seeds from which entrepreneurs grow. Hence, any program in entrepreneurship education should assign the highest priority to efforts to increase self-confidence in the students who are in the program. No other area of success is important.

Criteria #15: *The program should enable students to apply their knowledge and skill to a particular endeavor.*

A successful program in entrepreneurship education will enable students to get their teeth into the subject by enabling students to apply acquired knowledge and skills to a particular endeavor. Each student should have the opportunity to explore the school, community, and local economy in search of a particular entrepreneurial opportunity. Once identified, the student should have the chance to formulate and test ideas that result from the perceived opportunity. The student should be allowed to establish a plan for the initiative so that experience can be obtained in learning how to identify needed resources, how to mobilize resources, and so forth. Enabling the student to apply knowledge and skill to a particular endeavor will also expand the opportunity for establishing self-confidence in students and convincing each one that the ability is there.

Criteria #16: *The program should build to a potential "launch point."*

The work done in the program should provide the interested student with the opportunity to launch a particular initiative. This does not mean that the venture needs to be launched within the program. However, the program should build to the point that if the student wants to pursue the chosen entrepreneurial initiative, it will be possible to do so.

Criteria #17: *The program should enable and encourage group and team activities.*

It is surprising to many people that entrepreneurs are good team players. They realize that they can not do everything alone. They require effective and able support. Furthermore, they understand that for their dreams to be realized, they are likely to be dependent on the abilities of others. To foster such effective team play should be both a goal and an element of the entrepreneurship program. Students should be given opportunities to work in groups and as members of a team, learning how to share and transfer responsibilities.

Criteria #18: *The program should alert students to the common pitfalls and reasons for failed initiatives.*

There are many common problems that confront entrepreneurs. The causes of failure tend to be all too similar on many occasions. Students should be alerted to the common problems and their potential for failure.

In addition, students should be taught how to learn from failure. Most successful entrepreneurs have had failures along the way. At the same time, you will find that many entrepreneurs do not talk about these experiences as failures, but rather regard them as learning experiences, stepping stones to eventual success.

The effective entrepreneurship program will alert students to foresee problems and failures—indeed, even to expect failure. Most important, though, students should be taught how to accept, deal with, and learn from failure, and how to make every venture a positive one.

Criteria #19: *The program should place a heavy emphasis on "opportunities": what gives rise to them, how to identify them, and how to evaluate them.*

The essence of entrepreneurship is the opportunity. Most people believe that the idea comes first. In reality, most entrepreneurs perceive the opportunity first and formulate the idea as a result. Students should learn about the nature of opportunities—what constitutes an opportunity, what gives rise to opportunities, how to assess opportunities, and so on. Without an opportunity, there is no entrepreneurship. Without knowing how to find, assess, and utilize opportunities, there is no entrepreneur.

Criteria #20: *The program should expect the teacher to be entrepreneurial.*

The successful entrepreneurship program should not only enable the teacher to be entrepreneurial—it should expect the teacher to be entrepreneurial. Students are encouraged to pursue entrepreneurship via effective role models. There is no more available and effective role model than the educator. Not only is it important that information be conveyed to students in an entrepreneurial way, the teacher can serve as one of the most important role models by providing examples of new and innovative ideas.

Criteria #21: *The program should link entrepreneurship to innovation.*

Much of the work in entrepreneurship education has focused on the notion that entrepreneurship is the start-up of a new small business. Simply setting up a small business and doing what has been done in the past involves initiative and risk and takes hard work. However, if there is no innovative aspect to it, the true spirit of entrepreneurship—mobilizing resources into new, more productive uses—is lacking. Therefore, the program in entrepreneurship should focus on the need for an innovative aspect to an entrepreneurial endeavor and should challenge students to look for opportunities for initiatives that have not been done in the past. Challenge their creativity and really push for their entrepreneurial spirit to be at full throttle, not just in idle or seeking possibilities for replication. The spirit of entrepreneurship as presented in the program should have *innovation* written all over it.

Criteria #22: *The program should focus on the consideration and examination of "disequilibrium" as opposed to "equilibrium."*

As Schumpeter has noted, economics has traditionally shown a preoccupation with static equilibrium analysis. By being concerned with equilibrium economists neglect the forces that cause either a movement to or from equilibrium. Entrepreneurship is one of those forces. By focusing on equilibrium, economists assume away entrepreneurship.

The focus of entrepreneurship should be on the situation and causes of disequilibrium, not on equilibrium. Entrepreneurs thrive in and create disequilibrium. It would be highly incongruous to focus on equilibrium states. Disequilibrium should be the nature of the study arena.

Criteria #23: *The program should provide direction and guidance regarding the design of a conducive learning environment. The traditional learning environments will be inappropriate.*

Much of the attention for entrepreneurship education naturally focuses on content and teaching approach. However, the learning environment must be given its due. It seems inappropriate to expect the kind of instruction that has been discussed above to take place while students sit in regimented rows. If the learning outcome is to be dynamic, fluid, and relatively unstructured, then so should the learning environment. It will be important to develop a learning environment that is conducive to the spirit of entrepreneurship—one that is flexible, fluid, adaptable, changeable, and innovative. The context in which they learn should surprise the students as much as does the approach to teaching by continually forcing them into new circumstances and new perspectives.

Criteria #24: *The program should utilize case studies that are varied in terms of the nature of the entrepreneur, the type of initiative, and the degree of success.*

One of the objectives of an entrepreneurship program should be to open the eyes and ears of youth to the notion that entrepreneurs come in all sizes, shapes, colors, heights, sexes, and so on. To emphasize this, care must be taken when selecting the case studies for use in the program. Otherwise a stereotype may emerge for the students and may undo many of the other efforts that were taken to broaden their perspectives of who can and cannot be an entrepreneur.

Criteria #25: *The program should address behavioral dimensions of learning as opposed to just content.*

Much of the effort in entrepreneurship education in the past can, I believe, be justly criticized for being preoccupied with teaching the institutions—and primarily the institution of business. What is a business, and what is its role? The effort has been to teach the student about business and most particularly about small business. However, the new thrust, and one that I advocate, is to focus on the individual as opposed to the institution or enterprise. The aim is to reach the individual and to alter perspective and behavior; to change attitudes; to alter the way one looks at the world; and, finally to affect the way that one looks at and feels about oneself. Once the goal has been met and the individual is motivated and skilled, then the concern can be placed on the institutional learning. Until the education effort is successful in developing and motivating the entrepreneur, however, the institutional aspects of training, I believe, are premature and unconstructive. The entrepreneurship education program should first assign priority to the spirit, nature, and behavior of the individual and then to the nature and behavior of the enterprise.

These criteria represent my opinions regarding the important elements of a successful entrepreneurship education program. If they make you think, imagine, consider, wonder, and envision, then they will have served their purpose. One of the wonderful aspects of entrepreneurship education is that hopes, dreams, inspirations, and aspirations are part of the curriculum. No matter how great or how small, there is the belief that the world—or some small part of the world—can be better. What a marvelous challenge for an educator—to aim to instill such a spirit in young people and to attempt to equip them with the knowledge, skills, and judgment to help them succeed.

PART TWO

Entrepreneurship Education at the University Level

5

The Educated Entrepreneurs: A New Era of Entrepreneurial Education Is Beginning

Robert Ronstadt

The continued dialogue is worthwhile, but the decision has already been made. Entrepreneurship will be taught and students have chosen in large numbers to learn about starting new ventures and other topics associated increasingly with the emerging field of entrepreneurial studies.

No one, of course, can state unequivocally at this time that these "educated entrepreneurs" will be better entrepreneurs because they have studied entrepreneurship. However, no one can make comparable statements about many other accepted disciplines such as marketing, management, finance, economics, and so on. Nevertheless, strong indications exist that an entrepreneurial education will produce more and better entrepreneurs than were produced in the past. Tomorrow's educated entrepreneurs will know better when, how, and where to start their new ventures. They will know how to better pursue their careers as entrepreneurs, and how to maximize their goals as entrepreneurs, not just for themselves, but also for the betterment of society.

AN ACADEMIC BEACHHEAD IS ESTABLISHED

By 1985, entrepreneurship had established a secure beachhead as an academic discipline. This beachhead has expanded considerably over the past five years, and will continue to do so in the 1990s. As it expands, entrepreneurial studies will experience some basic changes. In fact, the transformation process has already started. New concepts and curricular approaches are being tested in the classroom; there have been significant departures from the past. This new pedagogy marks a new era of entrepreneurial education, and one purpose of this chapter is to describe its advent and explain its implications.

Several hundred business schools now offer one or more courses in entrepreneurship. About two dozen business schools offer programs in entrepreneurship (where a program is defined as multiple courses and other key resource commitments: funded chairs, entrepreneurship centers, outreach projects or courses, special annual events, networking groups, and so on). In addition, at least one business school has made entrepreneurship a required course. Two others offer it to freshmen as a substitute for a management elective or as an alternative to the introduction to business course.

An equally interesting fact is that entrepreneurship courses are offered not only at business schools, but increasingly at community colleges, junior colleges, and engineering schools. About fifty engineering schools offer entrepreneurship as an elective course (Vesper, 1984). Finally, I know of at least one university that offers entrepreneurship within its school of arts and sciences. This innovation makes sense. There is much that economists, historians, sociologists, anthropologists, philosophers, technologists, and other social scientists have to offer to a field that is interdisciplinary to its core. It is very possible that more schools of liberal arts will follow suit as they combat the shift in enrollments to schools and programs that specialize in "professional" education.

THE BEACHHEAD WILL EXPAND

However, even if the liberal arts adoption of entrepreneurship does not occur, the entrepreneurship beachhead will expand into an established and, ultimately, accepted field of academic inquiry. Basic socioeconomic forces will propel this expansion. They will dispel any thoughts that entrepreneurship is a fad, either as a growing career preference nationally or, at the college level, as an academic area.

At the national level, some fundamental changes are fostering a long-term preference for starting, operating, and harvesting new ventures. These include the following:

1. the institutionalization of the two-income family;
2. the growing recognition that larger organizations do not fulfill basic needs for autonomy and security;
3. the shift in womens' roles in economic life along with a parallel shift in the belief that women can be entrepreneurs, to the point that the current growth

in new ventures created by women is considerably higher than the rate of new ventures created by men;

4. a recognition by policymakers that smaller new ventures are critical producers of new jobs, exports, and innovations;

5. a desire by local government officials to avoid falling hostage to large corporations that may become a city or town's dominant employer;

6. a growing appreciation that the risks of venture failure have been grossly overstated and that entrepreneuring is not just the province of a few superstars or celebrity entrepreneurs;

7. an understanding that owning your own business still represents one of the few pathways left to the middle and lower classes to build wealth in an ever-increasing tax-conscious society that all too often penalizes the achiever who works for someone else;

8. a computer and information revolution that is presenting new venture opportunities while often lowering entry costs and other start-up barriers in many industries; and

9. the development of programs to study, teach, promote, and accelerate entrepreneurship in many nations around the world, giving credence to the belief that entrepreneurism is an international phenomenon, not just a national one.

ACADEMIC TRENDS AND ENTREPRENEURSHIP

The wheels of academia move slowly—most often too slowly. Nevertheless, once the wheels begin to churn in a particular direction, they do not easily change course. Academia appears to be moving in a very definite direction toward a new era of entrepreneurial education. Specifically, a number of recent events at the academic level suggest that interest in entrepreneurship will continue to grow for some time. These include the following:

1. A recognition that the short term/low risk focus of the "traditional MBA" type of business education is wrong—not only for potential entrepreneurs but also for potential managers (Hayes and Abernathy, 1980; Gilder, 1984; Behrman and Levin, 1984; Peters and Waterman, 1982; and Cheit, 1985)

2. A recognition or at least an acceptance that entrepreneurship is a process that can be learned and hence is teachable (Drucker, 1985)

3. A recognition among some key academic decision makers—business school deans—at the 1985 American Assembly of Collegiate Schools of Business (AACSB) conference that entrepreneurship is an important education innovation deserving of serious consideration and, where appropriate, adoption or expansion

4. The attendance of about a hundred potential new teachers of entrepreneurship at a special conference of pedagogy run concurrently with the 1985 annual Association of Collegiate Entrepreneurs (ACE) meeting in Dallas

5. The launching of the Babson/Price Fellows Program this summer, designed to deliver teaching information and skills to successful entrepreneurs who want to teach, along with several entrepreneur-in-residence programs at other schools which bring effective entrepreneurs into the classroom

6. The continuing desire among students and alumni for courses and programs in entrepreneurship. Surprisingly, many businesses and engineering schools still do not have a single course in entrepreneurship, and where single courses exist, students often lobby for more

7. The development of a growing number of course materials over the last five years that give potential and existing teachers more to teach on the subject (Ronstadt, 1984a; Stevenson, Roberts, and Grousbeck, 1985; Timmons, Smollen, and Dingee, 1985; and Vesper, 1980b)

8. A growing awareness among deans and alumni directors that their most generous alumni donors are individuals who have created their own businesses

9. The development of a growing body of research, most of it appearing over the last ten years (Ronstadt, 1985a; see also the eight volumes of *Frontiers of Entrepreneurship Research* [FOER], which contain approximately 375 empirically based research articles; Vesper, 1981, 1982; Hornaday, Timmons, and Vesper, 1983; Hornaday, Tarpley, Timmons, and Vesper, 1984; Hornaday, Shils, Timmons, and Vesper, 1985; Ronstadt, Hornaday, Peterson, and Vesper, 1986; Churchill, Hornaday, Kirchhoff, Krasner, and Vesper, 1987; Kirchhoff, Long, McLullan, Vesper, and Wetzell, 1988)

FROM FOLKLORE TO SYSTEMATIC RESEARCH

This last development is particularly important since the foundations of our knowledge about entrepreneurship will be reformulated by systematic research. Hard facts will be identified, along with useful concepts. This new information will find its way into the classroom, especially since many of the researchers are also entrepreneurship teachers. With time, the questions that ask whether entrepreneurship can or should be taught will be replaced increasingly by questions of *what* should be taught and *how?*

In fact, this replacement process has started. New facts and even a few new concepts, drawn from systematic research, are emerging and being married to new insights on pedagogy. The result is movement toward a new era or new school of entrepreneurship education. Before examining this new school, however, it is necessary to understand its roots.

THE OLD SCHOOL

The old school of entrepreneurship is not very old. The earliest courses date back to the 1940s. However, even by 1970 less than two dozen schools were offering entrepreneurship courses, as distinct from small business courses. Significant growth began, in the early 1970s. By 1975, about one hundred business schools had started entrepreneurship courses, that is, courses that focused primarily on new enterprise creation. Ten years later the total number of courses had nearly tripled among AACSB schools alone (Vesper, 1985).

Until recently, the content of these courses was quite similar to that of the earliest courses in entrepreneurship, and I believe it safe to say that the old school still exists today in many classrooms. Its earliest pioneers merit our warm regard for their innovative courage. Acceptance by their academic colleagues was weak at best, and many a career was damaged, or even destroyed, because the "new academic kid on the block" was not understood or was perceived as a threat to a system of management education that largely ignored business in favor of producing bureaucrats, euphemistically called *middle managers,* for the *Fortune* 500 and other large organizations (Shapero, 1982a). The fact that most graduates did not go to work for larger organizations or certainly did not spend the majority of their careers there was simply ignored by most of academia. After all, studying larger, established organizations was at least tolerable by one's academic colleagues, particularly those in nonmanagement disciplines. It was also easier, and more lucrative. Researching larger organizations led to consulting contracts, board positions, funded chairs, and other perks that corporate America was ready to fund. Over the years, the result was the evolution of a system of management education with an implicit value system that clearly favored the large organization versus the small, the established entity versus the new, the ongoing business versus the emerging, the follower versus the leader, and the steward versus the creator and risk taker.

Those who bucked this value system found a rough road. Advocates of entrepreneurship often found themselves vulnerable to attack, not only when they proposed such programs but also when they were being considered for promotion and tenure. When put on the spot, who could prove entrepreneurship was teachable, and that it needed to be taught? Couldn't marketing, business policy, finance, or some other established area handle it? Furthermore, what in entrepreneurship was researchable, anyway? From an intellectual and conceptual perspective, the academic pioneers had very little to work with but their experience and faith. Nonetheless, as Samuel Johnson noted long ago, "They all ill discover that think there is no land when they can see nothing but sea."

While "at sea," the early teachers of entrepreneurship took an extreme, action-oriented approach to the subject. The motto of the old school was decidedly "Go out and do it now." The business plan served as the academic heart of these courses. The rest of the curriculum was provided by experienced visitors who provided interesting stories, practical advice, and inspirational motivation.

The approach was entirely appropriate given the academic state of the art prior to the 1980s, but it possessed some serious drawbacks that have become evident with the passing of time and the advent of new information. Looking back, we can now see that the old school suffered from a bad case of ideological schizophrenia. It preached action and avoidance of "analysis paralysis," but its business plan assignment required 75 to more than 150 hours of analysis and writing. It preached "doing" versus "thinking," but then teachers advised their students not to start a venture right away, advising, "Better to wait. Work for someone else first for five to ten years and then start your own business, preferably when you're in your thirties."

Unfortunately, the schizophrenia went deeper. Despite exercises in "venture evaluation," a deep seated belief existed that human traits determined all outcomes. For many instructors (and their guests) this inner belief was distilled further to a single variable. For some it was perseverance, for others it was courage, "guts," ambiguity tolerance, creativity, achievement motivation, or some other factor. As a result, despite recommendations for first obtaining some experience, the classic advice for finding a venture opportunity ("Just look in the yellow pages for something interesting") had nothing to do with relying on experience. After all, human attributes were the sine qua non of entrepreneurship. Real entrepreneurs, if they truly had the "right stuff," would make a venture succeed, despite the environment, despite the structure of the concept, despite critical venture factors, and despite all else.

A NEW SCHOOL IS EMERGING

None of this advice conforms to our current knowledge about the entrepreneurial process. For instance, the best available evidence at this time indicates that many potential and existing entrepreneurs:

- Do not consider starting their entrepreneurial careers early enough
- Do not consider enough different ways to configure a venture, instead tending to get locked into a particular venture concept prematurely and then spending too much time doing a traditional business plan
- Do not consider explicitly the possibility and potential desirability of creating additional ventures and harvesting old ones. Instead they develop bad cases of "venture myopia"

In addition, we now know the following:

- Many generic kinds of entrepreneurs exist (meaning that simplistic prescriptions, which are usually based on the experiences or traits of one kind of entrepreneur, do not necessarily apply to other entrepreneurs).

- Entrepreneurs start their initial ventures at vastly different ages and for a variety of different reasons (which translates into a need for comparative knowledge about their distinctive needs and motivations in place of reliance on entrepreneurial quizzes that purport to yield *the* entrepreneurial profile).
- A need exists to create favorable environments for entrepreneuring (which translates into a need to educate non-entrepreneurs about the entrepreneurial process).

This new knowledge about entrepreneurship suggests a need for new and better pedagogical approaches. I believe that the new school of entrepreneurship which is emerging to fill this need is more consistent with entrepreneurial reality. Some key differences between the two schools are summarized in Figure 5.1.

The course content and approach of the new school has explicitly recognized and emphasized these new perspectives of the entrepreneurial process. These new views of entrepreneurship recognize that it is a career process in which

- multiple ventures are the rule more than the exception;
- many ways exist to configure or alter a new venture concept, and the initial concept is seldom the best one; and
- time is the scarce factor, not only in terms of the actual start-up and later operations but in terms of planning and investigating new venture opportunities.

ENTREPRENEURSHIP AS A CAREER PROCESS

Most people, even entrepreneurs, still fail to think of entrepreneurship as a career. Nevertheless, the creation and development of one or more new enterprises is a passage, a field of pursuit, a calling, and a way of life that fits the basic notion of a career. For some the passage is brief, but for many others it presents the bulk of their adult lives.

In either case, one reason for the lack of recognition about the career status of entrepreneurship is that the passage does not start at a similar time for those pursuing it. In fact, entrepreneurship is a career process that is started at vastly different times by its practitioners.

The educational ramifications of this "career unevenness" and career nonrecognition are serious, for among our current students, only a minority of all future entrepreneurs will suspect when they attend college that they will make entrepreneurship a major life pursuit. Of those who are considering entrepreneurship while at college,

- only a small minority will start right after graduating, and
- another small minority will wait but will anticipate their entrepreneurial careers by explicitly choosing to work for someone else in a position or industry that will prepare them for their future ventures.

Figure 5.1
The Old School Versus the New School of Entrepreneurship

The Old School Said:	The New School Says:
Don't think too much about the venture. Do it.	Successful entrepreneurs are critical thinkers, as well as action-oriented.
Find any opportunity. It doesn't matter what it is. Just get out there and do it.	Build and rely on experience: either personal, industry, or technical experience initially. Also, assess the need for "entrepreneurial experience."
Wait until you are thirty-five.	Any age can be the right age, but the odds of career continuance favor starting earlier, during the late 20s and early 30s.
Do a business plan first.	Takes too much time and is not appropriate for most ventures. Do a creative "venture feasibility analysis" and avoid getting locked into your initial concept prematurely.
Focus exclusively on the venture start-up, which is almost always the initial venture.	Entrepreneurship is a career, composed, more often than not, of multiple ventures. As such, other entrepreneurial issues exist besides getting the doors of the first venture open.
Rely heavily on outside guests and war stories to provide course content.	Classroom guests, particularly entrepreneurs, are the icing on the cake -- not the cake itself.
Little or nothing said about ethical assessment. At best, ethics are treated as an afterthought, and certainly not as a core issue of the course.	Ethical assessment is critical for long-term success as an entrepreneur and is a central analytic part of the course, rather than an afterthought.
Entrepreneurial success is a function of one necessary and sufficient condition -- the right human characteristics and traits.	Entrepreneurial success is a function of a viable combination of human, venture, and environmental conditions. It is a function not only of "entrepreneurial know-how" but also of "entrepreneurial know-who."

Unfortunately, the vast majority of people who become entrepreneurs will go to work for someone else without anticipating an entrepreneurial career. Evidence now exists that the lion's share of "career fatalities" will be within this latter group (Ronstadt, 1984b, 1985b).

The major implications are numerous. Single courses are not sufficient if the goal is to educate the majority of all potential entrepreneurs about entrepreneurship. Elective entrepreneurship courses reach only a minority of all future entrepreneurs. Unless these courses are required or other required courses are "entrepreneurialized," most future entrepreneurs will not be educated entrepreneurs.

At this juncture some critics would say "So what?" However, the hard truth, whether we like it or not, is that those individuals who for one reason or another are sensitized to the possibility of an entrepreneurial future, who start earlier, or who anticipate and prepare for starting, tend not only to become entrepreneurs at higher rates, but also tend to survive longer as entrepreneurs (Ronstadt, 1982, 1983, 1984b, and 1985b).

What, then, is the answer? Assuming that required entrepreneurship courses are not politically feasible at most schools, the next best option is to develop an entrepreneurship program containing multiple courses and an entrepreneurship major or concentration, plus other program components. The principal reason for a program is that it helps make entrepreneurship more visible to students as a career possibility.

For example, practicing entrepreneurs who did not take Babson's lone entrepreneurship course (before our program was introduced) were asked why they failed to sign up. A popular response was, "I didn't know at the time that such a course was even offered" (Hornaday, 1985). We need to reach out to sensitize students to entrepreneurship as a possible option.

ENTREPRENEURSHIP AS A MULTIPLE VENTURE PROJECT

A growing body of evidence is emerging indicating that entrepreneurship is a process in which multiple ventures are the rule more than the exception. A pervasive entrepreneurial phenomenon, the Corridor Principle, says that most entrepreneurs will see corridors leading to new venture opportunities that they could not see or exploit before getting into business. However, some entrepreneurs will not be able to pursue these opportunities, either by substantially modifying their existing venture or starting new ones, because they are trapped by their current business.

The major implications are as follows: Venture analysis should consider the likelihood, and even the desirability of multiple ventures or major modifications in the initial venture. Just as a managerial career is often a progression of jobs and positions, an entrepreneurial career is usually a progression of ventures or the creation of new ventures within the existing venture.

ENTREPRENEURSHIP AS A PROCESS OF MULTIPLE CONCEPT CONFIGURATIONS

In-depth studies of new venture creation reveals that entrepreneurship is a process that generally allows many configurations of a potential venture. Some configurations represent less risk and greater flexibility for taking advantage of the Corridor Principle without reducing potential rewards. Unfortunately, many new entrepreneurs get locked into a particular venture concept or configuration without considering more favorable options. A trade-off also exists between looking at one variation in great detail versus considering a larger number of variations, some of which may be relevant given the fact that ventures rarely follow the course detailed in traditional business plans.

The major implications are as follows: What is needed is a flexible and time-efficient planning mechanism that fosters creativity rather than detail, identifies options rather than a single course of action, is a realistic compromise between the twin dangers of under- and overanalyzing, and yet admits the dominance of uncertainty and our likely inability to foretell the future in a traditional business plan. The latter often requires over 150 hours to produce a good product. By contrast, a *venture feasibility plan* requires 30 to 35 hours of work. The heavy investment in time required by the traditional business plan is inappropriate for most budding and practicing entrepreneurs, whether they are planning their first venture or later ones. The possible exceptions, and they are a small minority, are those individuals planning high-growth ventures that require substantial infusions of venture capital. Separate courses should be established for those who need the time to develop a full-blown business plan.

ENTREPRENEURSHIP AS A PROCESS WITH LIMITED TIME FOR VENTURE INVESTIGATION

The old school of entrepreneurship recognized the importance of time, but it was emphasized in terms of the time it actually took to start and establish a new venture. The new school takes this notion a step further. Entrepreneurship is a process where the scarce factor is still the entrepreneur's time; however, the scarcity impacts directly on opportunity recognition, investigation, and development, not only before but also after starting the first venture.

The major implications are as follows: Time must be available to search for, identify, and explore new venture corridors. Such activity is needed in most instances to realize entrepreneurial ambitions and to experience at least a longer entrepreneurial career.

Figure 5.2
Selection Goals of Entrepreneurship Education

Courses Need to Teach:

1. Fact Versus Myth About Entrepreneurship

2. Reality Testing Skills

3. Creativity Skills

4. Ambiguity Tolerance Skills and Attitudes

5. Opportunity Identification Skills

6. Venture Evaluation Skills

7. Venture Start-up Action Skills

8. Venture Strategy Skills

9. Career Assessment Skills

10. Environment Assessment Skills

11. Ethical Assessment Skills

12. Deal-making Skills

13. Contacts--Networking Skills

14. Harvesting Skills

OBJECTIVES, COURSE STRUCTURE, AND NON-STRUCTURE

Given these observations, what specifically do courses in entrepreneurship need to teach future entrepreneurs? Figure 5.2 lists goals that I believe are particularly important given what we now know about the entrepreneurial process. This list, of course, can be expanded, and it should be expanded given the needs of specific audiences. (For example, a list of goals for nonbusiness students would include relevant marketing, management, finance, and similar goals.)

Given these goals, Figure 5.3 shows the conceptual structure of an en-

Figure 5.3
Curricular Design for Entrepreneurship Courses and Modules

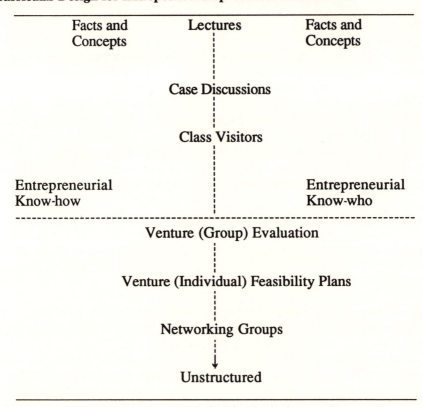

trepreneurship course at either the graduate or undergraduate level. It also represents the structure of an entrepreneurship program that involves multiple courses. The vertical axis shows that the course (program) proceeds from being more structured to extremely unstructured—to the point that individual initiative ultimately becomes the critical variable shaping the project and the outcomes. The rationale for this approach is the uncertain and often unstructured nature of entrepreneurial environments. I think it safe to conclude that the entrepreneurial environment for the vast majority of our graduates will be extremely unstructured and highly individual experience.

The horizontal axis in Figure 5.3 shows the course or program moving from "entrepreneurial know-how" to "entrepreneurial know-who." The need to understand networking and making contacts is a critical requisite for long-term entrepreneurial success. We know that there is some truth in the dictum, "It's not what you know but who you know." Nonetheless, past courses and programs have not explicitly programmed the development of "know-who" skills or fostered networks that last beyond the life of the course.

Contacts are developed through a variety of projects and organizations at Babson that have networking as a primary objective (though it may not always be an explicit or stated goal). Within my course, the venture evaluation project helps students make contacts and observe entrepreneurial know-how firsthand. It also gives them an opportunity to apply their entrepreneurial knowledge, the concepts and evaluative skills they have learned via lecture and case analysis. An organization called the Entrepreneurial Exchange fosters contacts and networking by bringing together undergraduate students, graduate students, alumni, and non-alumni who have a common interest in exchanging information about their entrepreneurial aspirations, pursuits, and services.

FROM COURSES TO MAJOR PROGRAMS

Many schools have launched entrepreneurship programs in recent years, but a few schools have clearly led the charge. Four of the latter are Babson College, University of Southern California (USC), Baylor University, and Wichita State University. I have designated these four because each school has developed an entrepreneurship program that has excelled along one or more dimensions compared to other programs, and each has something important to teach us about program development.

For example, USC has a superior program structure that operates relatively independently of its regular business program. It also has developed an extremely strong and integrated teaching team. Babson College has excelled at developing new materials, concepts, and courses generic to Entrepreneurial Studies. Wichita State has led the active development of the entrepreneurship know-who side. Its Association of Collegiate Entrepreneurs (ACE) is now a national organization that breeds deal making and contacts among budding entrepreneurs. Baylor University has developed courses and programs that give students more and better exposure to the unstructured side of entrepreneurship. Its Venture Assistance Program and its Innovation Evaluation Program extend and improve on traditional field studies programs or approaches utilizing small business institutes (which usually do not involve students in the start-up phase of a venture).

While each program has its differences, the people who have developed these four programs (Richard Bursick at USC, Robert Ronstadt at Babson, Fran Jabara at Wichita State, and Donald Sexton, formally at Baylor and now at Ohio State) have served together on several panels to discuss their programs. What follows is a distillation of their advice about creating an entrepreneurship program.

CRITICAL FACTORS FOR ENTREPRENEURSHIP PROGRAMS

A key fact is that nearly all entrepreneurial programs will be composed of selective courses, whether taken at the undergraduate or the graduate level. At its most basic level, this fact means that entrepreneurship courses must fit into an existing curriculum. Such accommodation is seldom easy to achieve politically or administratively, particularly when talking about a new program and multiple courses. Other professors will have staked out their turf in the competition for the usually limited and scarce elective course time of students. Unfortunately, the environment is particularly a zero-sum situation, and will be perceived as such by some people.

However, who will be hurt or helped is not clear. It is difficult to predict beforehand who will lose students and who will gain them. Such uncertainty inevitably serves as a breeding ground for opposition, which can surface from the flank or even the rear. These days it is hard to be immediately and openly hostile to entrepreneurship or any acknowledged innovation. It simply is not considered open-minded. Nevertheless, the negative opposition, as opposed to honest constructive criticism, will come.

You must recognize that in an academic and intellectual battle over entrepreneurship, you have some severe disadvantages. The field is new, it is hard to defend, and it has little conceptual substance because it is so young. Anyone can kill a new idea, and most of your colleagues will consider themselves knowledgeable even though their entrepreneurship IQs are woefully low. Consequently, you will face many self-styled experts who have never run a business or studied the field but who will still have forceful opinions about

- one's ability to teach entrepreneurship. "After all, aren't entrepreneurs born, not made?" (actually a wealth of evidence indicates the opposite)
- the need for a major or concentration. "It won't help students get a job." (Actually, quite the contrary seems to be the case, especially when entrepreneurship is taken as a joint or dual major with some other discipline. Many companies are seeking entrepreneurial types and, if they are not, then, as one student expressed it, "I really shouldn't be interested in them.")

During the pre-start-up phase of your entrepreneurship program you must

1. gain the total and unqualified support of your dean, president, or the acknowledged leader of your school. In short, you must have a political champion who will protect you and your program when sudden puffs of flack appear and their immediate source is unknown;
2. gain the active involvement of someone (probably an assistant or associate dean) who thoroughly knows the existing interrelationships between courses, their

scheduling, and the impacts of various kinds of prerequisites on the ability of students to take your proposed courses. This administrative champion will help you avoid many time-consuming mistakes as you design your program in the context of an existing curriculum;

3. avoid the label, small business. Unfortunately it is too easy to equate small business, management of smaller enterprises, or small business entrepreneurship with "unimportant business," the "management of potpourri," or "Fluff Management 101." Like it or not, small business courses have an uneven reputation that includes words like *gut.* Those of us in the field know that smaller enterprises are important along many dimensions. We recognize that there are meaningful differences in strategy and operations based on size. However, entrepreneurial studies can incorporate these positive aspects without picking up the negative baggage. Remember, size is not the issue. The distinctive focus of entrepreneurial studies is enterprise creation, simply because it is an area not being covered by other academic disciplines;

4. attempt to organize your program as separately as possible from the existing undergraduate and MBA (Masters of Business Administration) programs, particularly if you are in a university setting. There is no logical reason to assume that entrepreneurial education should be made to fit within the existing structure of an undergraduate or graduate school of management; and

5. organize your program in terms of the scheme presented in Figure 5.3 (i.e., structured to unstructured, entrepreneurial know-how to entrepreneurial know-who), and/or in terms of the venture initiation process. Avoid a "functional approach" that includes courses in entrepreneurial finance, entrepreneurial marketing, and so on. Sufficient knowledge does not exist to warrant such courses where good finance and marketing courses already exist or can be developed.

Once your program is launched, you must

1. maintain tight control across courses and sections as soon as more than one instructor is involved. Numerous faculty meetings will be needed so you will know the precise topics being covered in each class session. Again, because the field and its courses are not closely defined, the danger of duplication and redundancy is particularly acute. A close-knit team is vital to avoid serious and legitimate student complaints about subject duplication;

2. maintain a hard line on assigned readings and case assignments. Many entrepreneurial students will resist the structured end of the program, and will want to begin writing business plans immediately. Unfortunately, the road to knowledge is seldom an easy one; students must learn to walk before galloping, and you must be the one to exercise constraint;

3. stimulate awareness of entrepreneurship and your courses by class visits to required courses that occur early in the students' program. If possible, develop permanent entrepreneurship modules for these courses; and

4. develop outreach programs that bring students together with alumni and non-alumni who are entrepreneurs and professionals assisting entrepreneurs. Such associations will foster the know-who or networking side of entrepreneurship.

THE NEW ERA AND THE FUTURE

The interplay between research, course development, and teaching is a close one for entrepreneurship. As new concepts emerge from systematic research, case studies, or other in-depth clinical studies, the need to reformulate teaching approaches will become increasingly vital to maintain currency with knowledge about the entrepreneurial process.

Currently, I believe we are entering the early phase of a new era of entrepreneurship education. New knowledge about the process of entrepreneurship is suggesting new pedagogical approaches. Conversely, these new approaches must do a better job of conveying or transferring this new knowledge to tomorrow's entrepreneurs.

Transferring this knowledge will require the development of programs of entrepreneurship, and not just individual token courses. Like any new venture, these new programs in entrepreneurial studies must be given room to breathe, flexibility of movement in order to develop their educational products, and protection to grow and flower into a healthy maturity. Their success is critical, not just in terms of developing more and better independent entrepreneurs, but also in terms of fostering an entrepreneurial spirit, perspective, and approach among managers and employees that will rekindle our desire to excel, to be the best, and to innovate and pioneer. While it may be possible "to manage our way to economic decline" (Hays and Abernathy, 1980, p. 66), the opportunity also exists for us to entrepreneur our way to economic and social prosperity.

POSTSCRIPT 1990

Having left academia for the real world of entrepreneurship several years ago, I have an expanded perspective on the process of entrepreneurship and the relevancy of entrepreneurship education. What follows are my conclusions, based on the experience of running a high-growth venture for the last few years:

1. The concept of an educated entrepreneur is still valid. My experience tells me that entrepreneurial knowledge is a cornerstone for success. It does not insure success, but I believe it certainly improves the odds. A recent article in *INC.* magazine (*INC.*, 1989) discussed how much of our business success had come from our "doing" entrepreneurship and how much was due to my teaching of entrepreneurship over the last few years. However, I am convinced that most others would not have survived nor achieved the success our company has attained without what I had learned previously about the entrepreneurial process.

2. More should be taught about working with and for entrepreneurs. The perspective of most entrepreneurship courses is the perspective of the lead entrepreneur or the entrepreneurial team, and rightly so. How-

ever, many future entrepreneurs will work for other entrepreneurs before starting their own ventures. Other students taking entrepreneurship courses will never become entrepreneurs, but will work for one. What does it take to work for an entrepreneur, and what are some of the problems that can occur? How should employees (and team members) take advantage of opportunities? It seems to me that the perspective (and key issues) of some cases, lectures, guests, and so forth, should be those of people working with and for entrepreneurs.

3. More should be taught about ending a venture. There is a very real connection between starting a venture and ending one. How ventures are ended often determines whether another venture can be started. In a world where multiple ventures are the rule rather than the exception, knowing how and when to terminate a venture with skill and professionalism is mandatory knowledge for educated entrepreneurs.

4. More pertinent finance and marketing concepts need to be developed and taught. In some schools, separate courses in entrepreneurial finance and entrepreneurial marketing may not be feasible; nevertheless, more knowledge in these areas needs to be developed and integrated into entrepreneurship courses. The stock knowledge drawn from traditional finance and marketing courses is not sufficient for today's educated entrepreneur.

5. More emphasis needs to be placed on product and service excellence. Too much emphasis in entrepreneurship courses has been placed on the value of being a marketing-led company. The reaction to this myopia concerning product and technology has resulted in an overdependence on marketing. Having a truly superior product is still the best insurance against unforeseen events and marketing miscues. A more dynamic notion of what is needed to succeed with a new venture should find its way into the classroom. At times, a new venture must be marketing-led, but at other times the emphasis should be either on product, production, customer support, or finance.

6. More should be taught about raising funds from informal sources. Conversely, much less needs to be covered about the professional venture capital industry. How to approach and work with professional venture capitalists is simply irrelevant for 99.9 percent of all entrepreneurship students. Most entrepreneurs will have to secure funding by their own resources from family or friends. Venture capitalists are usually only interested in backing winners who have moved beyond start-up into an accelerated growth phase.

7. More should be taught about superior venture design and implementation and less time spent on writing business plans. Business plans are important, but learning how to write a good one takes too much time (literally hundreds of hours). Most business plans written by students (except in courses devoted largely to the business plan) are not worth much

in terms of educational value. Set up a separate course for those individuals committed to writing a real business plan. For introductory courses, the time spent on business plans (including time-consuming presentations) is better spent elsewhere. Remember, a great business plan is insufficient without ongoing, superior venture thinking and implementation. Change and unforeseen events will dominate, and the time to continually rewrite business plans simply is not available. Schumpeter was right: We do plan too much, and think too little.

8. Finally, more effort is needed to establish *required* entrepreneurship courses for all college students. I am not just referring to all business students, but rather all college students. A recent poll of 900 members of the undergraduate class of 1993 by the *Boston Globe* (1989) revealed that an astounding 14 percent of students in the Northeast were considering an entrepreneurial career. This percentage was considerably higher than the numbers wishing to go into government, social work, law, medicine, engineering, computer-related fields, or the arts.

As we look back at the 1980s, we can already see this decade as a time when *elective* entrepreneurship education has become intellectually accepted and institutionalized in academia. What does this mean? It means that college doors were opened for a relatively small number of predominantly business school students who were fortunate to realize the need for one or more elective entrepreneurship courses. The number of students taking such a course grew to a few thousand by the end of the decade. Undeniably, this growth represented real progress.

However, to create an entrepreneurial society in this nation, an environment where entrepreneurship is institutionalized and woven into the country's future landscape, we need to reach hundreds of thousands of students each year. Clearly, not all will become entrepreneurs, just as everyone who takes a science or fine arts course does not become a scientist or artist. Nonetheless, every member of our society needs to understand the process of entrepreneurship and how wealth is created.

Certainly this is a big task, but don't be frightened to think big, and don't let the nay-sayers in academia say it cannot or should not be done. Take courage, and let's move ahead. The job of creating educated entrepreneurs is far from over.

NOTE:

Major portions of this chapter were previously published under the same title in the *American Journal of Small Business,* Spring 1987, and are now reproduced with permission.

REFERENCES

Behrman, Jack N., and Richard I. Levin. 1984. "Are Business Schools Doing Their Job?" *Harvard Business Review* (January–February): 140–147.

Cheit, Earl F. 1985. "Business Schools and Their Critics." *California Management Review* (Spring): 43–62.

Churchill, Neil C., John A. Hornaday, Bruce A. Kirchhoff, O. J. Krasner, and Karl H. Vesper, eds. 1987. *Frontiers of Entrepreneurship Research.* Wellesley, Mass.: Babson College, Center for Entrepreneurial Studies.

Drucker, Peter F. 1985. *Innovation and Entrepreneurship: Practice and Principles.* New York: Harper and Row.

Gilder, George. 1984. *The Spirit of Enterprise.* New York: Simon and Schuster.

Hayes, Robert H., and William Abernathy. 1980. "Managing Our Way to Economic Decline." *Harvard Business Review* (July–August): 66–77.

Hornaday, John A. 1985. "Alumni Opinions of the Value of the Curriculum in General Business and in Entrepreneurship Courses." In *Frontiers of Entrepreneurship Research,* edited by J. A. Hornaday et al., pp. 560–565.

Hornaday, John A., Jeffry A. Timmons, and Karl H. Vesper, eds. 1983. *Frontiers of Entrepreneurship Research.* Wellesley, Mass.: Babson College, Center for Entrepreneurial Research.

Hornaday, John A., Fred A. Tarpley, Jr., Jeffry A. Timmons, and Karl H. Vesper, eds. 1984. *Frontiers of Entrepreneurship Research.* Wellesley, Mass: Babson College, Center for Entrepreneurship Research.

Hornaday, John A., Edward B. Shils, Jeffry A. Timmons, and Karl H. Vesper, eds. 1985. *Frontiers of Entrepreneurship Research.* Wellesley, Mass: Babson College, Center for Entrepreneurship Research.

Kierulff, Herbert. 1974. "Education for Entrepreneurship." *AACSB Bulletin* 10, no. 3 (April): 6–14.

Kirchhoff, Bruce A., Wayne A. Long, W. Ed McMullan, Karl H. Vesper, and William E. Wetzell, Jr., eds. 1988. *Frontiers of Entrepreneurship Research.* Wellesley, Mass: Babson College, Center for Entrepreneurial Studies.

Peters, Thomas J., and Robert H. Waterman, Jr. 1982. *In Search of Excellence: Lessons From America's Best Run Companies.* New York: Harper and Row.

"Rewriting the Book on Entrepreneurship." 1989. *INC.* August, pp. 86–93.

Ronstadt, Robert. 1982. "Does Entrepreneurial Career Path Really Matter?" In *Frontiers of Entrepreneurship Research,* edited by K. H. Vespar, pp. 540–567.

———. 1983. "The Decision NOT to Become an Entrepreneur." In *Frontiers of Entrepreneurship Research,* edited by J. A. Hornaday et al., pp. 192–212.

———. 1984a. *Entrepreneurship: Text, Cases and Notes.* Dover, Mass: Lord Publishing.

———. 1984b. "Ex-Entrepreneurs and the Decision to Start an Entrepreneurial Career." In *Frontiers of Entrepreneurship Research,* edited by J. A. Hornaday et al. pp. 437–460.

———. 1985a. *Entrepreneurship Bibliography.* Dover, Mass: Lord Publishing.

———. 1985b. "Every Entrepreneur's Nightmare: The Decision to Become an Ex-

Entrepreneur and Work for Someone Else." In *Frontiers of Entrepreneurship Research,* edited by J. A. Hornaday et al., pp. 409–434.

————. 1987. "The Educated Entrepreneurs: A New Era of Entrepreneurial Education Is Beginning" *American Journal of Small Business* 11, no. 4 (Spring): 37–53.

Ronstadt, Robert, John A. Hornaday, Rein Peterson, and Karl H. Vesper, eds. 1986. *Frontiers of Entrepreneurship Research.* Wellesley, Mass: Babson College, Center for Entrepreneurial Studies.

Shapero, Albert. 1982. "Are Business Schools Teaching Business?" *INC.* 4, (January): p. 13.

Stevenson, Howard H., Michael J. Roberts., and H. Irving Grousbeck. 1985. *New Business Ventures and the Entrepreneur.* 2d ed. Homewood, Ill.: Irwin.

"Survey: For N.E. Freshman, Fulfillment Outranks Money." 1989. *Boston Globe,* October 1, pp. 1, 26.

Timmons, Jeffry A., Leonard E. Smollen, and Alexander L. M. Dingee, Jr. 1985. *New Venture Creation.* 2d ed. Homewood, Ill.: Irwin.

Vesper, Karl 1980. *New Venture Strategies.* Englewood Cliffs, N.J.: Prentice-Hall.

————. 1984. *"Summary of Entrepreneurship Course Survey."* University of Washington, (April).

————. 1985. "New Development in Entrepreneurship Education." In *Frontiers of Entrepreneurship Research,* edited by J. A. Hornaday et al., pp. 489–497.

———— ed. 1981, 1982. *Frontiers of Entrepreneurship Research.* Wellesley, Mass.: Babson College, Center for Entrepreneurial Studies.

6

Post-Secondary Entrepreneurship Education for the Practicing Venture Initiator

W. F. Kiesner

The decade of the eighties is clearly a period during which the academic community recognized the entrepreneurial and small business sector as a viable target market of interest and opportunity for academic research and education programs. Colleges and universities by the hundreds initiated courses and programs in entrepreneurship for traditional students as well as actual entrepreneurs and business venturers. The impressive and rapid growth of entrepreneurial education as a major and accepted academic subject area on college campuses during the past ten years gives testimony to the fact that the thrust of entrepreneurship as a subject area has been successful.

However, mere growth in numbers of programs and students, traditional and nontraditional alike, does not guarantee that all of these programs are working well, nor does it insure that the academic community has optimized the quality and methodology of efforts aimed at both practicing and potential entrepreneurs. Entrepreneurship education is a new field for educators, and though it has enjoyed tremendous growth in the past decade, there is a great deal to be learned about the education of the smaller business venturer. Entrepreneurs are indeed a different breed that demands special attention and innovative approaches if the academic community is to satisfy its desires, special needs, and idiosyncrasies with regard to training and education.

This chapter reports on a number of research studies of entrepreneurs

Table 6.1
Overall Satisfaction Levels with Small Business Training from All Sources

	Owner	Faculty
Mean Response	4.85	3.97
Positive Response Percent (7-6-5)	59.7%	35.6%
Neutral Response Percent (4)	23.7%	24.4%
Negative Response Percent (3-2-1)	16.6%	40.0%

and educators that this author has undertaken over the past several years in an attempt to understand the special situation of entrepreneurs as consumers of formal and informal education and training programs. These studies focus on training and education programs for practicing entrepreneurs and small business owners who are not enrolled in traditional college courses. This chapter is based on the results of several studies of entrepreneurs (a total of 692 entrepreneurs responded to the studies) as well as a study of the views of 316 college and university professors active in the area of small business and entrepreneurial education. While preliminary, these studies indicate what works and what does not, and provide guidance for entrepreneurship educators working with practicing venture initiators.

SATISFACTION LEVELS WITH EXISTING EDUCATION AND TRAINING PROGRAMS

As can be noted in Table 6.1, the entrepreneurs seemed a great deal more satisfied with the educational programs being offered to them, by all sources, than were the faculty. These responses were based on a 7-point Likert Scale where a response of "7" meant "extremely pleased" and a response of "1" indicated the respondents were "extremely unhappy."

Whether owners are actually qualified or capable of determining what they should be receiving in the area of training and education is a valid question, yet their satisfaction with the educational programs being offered gives valuable insight into what educational products they wish to consume. In contrast, the educators are purported to be on the leading edge of knowledge in the latest methods, techniques, concepts, and problems in business. Consequently, the disparity in satisfaction levels with regard to entrepreneurship training is of tremendous interest. Insight into the reasons for these differences will come from the review of the information and survey results that follow.

Table 6.2
Important Sources of Assistance and Training

Source of Help	Owner Ranking	Faculty Ranking
Accountants, lawyers, etc.	1	2
Advice from customers	2	8
Other small business owners	3	3
Business magazines	4	10
Trade associations	5	5
Your bank	6	6
Suppliers	7	7
Consultants	8	1
Colleges and universities	9	4
Chambers of commerce	10	11
Big firm executives	11	12
Small Business Administration	12	9

IMPORTANT SOURCES OF ASSISTANCE AND TRAINING

The owners and faculty were asked to rank the most important sources of assistance available to the small business owner. The results provide interesting insights into the thinking of both groups, and are noted in Table 6.2. There is no question: The faculty and owners did not share identical views.

The educators clearly rated their own offerings to the entrepreneurs as being of much greater value to the small business community than did the owners. This was demonstrated by the ratings of colleges and universities and of consultants. Among business owners, college and university programs were ranked ninth out of twelve. By faculty, they were ranked fourth. Consultants received the top rating from faculty but were ranked ninth by business owners. (Keep in mind that most university teachers also moonlight as consultants.) The faculty must clearly take into account the business owners' negative reactions to them as they design and develop programs and formats for training entrepreneurs.

THE VALUE OF COLLEGE TRAINING TO
THE SMALL BUSINESS COMMUNITY

Despite the relatively low rating that college and university training received (Table 6.2), the owners did indicate that the programs were of

Table 6.3
College Courses and Programs Helped Increase Owner's Skills and Knowledge

	Owners	Faculty
Mean Response Level	5.16	5.70
Positive Response Percent (7-6-5)	68.3%	88.6%
Neutral Response Percent (4)	17.1%	7.0%
Negative Response Percent (3-2-1)	14.6%	4.4%

value (Tables 6.3 and 6.4). Owners who had taken courses from colleges and universities were asked to evaluate those courses with regard to several specific results measurements. Faculty members were asked to give their opinion of the value of college courses to the entrepreneurs based on the same criteria.

Both faculty and owners had relatively positive feelings about the value of college and university programs to the small business owner. However, business owners were definitely not as excited about the value of the programs they experienced in the academic sector as were academics.

Table 6.3 shows that 68.3 percent of the owners felt positively about these programs, while almost 90 percent of the academics did. There should be serious concern and program review caused by the fact that only about one-half of the respondents indicated that the programs they took at the academic institutions helped them to identify problems (see Table 6.4) and make changes (see Table 6.5). Training for entrepreneurs should be made immediately applicable to their businesses. The survival rates for

Table 6.4
College Courses and Programs Helped Identify Problems in the Owner's Business

	Owners	Faculty
Mean Response Level	4.67	5.47
Positive Response Percent (7-6-5)	54.2%	82.6%
Neutral Response Percent (4)	15.3%	10.1%
Negative Response Percent (3-2-1)	30.5%	7.3%

Table 6.5
College Courses and Programs Caused Changes in the Owner's Business

	Owners	Faculty
Mean Response Level	4.63	4.88
Positive Response Percent (7-6-5)	51.4%	60.5%
Neutral Response Percent (4)	13.5%	25.8%
Negative Response Percent (3-2-1)	35.1%	13.7%

new ventures dictate that vague or theory-oriented offerings are not what entrepreneurs need or desire.

Despite the fact that the initiators had some misgivings with regard to the value of their educational experiences, they still retained an overall positive view towards the colleges and universities, as noted in Table 6.6. While they exhibited some misgivings about the immediate applicability of the courses they had taken, the owners had a generalized appreciation of the potential value of colleges and universities as a resource that can, and should, provide them with all the latest techniques and solutions to the problems they face alone every day (see Table 6.7).

Though these results may initially appear to be contradictory, they do indicate that the entrepreneurial community has a generalized, overall appreciation of the potential of the academic community to help them, but that as the entrepreneurs evaluate specific offerings they have taken and assess the direct values to themselves as business owners, they have some reservations. It is not unlike the consumer who looks at a new automobile as something that would be great to buy, but then finds out after the sale there is not enough room in the car and the engine is not big enough. Small business owners are saying they want more bottom line in college courses.

Table 6.6
College Courses and Programs Helped the Owner's Business

	Owners	Faculty
Mean Response Level	5.08	5.42
Positive Response Percent (7-6-5)	62.1%	80.7%
Neutral Response Percent (4)	15.2%	13.0%
Negative Response Percent (3-2-1)	22.7%	6.3%

Table 6.7
Should an Owner Attend College and University
Entrepreneurship Courses?

	Owners	Faculty
Mean Response Level	5.66	6.05
Positive Response Percent (7-6-5)	79.8%	92.3%
Neutral Response Percent (4)	12.0%	5.4%
Negative Response Percent (3-2-1)	8.1%	2.3%

To prevent the erosion of the initial positive perception, the academic institutions must make strong efforts to fine-tune their programs to more specifically fulfill the immediate needs and desires of entrepreneurs. When half the business owners attending courses at colleges indicate that the product offered did not have an immediate impact on their business, a drastic improvement is needed to make the courses more results-oriented. The faculty must recognize and accept this problem, and take special action to insure that course offerings are directly and immediately applicable to the daily operations of the entrepreneur's firm. Beyond that, teachers must also demonstrate how classroom subjects are applicable, and how methods and theories can and should be immediately implemented by the owner. The product must be strengthened, and then its improved value must be marketed and sold to the entrepreneurs (consumers).

THE MOST IDEAL ENTREPRENEURSHIP TRAINING AND DEVELOPMENT METHOD

Both faculty and owners were asked to identify what they considered the most ideal methods for conducting effective programs for the business venturer. Once again the faculty view differed substantially from that of the owners.

According to Table 6.8, of the eight training methods investigated, "Group discussions led by small business people," was ranked number one by owners and only number six by faculty. Both groups did agree that "lectures by faculty" and self-study programs were the least preferred. The disparity between the owner and faculty rankings should lead to a recognition that the owners want expert advice but do not necessarily accept college and university teachers as experts! This does not rule out the success of college and university courses, but it does point to a need to use outside experts as a resource in the classroom or for college faculty to establish their credentials as experts during the course. If the teachers do not have

Table 6.8
Most Ideal Method of Training for Entrepreneurship

	Owners	Faculty
Group discussions led by small business people	1	6
Lectures by experts, lawyers, accountants, etc.	2	5
Specific problems clinic	3	1
Working with a consultant	4	2
Special college courses for small business	5	3
Discussions led by university small business faculty	6	4
Lectures by college faculty experts in small business	7	7
Self-directed, self-study programs	8	8

direct hands-on business experience and demonstrate it in their presentation, the entrepreneurs will not accept them as experts.

PREFERRED SOURCES FOR FORMAL ENTREPRENEURSHIP COURSES AND PROGRAMS

The owners who had taken formal training courses or programs were asked what the most preferred source for this training was. Table 6.9 presents the results.

According to this research, trade and professional associations are the preferred source for entrepreneurial training. This may reflect their credibility and familiarity with the industry. Certainly these groups can target their programs with specific applications to situations with which the entrepreneur is familiar. Colleges must often offer courses to all comers. This may limit their capacity to deal with the industry-specific issues of entrepreneurs. Once again it would appear that the entrepreneur's desire for hands-on, bottom-line expertise is showing up in this study.

It is also important to note that two- and four-year colleges as well as universities have made a strong entry into this market, with a penetration of approximately 25 percent of owners preferring training from them. Maintaining and improving that level of penetration is dependent on how the academic community adapts and responds to the owners' desires and needs.

Table 6.9
Preferred Training Source

	% Responding
Trade and professional associations	42.6%
Four-year colleges	18.8%
Private, for pay, seminars	9.0%
Two-year colleges	6.1%
Chambers of commerce	5.3%
Small Business Administration (SBA)	3.7%
Bank	2.9%
Suppliers	2.5%
Government (non-SBA)	2.5%
Franchisers	2.0%
Consultants	1.6%
All other sources	2.9%

REASONS FOR NOT USING TRAINING FROM ANY SOURCES

The entrepreneurs were asked to indicate why they had not taken training programs from any source. The reasons given in Table 6.10 are of interest, and can give some understanding of the critical concerns of the potential customers for the offerings of colleges and universities.

Table 6.10
Reasons for Not Using Training

Reason	Percent Responding
No time, too busy	47.3%
Don't need	21.9%
Nothing sounds of interest or useful	7.9%
Not aware of useful courses	6.1%
Lazy, never get around to it	4.4%
Too costly	4.4%
Not at a convenient time	1.8%
Courses not productive	1.8%
All other responses	4.5%

Table 6.11
Disadvantages of College and University Entrepreneurial Training

Response Category	% Responding
Faculty has no field or practical experience	32.9%
Colleges too impractical, too intellectual	18.8%
Colleges have no time to do it right	11.3%
Won't be relevant, colleges can't think small	7.5%
College teaching is too generalized	7.5%
Will be too costly	2.5%
Colleges only able to teach big company people	2.1%
No qualified or capable instructors	1.7%
Too big a risk to their reputation with colleges if they fail	1.3%
Colleges are not general enough	1.3%
On-the-job training is better	0.8%
Professors don't treat the small business owner as equal	0.4%
No disadvantages	5.0%
All other responses	7.1%

Clearly, the conservation of limited time is of critical importance to the entrepreneur. Traditional quarter- or semester-long courses will not be popular. The results noted in this table also point up the value of proper marketing to the consumers of program offerings. Almost 22 percent felt they had no need for additional training. Making the owners aware of offerings and convincing the owners of their value is a lesson the academic community must learn. Academics must practice what they preach and market their product offerings more effectively.

DISADVANTAGES AND ADVANTAGES OF UNIVERSITY ENTREPRENEURIAL TRAINING

Owners were asked to list the major disadvantages of college and university programs, as well as the major advantages. The most frequent responses are listed below in Tables 6.11 and 6.12.

A good deal can be learned by what is said in these tables, both in support of the involvement of colleges and universities in entrepreneurship training, and in opposition. Note how many of the small business respondents listed advantages accruing to the colleges rather than to

Table 6.12
Advantages of College and University Entrepreneurial Training

Response Category	% Responding
Provide good basics, overall framework and tools	21.3%
Have the latest ideas	15.6%
Broad diversity of ideas, fields, and resources	8.5%
Faculty will gain valuable experience and learn	8.1%
Lots of talent, experts at colleges	4.3%
Will provide good PR for the colleges	4.3%
Helps the community	3.3%
Can interact and exchange experiences	2.4%
Colleges will get donations	2.4%
Provides centralized, concentrated learning	2.4%
Will provide a new market for schools	2.4%
Strong library research ability	1.9%
Good income for colleges	1.4%
All other responses	21.8%

themselves as entrepreneurs. The owners showed a certain level of fear of large institutions such as colleges and universities, and a belief that educators do not have useful knowledge and experience in the real world of running a small firm, or even an appreciation of the entrepreneur as a viable subject for attention. The owners clearly perceived that the faculty was out of touch with the specific problems of entrepreneurs. They also appeared to be somewhat convinced that teachers lack the practical experience necessary for credibility in the entrepreneurs' eyes.

A popular joke in entrepreneurial circles that always elicits knowing nods of acceptance and only slightly muffled guffaws is the time-worn statement that "Those who can, do; those who can't, teach." It matters not that faculty members may violently disagree with this old joke, and will attempt to offer extensive and erudite refutation. The only thing that matters is what the entrepreneurs, or potential consumers, perceive and believe about products offered by the college and university faculty. The fears represented by this old joke have not been dispelled, at least not by the college and university courses and programs that were taken by the participants in this research.

Table 6.13
Best Time to Take Training

Timing Option	% Responding
One evening per week	32.1%
Weekend (two days)	17.5%
Weekend (one full day)	14.9%
Saturday	12.1%
One morning per week	9.5%
One afternoon per week	7.3%
Sunday	4.8%
Other	1.9%

Small business owners clearly perceived college and university offerings to be oriented toward big business rather than venture initiators. Those teachers at postsecondary institutions should ask if this perception is correct for their offerings, and, if not, how it can be overcome. Probably increased visibility in the small business community through speeches and presentations plus membership in groups where entrepreneurs are members are the best ways to increase both visibility and credibility.

THE BEST TIME FOR ENTREPRENEURIAL TRAINING PROGRAMS

Entrepreneurs were asked several questions about the best timing for course offerings. Their responses are presented in Tables 6.13 through 6.17.

From these results it appears that the owners want programs at off-work time periods. Unfortunately, these may not always conform with the desired work times of the faculty. Less than 20 percent of responding owners wanted the programs offered during normal working hours (according to Table 6.13). The owners showed overwhelmingly that they preferred having these programs at off-work times. Thus, when they indicated that 9:00 A.M. was the best starting time or that 5:00 P.M. the ideal ending time, the vast majority of the owners were referring to weekend programs. If the preference for off-work hours is kept in mind, what might appear to be an inconsistency in the responses shown in the different programs will be eliminated.

According to Tables 6.14 and 6.15, owners were quite willing to start their training programs early in the morning and stay late. It also can be

Table 6.14
Best Course Starting Time

Starting Time	% Responding
9:00 a.m.	24.0%
7:00 a.m.	23.7%
8:00 a.m.	21.3%
6:00 p.m.	12.7%
10:00 a.m.	5.7%
2:00 to 5:00 p.m.	5.3%
1:00 p.m.	2.7%
11:00 a.m. or 12:00 noon	1.9%
8:00 p.m. or later	1.8%

concluded that weekday programs should be early in the week. The end of the work week is the least popular, no doubt because of the demands of the business. The entrepreneurs were not afraid of staying late in the evening for a program, nor were they excessively upset by giving up their weekend time for programs offering real value.

Table 6.17 reveals that early in the year seems to be the most popular time for owners to take training programs and courses. Course offerings near holidays, during vacation months, or near tax deadlines probably will

Table 6.15
Best Course Ending Time

Starting Time	% Responding
10:00 p.m.	20.3%
9:00 p.m.	15.1%
5:00 p.m.	14.4%
4:00 p.m.	11.4%
Noon	10.3%
6:00 to 8:00 p.m.	7.4%
3:00 p.m.	7.0%
1:00 to 2:00 p.m.	3.0%
9:00 to 11:00 a.m.	3.0%

Table 6.16
Best Day of the Week for Courses

Day of Week	% Responding
Tuesday	26.2%
Saturday	24.5%
Wednesday	20.5%
Monday	14.8%
Thursday	7.4%
Friday	3.9%
Sunday	2.6%

be less successful. September, a post-vacation month before the holiday season, was also popular.

ACADEMIC CREDIT OR NO CREDIT

The entrepreneurs indicated that they were not particularly interested in receiving formal college credit for their college and university training

Table 6.17
Best Month of the Year for Courses

Month	% Responding
January	23.5%
February	15.7%
September	11.3%
June	8.7%
March	7.0%
May	6.1%
October	6.1%
November	6.1%
July	6.1%
April	3.5%
August	3.5%
December	2.6%

Table 6.18
Desire for College Credit

Response Option	% Responding
College degree credit	11.7%
Certificate in small business management	36.3%
Unimportant, does not matter	52.1%

programs, as noted in Table 6.18. This is a clear indication that providers of courses do not need to be concerned with formal college credit. Entrepreneurs seek training for knowledge, not credentials. Nonetheless, issuing some type of certificate will be favorably received by a significant minority of the potential participants.

IMPORTANT SUBJECT AREAS FOR ENTREPRENEURSHIP TRAINING AND DEVELOPMENT

The entrepreneurs and faculty were asked what specific subjects they considered most important for courses aimed at entrepreneurs. These responses are recorded in Table 6.19. The similarities and disparities between their responses are interesting, and can give entrepreneurship educators valuable knowledge about how the small business owner thinks about training and developmental needs. Certainly these needs would vary depending on a number of demographic factors, but they are a valuable indicator.

The difference in the rankings of subject areas such as computers, leading and managing people, inventory, and access to capital are of particular interest. The disparity in the ratings between the owners and faculty with regard to computers is striking. Faculty must recognize the value and importance of the computer for even the smaller business owner. Perhaps the faculty does not recognize, or accept, the smaller business owners' need for, or capability to use, computers. If this is the case it is unfortunate, and such attitudes must be corrected. This ranking may give credibility to the entrepreneurs' contention that faculty are out of touch with the realities of the world in which the entrepreneur and venturer operates.

Similar observations might be made when we consider the disparity between the faculty view and the owner's view with regard to the value of training and development in leading and managing people. One might conclude that the faculty take too seriously the common view of the entrepreneur as a rugged individualist who does not need others' help in building a business, while the owners are clearly saying they need and want help

Table 6.19
Important Subject Areas for Entrepreneurship Training

Response Area	Owner Ranking	Faculty Ranking
Budgeting and cash flow	1	1
Leading and managing people	2	7
Understanding financial statements	3	2
Computers for small business	4	11
Advertising, PR, promotions	5	5
Accounting, bookkeeping	6	3
Tax planning	7	9
Marketing, product development	8	8
Access to capital, loan packaging	9	4
Business law, contracts	10	13
Incentive plans, retirement plans	11	14
Inventory control, production control	12	6
How to buy or sell your small business	13	12
Business site location	14	10
Import-export for small business	15	15

in the area of managing and leading people. Educators should respond to this.

A comment must be made on the surprisingly low ranking given to international trade by both the entrepreneurs and the academics. The world is rapidly moving toward global markets and international cooperation and interdependence, with regional specialization. This applies to both large and small firms. Firms that do not respond to the dramatic shift toward international trade and marketing face potentially severe negative impacts on their operations. Perhaps the entrepreneur does not recognize this yet, but certainly the academic community should unless they fail to perceive the smaller firm as having the capability for a potential niche in world markets. This kind of short-sighted thinking with respect to the potential of smaller firms in the international market (in contrast to the action being taken in other countries such as Japan) can have potentially severe results on America's economic future. Even if entrepreneurs do not recognize the potential of international markets for the smaller firm, certainly it is incumbent on the faculty to guide them into this area.

A PROFILE OF ENTREPRENEURS MOST LIKELY TO USE COLLEGE AND UNIVERSITY TRAINING

In basic marketing courses professors often teach students to study the market, and determine the demographics of those consumers most likely to purchase their products. However, faculty and academic institutions seldom practice what they preach to their students. The literature shows very little research about who the customers are for college and university entrepreneurship training programs. To gain a better insight into the potential market for training, a total of forty-three demographic variables were studied. Entrepreneurs who did, and did not, make use of college and university small business and entrepreneurial offerings were compared. Different questions were used, and weighed, to arrive at a ranking of those individuals most likely to use college courses and programs. The questions dealt with the following:

• The owner's generalized opinion of the value of college training to owning a business

• The desirability of using college and university training and programs after one has entered the entrepreneurial ranks

• The amount of college and university entrepreneurial programs the owners had participated in

• Their opinion of the value of those courses

The results appear in Table 6.20.

Demographic factors such as prior education, age, industry, race, success in a prior business, and years in business have significant impact on the likelihood of an entrepreneur making use of college and university programs, and at times exert a reverse influence to what might be expected. Size of firm, sex, and number of prior businesses initiated tended to have lesser impact, though there are exceptions. It will be valuable to consider these demographic factors when targeting college and university entrepreneurial programs at specific market segments. For example, minorities such as Hispanics and blacks clearly have a substantially higher propensity toward college and university training for small business ownership than do orientals or Caucasians. Those with the most advanced graduate degrees, along with the youngest individuals are the most likely to be consumers of college and university entrepreneurial training. Industry-wise, those in the retailing industry have a much greater interest in college and university programs than do those in wholesaling, construction, and the service industry. Is this the result of a perceived need (or lack of need) for help, or the availability (or lack of availability) of programs with direct content and applicability? Considering the rapid growth in importance of the service sector in the U.S. economy, one must certainly be concerned at the relatively low level of value this sector puts on the value of the academic community in providing training and assistance for entrepreneurs in this field.

Table 6.20
A Profile of Entrepreneurs Most Likely to Use University Training Programs

Demographic Variable	Weighted Rank
Under 25	1
16 to 25 years in business	2
In retailing	3
Black ethnic origin	4
26 to 50 employees	5
In finance industry	6
Owned more than 3 prior businesses	7
4 to 7 employees	8
No prior business ownership	9
Hispanic ethnic origin	10
Holds graduate degree	11
8 to 15 employees	12
Over 100 employees	13
Construction industry	14
Age 36 to 45	15
Female	16
Some graduate school education	17
Age 26 to 35	18
Over 25 years in business	19
Manufacturing industry	20
1 to 3 years in business	21
Never failed in prior business	22
Male	23
Caucasian	24
1 to 3 employees	25
4 to 8 years in business	26
Professional industry	27
College graduate	28
Age 46 to 55	29
Age 56 to 65	30
Owned 1 prior business	31
9 to 15 years in business	32
Owned 2 to 3 prior businesses	33
51 to 100 employees	34
Under 1 year in business	35
Wholesale industry	36
Oriental ethnic origin	37
Failed in prior business	38
Transportation industry	39
Age over 65	40
Service industry	41
High school education	42
16 to 25 employees	43

THE MOST IMPORTANT ENTREPRENEURIAL SUCCESS TRAITS

In gaining an understanding of the entrepreneur or customer for college and university training and education, it is important to learn what entrepreneurs consider the most important traits to be a winner in their own business. Gaining an understanding of these traits is a useful exercise for the educator, and proves valuable in the classroom in stimulating discussion and studying what characteristics business initiators might want to develop. The results of the following study will be of value to faculty in understanding just how the entrepreneur, their prospective customer, thinks. A total of 249 owners responded to a survey question that asked them to rank, on a Likert Scale, the value of various traits to their success as an entrepreneur. The responses were then weighed by the number of owners ranking that trait. There was only a slight difference between the weighted rank and the unweighted rank, so the weighing had little impact.

In reviewing the results in Table 6.21, note that several well-known and accepted myths and misunderstandings are shattered by the data, including the myth that the average entrepreneur is a money-grubbing Scrooge or stereotyped J. R. Ewing. Honesty and ethics receive a very positive ranking by the entrepreneurs, contrary to the popular opinion of the media. The relative rankings of such items as attractive appearance, desire for wealth, ambition, intelligence, creativity, innovation, the "people-oriented" traits, and energy and drive are seen as important, and should be used in stimulating discussion in the training classroom.

The results given in Table 6.21 are of value in the classroom and in providing programs for entrepreneurs in several different respects. Initially, it is of value to open the entrepreneur's eyes to the tremendous importance of such traits as energy, perseverance, drive, and ambition to the potential success of the firm. Too many fledgling entrepreneurs have a dream-world view of how easy it is to start a business and immediately reap phenomenal wealth. Such mistaken views can certainly be raised and clarified simply by looking at the rankings in this study concerning the critical factors the entrepreneurs rank most highly.

A number of the factors rated highly by the entrepreneurs in this study can, and should, be taught. This analysis of success traits is of value in providing insight into some of the factors entrepreneurs hold most dear, and would be most interested in developing through training and developmental programs at colleges and universities. While the entrepreneurs may already possess some of these traits, they can be honed and strengthened in the classroom.

Objective traits such as "people skills," delegation, creativity, innovation, and knowledge of the field can be taught and developed. More subjective traits such as perseverance, energy, honesty, ethics, drive, ambition,

Table 6.21
Importance of Various Traits to Being a Successful Entrepreneur

Trait	Rank	Mean Likert Response
Energy	1	6.730
Perseverance	2	6.721
Drive	3	6.696
Ambition	4	6.639
Knowledge of field (streetwise)	5	6.502
Honesty and ethics	6	6.425
Ability to work with people	7	6.274
Personal self-control	8	6.146
Ability to delegate authority	9	6.065
Independence	10	6.065
Creativity	11	6.008
Support of family	12	5.984
Excellent health	13	5.951
Aggressiveness	14	5.911
Innovation	15	5.805
Intelligence	16	5.714
Tough-skinned	17	5.244
Need to control events	18	5.089
Attractive appearance	19	5.028
Need for autonomy	20	4.958
Need to prove self	21	4.543
Strong desire for wealth	22	4.430
Strong desire for power	23	3.849
Powerful ego	24	3.764

and independence may be more inherent, "soul-and-heart" traits. However, one can certainly raise a strong case for the fact that these types of traits can be discovered, stimulated, and motivated through training and development programs. The consumption of motivational courses and programs by entrepreneurs gives testimony to their perception and belief that these types of programs are beneficial. A program combining the development and teaching of the more objective skills and the stimulation and motivation of the entrepreneur's subjective traits will result in a valuable educational experience.

SUCCESSFUL ENTREPRENEURSHIP EDUCATION IN THE NEXT DECADE: ADAPTING TO THE NEEDS AND DESIRES OF THE ENTREPRENEURIAL MARKET

Entrepreneurs and, more recently, faculty at colleges and universities have been enjoying the fruits of the "Age of the Entrepreneur" for some fifteen years. The tremendous interest in entrepreneurship in the United States and the entire world has resulted in millions of new firms being started. It has spawned hundreds of entrepreneurial courses and programs in colleges and universities throughout the world. Entrepreneurial studies have, in many schools, joined the more venerable, traditional, and accepted subject areas of economics, accounting, finance, marketing, and management, and are taking on the characteristics of full academic program areas and majors. Entrepreneurship at college campuses is in much the same position that computer science was a decade ago.

To a great degree academics are still in the "adolescent" stages of the field, particularly when it comes to sophisticated research, fully understanding the idiosyncrasies of the entrepreneur (who is the potential customer), and developing fully effective, results-oriented courses, seminars, and programs. If collegiate entrepreneurial education is to grow toward maturity as an academic field, we must continue to research the principal participants, the entrepreneurs, and gain a better understanding of who they are, how they function and think, and what they need and want in support and training from the academic sector.

This chapter provides some insight into the special desires and wants of the entrepreneur, and it is expected that it will prove useful in providing the academician with guidelines for avoiding mistakes in developing entrepreneurial courses and programs. The academic community is a tremendous resource that is not fully trusted, or utilized, by the entrepreneur. Faculty, colleges, and universities must properly apply their expertise and knowledge of entrepreneurial activity to make training more efficient, predictable (with regard to outcome), and successful. How this knowledge is applied and delivered to the entrepreneur is of critical importance. The academic community must listen to what the entrepreneur says, and must adapt their insights accordingly.

RECOMMENDATIONS FOR ACADEMIC ACTION

From the information developed in this chapter it is possible to develop a list of actions that the academic community should take to improve the effectiveness (and the perceived effectiveness, in the eyes of the entrepreneur) of their products and offerings in the area of entrepreneurial education and development. A list of the obvious and less obvious conclusions includes the following proposals:

1. Faculty and academic institutions must pay attention to what the entrepreneur desires. Right or wrong, venturers will not purchase products (courses or programs) that they do not perceive as valuable. Target marketing of consumer-desired products is essential.

2. The academic community must accept the fact that the entrepreneur does not value faculty and the colleges and universities as a resource as strongly as the faculty and schools value themselves. Action must be taken to change this negative perception.

3. The academic community must package, market, and sell its offerings in a format and at a time that are palatable to the entrepreneurs, who are nontraditional students.

4. Educators must gain hands-on small business and entrepreneurial experience if the entrepreneur is going to accept them as experts and valuable resources. They must prepare and package themselves in a manner that will increase their believeability and entrepreneurial trust.

5. Colleges and universities must target their course content and marketing at those demographically identifiable entrepreneurial segments most inclined toward purchasing the academic products.

6. Academic institutions and faculty must realize that the entrepreneur has an inherent appreciation of the potential value of academia. They must, however, develop and design their products, and the related delivery mechanisms, to fulfill the perceived needs and desires of the entrepreneurs, and pacify their fears that teachers are inexperienced and disinterested in the small business sector.

7. Courses and programs must be results-oriented. Consumers of such programs must be able to return to their businesses and immediately apply what they have learned to better their operation. Courses and programs must have the bottom-line applicability and content that the owner desires.

8. Faculty must use information about the entrepreneurs' perception of the most valuable success traits as a guide for course development, and as a stimulant to class discussion.

9. Courses must be totally relevant to the entrepreneurial experience, and must also appear relevant. They must be taught by faculty with actual small business entrepreneurial experience.

10. The courses should be industry- and market-specific.

11. Perks such as college credit are of little relative importance to the consumers of entrepreneurial education.

12. Short, quick, hard-hitting courses, during nonworking hours, are perceived by the entrepreneurial community as being of most value.

7

Entrepreneurship Education at the Collegiate Level: A Synopsis and Evaluation

Calvin A. Kent

It is impossible to pinpoint when collegiate courses and programs in entrepreneurship education were first offered. It is certain, however, that entrepreneurship education, as a significant component of university curriculum, is of rather recent origin. The last decade has seen a virtual explosion of entrepreneurship programs on college campuses across the nation. Over the years, George Solomon has conducted a series of surveys on small business and entrepreneurship education courses offered on college and university campuses. His first nationwide survey in 1979 netted 117 colleges that indicated some form of entrepreneurship education activity. In 1983, 263 colleges and universities responded that they were conducting such programs. In 1986, the figure was 417 (Solomon, 1988). The 400 percent growth rate in collegiate programs in entrepreneurship over the last decade is an understatement, as it only includes those institutions that responded to his survey. Undoubtedly, other schools offer something in the area, but chose not to respond. This growth in entrepreneurship education may be the most significant trend in collegiate schools of business over the past ten years. The growth has been particularly strong at the smaller and medium-sized universities (Zeithaml and Rice, 1987).

At the postsecondary level, entrepreneurship education takes several forms:

1. Courses and programs for traditional undergraduate and graduate students
2. Courses and programs for nontraditional students such as practicing and potential entrepreneurs who are not currently involved in an academic program leading to a degree
3. Courses designed to train teachers of entrepreneurs at the secondary and postsecondary level, including vocational/technical schools and junior colleges
4. Courses and programs for those seeking to work with entrepreneurs such as bankers, CPAs, consultants, government officials, insurance agents, and lawyers

In addition, a wide variety of supporting entrepreneurship education activities have flourished at college campuses. Among these are

- Student entrepreneur clubs
- Student seminars at secondary and postsecondary schools
- Programs designed to recognize outstanding entrepreneurial achievement

Research in entrepreneurship has also blossomed. Once relegated to the lowest rung of the academic ladder, research into the process of entrepreneurship and entrepreneurship education is now not only accepted but respected. The pattern of entrepreneurship research is uneven, and to a large extent entrepreneurship education is still flying by the seat of its pants due to a lack of an adequate research base on which to develop curriculum and approaches.

The purpose of this chapter is to review what has transpired in collegiate entrepreneurship education and the findings of researchers who have investigated these programs and processes.

COURSES FOR TRADITIONAL UNDERGRADUATE AND GRADUATE STUDENTS

Before the 1970s, it was most likely that undergraduate and graduate students enrolled in collegiate schools of business would have had little opportunity to study entrepreneurship. While some colleges offered a single course in small business management, it was rarely required and even more rarely respected. By the end of the 1970s, however, this had all changed. This was not due to innovative genius on the part of college administrators, but rather to rising student demand. In addition, college presidents and deans began to recognize that their most prolific and potentially biggest donors were often entrepreneurs who were willing to support entrepreneurship programs on college campuses through scholarships, contributions, endowed chairs, and centers. It is not surprising that many of the more prestigious entrepreneurship programs now bear the names of the entrepreneurs who endowed them.

ENTREPRENEURSHIP AND SMALL BUSINESS MANAGEMENT COURSES

There is a tendency at the collegiate level to confuse small business management with entrepreneurship. As Carl Zeithaml and George Rice point out, they are not the same thing, but they are so closely related that one can not be studied without studying the other (Zeithaml and Rice, 1987).

Lawrence Klatt performed an investigation based on 120 returns from two- and four-year colleges and universities offering graduate degrees (Klatt, 1988). He defined course offerings as to small business management and entrepreneurship. For the purposes of his survey,

a small business management course is one which concentrates on the starting of a small business, its operations and its problems, and an entrepreneurship course is one which focuses on entrepreneurs as individuals, their role in business and society and entrepreneurial studies. (Klatt, 1988, p. 104)

Entrepreneurship courses were "concerned with innovation and new ventures rather than the management of a business once it was in operation" (Klatt, 1988, p. 104). He found that ninety of the schools offered at least one course in small business management, but only forty-two offered one or more courses in entrepreneurship. Forty-six did report one or more courses that were a combination of small business and management.

In addition, the survey indicated that most two-year colleges offered only a single course in small business management. Four-year colleges and universities generally offered at least a second course in small business management or entrepreneurship. Only twelve schools offered three or more courses in small business management, two offered three courses or more in entrepreneurship, and only one offered three or more courses that combined elements of both small business management and entrepreneurship. Seventy percent of these schools offered their courses as electives; only 30 percent of the schools required entrepreneurship as part of a major.

Structure of Entrepreneurship Courses

The question then arises, "What is being taught in the entrepreneurship curriculum?" According to a study completed by Karl Vesper, the basic entrepreneurship program structure in most schools includes

- venture design projects
- case studies
- readings
- lectures by guest speakers and the instructors (Vesper, 1985)

Vesper's findings were consistent with the later study performed by Klatt, who also found that most small business and entrepreneurship courses were organized around guest lecturers, student consultation with practicing entrepreneurs, the development of business plans, field trips, use of video and films, and special readings (Klatt, 1988).

Robert Ronstadt has suggested that the content of entrepreneurship courses is changing (Ronstadt, 1986). He contends that in the past too much emphasis was placed on the preparation of a detailed business plan and too little directed toward other skills and insights. In addition, he criticizes the programs of the past for making too heavy a use of outside speakers who related old war stories as the principal content of these courses.

Studies of the effectiveness of current offerings in entrepreneurship education have been conducted by Donald Sexton and Nancy Bowman. These studies involved identifying the psychological characteristics of entrepreneurs and entrepreneurial students in order to recommend a new structure for courses in entrepreneurship that will increase course effectiveness. Sexton and Bowman suggest that courses should be relatively unstructured and should "post problems which require a novel solution under conditions of ambiguity and risk" (Sexton and Bowman, 1984, p. 24). The use of case studies was recommended as the best pedagogical approach.

Sexton and Bowman's studies of the psychological characteristics of entrepreneurs revealed that entrepreneurship students prefer independent efforts, individual activities, and individual analyses of situations. Their findings suggest that individual projects may be more effective than group activities. This is not surprising since most entrepreneurs work alone. Working with existing entrepreneurs was also seen as a highly desirable activity.

Textbooks and Materials

Klatt (1988) surveyed 220 colleges and universities that offered courses in entrepreneurship. As part of that survey, questions were asked about texts and other materials used in college courses.

Most instructors in the survey were pleased with the textbooks in entrepreneurship which had been developed to this point. Seventy percent of the respondents rated the texts satisfactory. The respondents' comments indicated a need for improvement in supplementary materials, such as teachers' manuals, test banks, and cases. According to this survey, the existing college texts apparently would profit from more practical examples, less theoretical discussion, more comprehensive case studies, and a higher-level approach which would be more challenging to the students.

Donald Hess (1987) conducted a survey of small business owners to determine their activities and training needs. These results were then compared to the coverage in ten major small business/entrepreneurship texts. He concluded that the texts devoted too little coverage to marketing and selling and too much to finance and accounting. In addition, too much emphasis was given to inventory management and too little to production. In the area of finance, too many pages were devoted to accounting and tax topics while financial planning and budgeting were neglected. Perhaps the greatest area of neglect was in the area of manager/employee training and education. His conclusion was that most courses followed textbook coverage and reflected the textbook weaknesses. He felt that textbooks would be improved if writers and publishers were in better communication with practitioners.

Course Content

There is one criticism that can be levied against current collegiate courses in entrepreneurship education as presented to traditional undergraduate and graduate students. Most of these course offerings are found in schools of business and tend to be located in departments of management or strategic planning with some in allied fields such as marketing and finance. None of the existing curriculums in entrepreneurship appear to be complete. Many aspects of entrepreneurship are ignored. Rarely are courses offered in entrepreneurial history, despite substantial research in the area and a growth in textbooks that now emphasize the contributions of entrepreneurs to the growth and development of the American economy (Perkins and Walton, 1985; DiBacco, 1987; Gunderson, 1989).

In addition, courses in entrepreneurship and economics seem to be lacking. This is probably due to the failure of economists to adequately integrate entrepreneurship into economic theory. Materials and texts that would constitute the core of a course in entrepreneurship economics are lacking, but this does not mean that they should not be developed. The key position of the entrepreneur in promoting economic growth, in both developed and underdeveloped countries, constitutes an added dimension that should be pursued (Kent, 1982; Broehl, 1982).

The study of how entrepreneurship affects and is affected by the social environment is another sadly neglected area. The sociology of entrepreneurship has been one of the earliest areas of research and investigation (Shapero, 1984; Shapero and Sokol, 1982; Harwood, 1982). Despite the continued interest of sociologists in this area, their insights rarely find their way into the collegiate entrepreneurship curriculum.

If entrepreneurship is to become a full-fledged discipline, capable of standing on its own merits rather than as an adjunct to existing majors in the business school, then a more broad-based approach to the collegiate entrepreneurship curriculum must be pursued.

Practical Experiences

The vast majority of the schools with entrepreneurship programs also have Small Business Institutes (SBI), conducted under the Small Business Institute program of the U.S. Small Business Administration. The SBI program began in 1972. Student teams work with small business firms providing consulting services. These teams are under the supervision of a faculty member who monitors their progress and evaluates their work. The Small Business Administration (SBA) pays a small fee for each completed case. These SBA programs may have been the forerunners of entrepreneurship education at most colleges and universities.

The Venture Assistance Program at Baylor University is somewhat unique in that it limits its consulting activity to working with start-up entrepreneurs rather than already existing businesses. Its emphasis is on business planning and establishment of new firms as opposed to dealing with problems of businesses already established, which is the emphasis of most SBI programs. This approach appears to be superior as it allows the students to participate in all aspects of the venture initiation process rather than limiting themselves to just a single problem of an established concern.

There have been no empirical studies distinguishing between successful and unsuccessful SBI programs. From the anecdotal evidence the following characteristics of successful programs appear correct:

The degree of involvement of the faculty supervisor. The more closely the faculty member works with the students on the case, the greater the likelihood of success, in terms of a project both useful to the business and satisfactory to the students.

The type of problem being addressed. Many SBI projects are of limited scope, dealing with only a specific problem such as how to set up an inventory control system, how to implement a computer-based information system, or how to control accounts receivable. While useful, these will be less likely to appeal to entrepreneurial students than would cases that involve them in the strategic planning of a start-up where they can integrate the specific knowledge gained from a variety of courses.

The motivation of the students. Students without motivation are likely to produce cases of little value. Instructors can maintain motivation through their own involvement, rigorous grading, and the proper matching of student interest and ability with the business problem.

The background of the students. Students should not be given projects for which their academic backgrounds leave them unqualified. While students should be challenged by a case to find new information and methods for problem solving, they must have adequate class preparation to handle the assigned task.

When properly constructed, integrated, and supervised, SBI programs are a valid complement to a collegiate program in entrepreneurial studies.

Research must be done on how to increase the effectiveness of these programs and how to integrate them into the entrepreneurial curriculum.

Program Structures

A review by this author of 63 college and university programs in entrepreneurship revealed a pedagogical tension that has developed in the field. These findings are consistent with those of Vesper (1985), Zeithaml and Rice (1987) and Klatt (1988). Collegiate entrepreneurship education programs tend to be of two types. The first is the *composite model*. The entrepreneurship curriculum consists of a series of courses taught out of the traditional academic department. The names of these courses indicate their content; "venture finance," "new venture marketing," "venture accounting," "computers for small business," "strategic management of new ventures," and "venture taxation," to name the more usual course offerings in the composite program. In these schools the student typically takes an introductory course in either entrepreneurship or small business and then a series of courses from the above-mentioned list. There is usually a capstone course that requires the students to prepare a business plan. In addition, under these programs students are frequently required to participate as consultants to existing small businesses, usually through a small business institute (SBI) program.

The second type of program uses the *integrated model*. Usually in these cases a department of entrepreneurship or entrepreneurial studies has been established that offers its own courses independent of the traditional academic departments. These courses integrate the insights that the student will have learned from the more traditional introductory courses in accounting, finance, marketing, and management, and has the student apply these principles in courses that require their integration.

There may be some strong reasons to prefer the second approach.

1. Teachers in traditional academic departments who are assigned courses in entrepreneurship may not have a strong interest in the field. If this is not a personal interest of theirs, then the enthusiasm that would characterize the integrated approach may be lacking. Under the integrated approach, professors would have as their principal teaching and research focus entrepreneurial studies, and would, therefore, be more likely to see it as important and to maintain familiarity with the most up-to-date research.

2. A separate department in entrepreneurial studies is likely to receive more attention from administrators and other college officials. It implies a higher level of commitment and also gives the administrator of the entrepreneurial studies program more clout with the staff, as their principal teaching responsibilities will rest in the entrepreneurship department and their performance will be evaluated principally on how well they perform in that environment.

3. The integrated approach can more easily eliminate the problems of gaps and overlapping. Considering the turf-conscious nature of most academic departments, it may be difficult to have the necessary flexibility to quickly adapt to new ideas and to integrate new concepts when the responsibility for the curriculum is fragmented.

COURSES FOR NONTRADITIONAL STUDENTS

Colleges and universities often find themselves providing seminars and short courses for potential or practicing entrepreneurs. These are often done through centers or institutes which are nonacademic units of the college or university. The effectiveness of these programs is reviewed by W. F. Kiesner in Chapter 6 of this book. Quite often the college or university finds itself in partnership with a private group such as a chamber of commerce or a private company whose product becomes the content of such seminars.

These seminars take two forms. Often the two forms are blended into a single package that may encompass from one to three days. The first form can be called the *networking model.* Principally these programs bring potential entrepreneurs in contact with practicing entrepreneurs. The practicing entrepreneurs tell their stories and answer questions from the participants. Usually this is done in a panel format in which the practicing entrepreneurs address a particular subject or topic.

Often these seminars do not provide a great deal of specific content or training. Much of their value is inspirational. Potential entrepreneurs see others who have succeeded in establishing their own ventures and come away with the feeling that, "If they can do it, so can I." In addition, potential entrepreneurs often feel that they benefit from having their own specific questions answered in the informal exchanges that take place after the formal sessions, at meals, or in the corridors. Another type of success claimed for these networking seminars is the establishment of contacts that may be useful to practicing entrepreneurs when their own ventures are launched.

The second type of program is the *skills seminar.* Here specific problems faced by the entrepreneur are addressed, usually by those with formal training or credentials in the area. College faculty are often utilized, as are accountants, lawyers, bankers, marketing managers, production engineers, and financial consultants. These experts make presentations on specific problems or topics in their fields of expertise. One of the best known and most highly regarded of these types of seminars are those conducted by John Welsh and Jerry White from the Carruth Center for Entrepreneurship at Southern Methodist University. Their program consists of an intensive course in financial management for owner/managers. Particular emphasis is placed on financial analysis including cash flow, break-even, profit and loss, and using financial statements as management tools. Because of the more academic orientation of the skills seminars, colleges and universities are more likely to be successful with these types of programs than with the networking model.

There has been very little research done on the effectiveness of these programs. Nevertheless, their continued popularity and resulting growth testify that the market placed high value upon them. In Kiesner's study (1987), he asked the owner/managers to rank among eight alternatives what they considered to be "the most ideal training method." The owners viewed small group discussions led by small business people as the most ideal, followed by lectures by experts, specific problem clinics and workshops, working with a consultant, special college courses for small business, discussions led by university small business faculty, lectures by small business faculty experts, and self-directed/self-study programs, in that order. It is worthy to note that less than 10 percent of Kiesner's sample found special college courses for small businesses to be effective. However, as Kiesner commented,

it is important to note that the vast majority of the ideal notions of the owners dealt with non-traditional formats (at least non-traditional to colleges and faculty types) such as group discussions and working with experts. The owners are saying they want to be treated in a special way as special people and they want to have a part in the programs and be treated as equals. They do not want to be lectured by those they believe are not quite as expert in the areas of small business as they. Faculty must recognize this problem and adjust their actions and offerings because of it. (Kiesner, 1987, pp. 134–135)

Collegiate-Based Programs for Student Entrepreneurs

The growing interest in entrepreneurship education on college campuses has fostered the growth of student organizations designed to encourage students to entrepreneur, promote networking, allow students to associate in more depth with practicing entrepreneurs, and allow students to develop business plans that they will implement when their formal education is completed.

In this regard, the achievements of the Association of Collegiate Entrepreneurs (ACE) are impressive. ACE is a nonprofit organization that was formed in 1983 to help young people, students, and young entrepreneurs network and learn from one another. ACE sees its strength as coming from its triangular organization. The base of that triangle comprises the student members, who are enrolled in entrepreneurship programs across the nation and organized into local chapters, usually under the sponsorship of a faculty adviser. The second side of the triangle is made up of the young entrepreneurs who are in the ACE 100. These young entrepreneurs are ranked on the basis of gross revenues generated by their companies and are to be under thirty years of age. The third side of the triangle consists of the faculty members who are teaching entrepreneurship courses on the campuses with ACE chapters.

Currently, two hundred universities are participating in ACE and the membership in ACE represents over forty countries. The highlight of ACE activity is its annual convention, which draws more than one thousand students, faculty, and young entrepreneurs from across the nation and world. Students present projects, and network with each other and with the young entrepreneurs. The young entrepreneurs serve as speakers, discussion leaders, and advisers to the students. The faculty present papers and engage in symposiums on teaching methodology and research needs in the field.

Another organization that has as one of its objectives the development of the entrepreneurial spirit is Students in Free Enterprise (SIFE). SIFE chapters now exist at 246 colleges in thirty-five states involving over eighteen thousand students and eight hundred faculty members. The SIFE program has two prongs. The first prong consists of seminars in leadership training and skills which are conducted around the nation for chapter members. The second prong comprises a series of regional contests leading to a national competition. In this competition SIFE students are evaluated on the basis of the projects they conduct each year. The goal is to promote a better understanding by the general public of the operation of the free enterprise system and the entrepreneurial genius that underlies it. While not concerned with the technical aspects of entrepreneurship, the SIFE competition encourages students to be entrepreneurial in devising new programs to communicate to the widest possible audience. Many SIFE chapters have as one of their components providing assistance to small businesses; many others have devised programs or presentations to students in elementary and secondary schools on the process of entrepreneurship and the role of the entrepreneur in the private enterprise economy. Cash awards are made to the winning teams at both the regional and national level.

CRITIQUE OF COLLEGIATE PROGRAMS

Collegiate programs for both traditional and nontraditional students suffer from one fault: They tend to focus primarily on traditional management skills and imparting technical expertise to their students. The growing literature in the psychology of entrepreneurs demonstrates that entrepreneurs have different psychological characteristics and attitudes than does the general population as a whole. Little attention is paid in entrepreneurship education to identifying the students who have entrepreneurial potential and in providing the educational environment that will reinforce and create those characteristics among students who do not possess them.

Entrepreneurship education at the collegiate level has apparently proceeded on the assumption that entrepreneurs are born, not made; therefore, training is provided for students with preexisting characteristics and attitudes. Unfortunately, little is done to generate those characteristics and attitudes among students who may not now possess them.

This approach severely restricts the potential supply of entrepreneurs to the economy. This may be particularly true among minority communities where role models are lacking. There the opportunity to work with entrepreneurs is virtually nonexistent, and self-images are generally deficient because of the environment in which the students live and learn. It is surprising that so much research has been done on the psychology of entrepreneurs and yet so little has been translated into structuring courses or devising ways of transmitting the necessary attitudes and insights to potential future entrepreneurs.

REFERENCES

Broehl, Wayne G. 1982. "Entrepreneurship in the Less Developed World." In *The Encyclopedia of Entrepreneurship,* edited by C. A. Kent, D. L. Sexton, and K. H. Vesper. Englewood Cliffs, N.J.: Prentice-Hall, pp. 257–269.

DiBacco, Thomas V. 1987. *Made in the USA: The History of American Business.* New York: Harper and Row.

Gunderson, Gerald. 1989. *The Wealth Creators: An Entrepreneurial History of the United States.* New York: Truman Talley Books, E. P. Dutton.

Harwood, Edwin. 1982. "The Sociology of Entrepreneurship." In *The Encyclopedia of Entrepreneurship,* edited by C. A. Kent, D. L. Sexton, and K. H. Vesper. Englewood Cliffs, N.J.: Prentice-Hall, pp. 91–98.

Hess, Donald W. 1987. "Relevance of Small Business Courses to Management Needs." *Journal of Small Business Management,* 27 (January): 26–34.

Kent, Calvin A. 1982. "Entrepreneurship in Economic Development." In *The Encyclopedia of Entrepreneurship,* edited by C. A. Kent, D. L. Sexton, and K. H. Vesper. Englewood Cliffs, N.J.: Prentice-Hall, pp. 237–253.

Kiesner, W. F. 1987. "The Value of Various Sources of Small Business Management Assistance from the Viewpoint of Owners and Faculty." *The Journal of Private Enterprise* 3 (Fall): 130–137.

Klatt, Lawrence A. 1988. "A Study of Small Business/Entrepreneurial Education in Colleges and Universities." *The Journal of Private Enterprise* 4, (Fall): 103–108.

Perkins, Edwin J., and Gary M. Walton. 1985. *A Prosperous People: The Growth of the American Economy.* Englewood Cliffs, N.J.: Prentice-Hall.

Ronstadt, Robert. 1986. "The Educated Entrepreneur: An Era of Entrepreneurial Education Is Beginning." *The Journal of Private Enterprise* 2 (Fall): 67–80.

Sexton, Donald L., and Nancy E. Bowman. 1984. "Entrepreneurship Education: Suggestions For Increasing Effectiveness." *Journal of Small Business Management* 22 (April): 18–25.

Shapero, Albert. 1984. "The Entrepreneurial Event." In *The Environment for Entrepreneurship,* edited by C. A. Kent. Lexington, Mass.: Lexington Books, pp. 21–40.

Shapero, Albert, and Lisa Sokol. 1982. "The Social Dimensions of Entrepreneurship." *The Encyclopedia of Entrepreneurship,* edited by C. A. Kent, D. L. Sexton, and K. H. Vesper. Englewood Cliffs, N.J.: Prentice-Hall, pp. 72–88.

Solomon, George T. 1988. "Small Business Management and Entrepreneurship Education in America: A National Survey Overview." *The Journal of Private Enterprise* 2 (Fall): 109–117.

Vesper, Karl H. 1985. "New Developments in Entrepreneurship Education." In *Frontiers of Entrepreneurship Research,* edited by J. A. Hornaday, E. B. Shils, J. A. Timmons, and K. H. Vesper. Wellesley, Mass.: Babson College, Center for Entrepreneurship Research, pp. 489–497.

Zeithaml, Carl E., and George H. Rice, Jr. 1987. "Entrepreneurship/Small Business Education in American Universities." *Journal of Small Business Management* 25 (January): 44.

8

Family Business: A New Wave for Business Schools

Craig E. Aronoff and Mary B. Cawley

In the mid-1970s, programs devoted to private enterprise education proliferated on college campuses. By the early 1980s, entrepreneurship had become the hot topic in business schools. Academic attention spawned a tremendous number of entrepreneurship programs and spurred a tremendous amount of thoughtful, insightful writing and research. Popular magazines like *INC.* and *Venture* developed to serve the entrepreneurial market.

A new wave, however, is now clearly on the horizon and will break dramatically into academic programs in the early 1990s. It is the fusion of America's two most potent institutions: family and business. Family businesses are an endlessly fascinating phenomena. All the complex drama of family relations and business enterprise are contained within them. Like families, they are human and personal—but as businesses they are concerned with the bottom line. They often are equally concerned with family values and value-added.

Given these weighty themes, the public's great interest in family business is not surprising. Unfortunately, much of this interest is of a somewhat prurient nature. Television shows like "Dallas" and "Dynasty" deal primarily with the dirty linen of fictional family enterprises. Disaffected heirs of business families write books that sell briskly. Progenies of the Reynolds tobacco and Bingham publishing families recently have produced best-selling books that titillated public interest by exposing family secrets and business politics (Reynolds and Schactman, 1989; Bingham, 1989). Newspapers headline prominent business families' internecine battles. Gallo brothers Ernest and Julio sued brother Joseph for trademark infringement. The Koch boys of Koch Industries, the second largest closely held company in the United States, engaged in a bitter, name-calling power struggle. Family members chose up sides and went to war at U-Haul.

Academics may also be attracted to family businesses by their dramatic elements, but hopefully that will not be our primary motivation. Instead, we should be primarily driven by our recognition (albeit belated) of the economic, social, and cultural importance of family businesses. As much as 90 to 95 percent of American businesses are family-controlled, including one-third of the *Fortune* 500. They account for half the nation's jobs and 40 percent of the gross national product (GNP) (Ward, 1987). Eighty percent of America's millionaires have ownership of a family business as their principal asset. Family-business owners are prominent in the social, civic, philanthropic, political, and cultural lives of every American community, large or small.

Academic programs designed to serve family businesses are already proliferating. An April 1988 study identified fifteen institutions of higher learning as in some way responding to the family business interests (Ward, 1988). Our review suggests that the number more than doubled in the next year (Aronoff and Cawley, 1989). The Family Firm Institute, whose members include professionals and academics focused on family businesses, was founded in 1986. Its membership tripled between 1987 and 1988 (Family Firm Institute, 1989).

The literature on family business has been developing fairly rapidly as well. While Greek tragedies and Shakespeare's plays contain lessons relevant to the subject, contemporary academic publication has become frequent only in the past ten years. The outlets most frequently used by those publishing research on family business include *Journal of Small Business Management, Organizational Dynamics, Business Horizons,* and *Harvard Business Review.* An academic journal, *Family Business Review,* began publication in 1988 and is enjoying wide circulation. Many popular magazines have already begun to exploit the family-business market. *Business Week,* among others, circulates a newsletter targeted at family businesses, and other magazines like *Nation's Business, Forbes,* and *Inc.* regularly include features on family firms. Even more print coverage is sure to develop.

Leading university-based writers include John Ward (Loyola University of Chicago), Ivan Lansberg (on leave from Yale University), Neil Churchill (Babson), Justin Longnecker (Baylor), Gibb Dyer (Brigham Young), Peter Davis (University of Pennsylvania), Jeff Barach (Tulane), and Amy Lyman (University of California-Davis). Others who have made substantial contributions include Leon Danco, Richard Beckhard, Donald Jonovic, David Bork,

Barbara Hollander, and John Davis. Sharon Nelton, writing primarily in *Nation's Business,* is the journalist who has made the greatest contribution to the field.

DEFINING FAMILY BUSINESS

Just what is a family business, and how is it defined? The usual definitions deal with percentages of ownership or control in family hands, overlaps between stockholders and management, and other technical considerations. While these definitions have great merit, they have never been entirely satisfying. Too much of the family-business phenomenon is emotional and cultural for a definition to suffice absent consideration of values or attitudes (Aronoff, 1988b).

The theoretical underpinning of work in the family business field grows from systems theory as it relates to families and businesses. During the late 1970s and the early 1980s, a systems model evolved (see Figure 8.1). The model consists of three intersecting circles representing family, management, and ownership dimensions of family businesses. Variations of this depiction have become almost generic to any description of family business complexity (Tagiuri and Davis, 1982). The complex phenomena created by these overlapping systems is precisely what makes the family business a complicated but exciting topic, full of opportunities for academic contributions.

ACADEMIA AND FAMILY BUSINESS

Academic responses to new areas of opportunity traditionally involve teaching, research, and service. The same is true of family business (see Table 8.1).

What is unusual in relation to family business, however, is that the service component in many ways runs ahead of research and teaching. This phenomenon seems at least partially driven by the nature of the opportunities represented by the family business *market.* Moreover, the complex characteristics of that market create unusual difficulties for traditional research or instructional approaches.

Family businesses are full of intelligent, successful people with a great deal of practical knowledge. The way they process knowledge is not necessarily the way academics typically process knowledge, nor is the family business student a traditional student. These students may encompass several generations, several management levels, several levels of family-business involvement, varying degrees of educational achievement, and many separate perspectives. These students share in common only the family and the business.

To have a significant positive impact on family business may require

Figure 8.1
Family Business Model

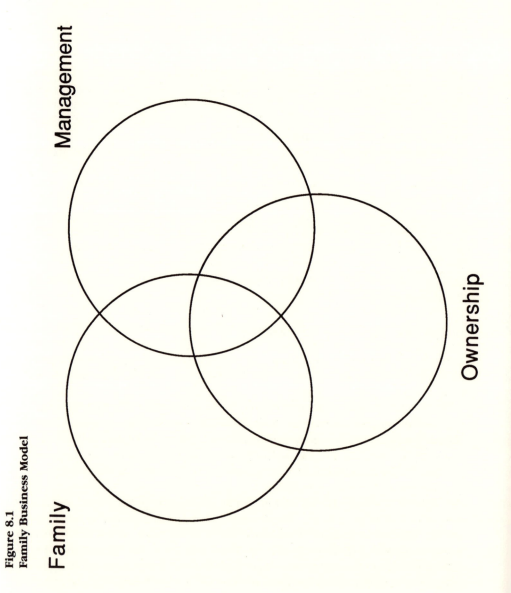

Management

Ownership

Family

Table 8.1
Some College and University Responses to Family Business

Institution	Teaching	Research	Service	Other [1]
Arizona State U-West			*	
Babson College	X -	X		
Baylor University			X	
Boston University	X + -	X		
Brigham Young	X + -	X		
Christian Brothers			X	
DePaul University	X	X		
Fairleigh Dickenson	* + -	*	X	
Georgia State		X		
Georgia Tech				X
Hillsdale College		X		
Jacksonville University		X		
Kennesaw State		X	X	
Montana State	X -			
Oregon State	X + -	X	X	
Sonoma State		X		
Tulane	X + -	X		
U. of Alabama		*		
U. of Baltimore				X
U. of Cincinnati	*	*	X	
U. of Connecticut				X
U. of S. Carolina		X		
Washington and Lee	*	X	X	
Wharton		X	X	
Yale	X	X		

Source: Chair of Private Enterprise, Kennesaw State College. Telephone Survey, August -- September 1989.

1   occasional programs or sponsorship

X   existing; * proposed; + graduate level; - undergraduate level.

both reaching beyond institutional walls and breaking down traditional academic barriers. If academicians want to help family businesses and business families toward business and family healthfulness, then educational programs must be both multidimensional and multidisciplinary.

Aspects of a family-business program should include management development, interpersonal communications, strategic planning, conflict resolution, financial planning, family systems, retirement and transitional planning and much more. Relevant disciplines may include anything from accounting to religion and cultural anthropology to gerontology.

This breadth is obviously difficult to achieve in a traditional academic context of curriculum development, standard credit course offerings, and the like. Nonetheless, some institutions are developing traditional course offerings related to family business.

TEACHING

Instruction centered on family business is integrated into the traditional business curriculum in a variety of ways, with most falling under the umbrellas of entrepreneurship, organization behavior, and management. In many instances, course development evolved as a result of a faculty member's personal family background or in consulting experience with or research projects related to family-run firms. This evolutionary process in itself hints at another inherent problem that impedes the development of family-business courses. Instructors with relatively narrow academic backgrounds have difficulty dealing with issues of family/business overlap.

At Montana State University, family business issues are incorporated into units of existing undergraduate classes in the school of business. Babson College, Boston University, and Oregon State University, on the other hand, each offer at least one undergraduate course focused on family business management. Brigham Young University, Tulane, and the University of California offer at least one—and in some instances, more—graduate-level courses. In all present course offerings, primary teaching methods include case analyses, seminars, and readings from relevant academic or popular literature.

Several institutions are studying the feasibility of family-business courses or have courses currently under development. A family-business course will be offered soon at DePaul University as part of its undergraduate entrepreneurship curriculum. Washington and Lee is in the process of developing a course that will be multidisciplinary, pulling together management, psychology, humanities, and law (Aronoff and Cawley, 1989).

Traditional academic approaches are most likely to be effective where there are reasonable numbers of undergraduate or graduate students who are the offspring of family-business owners and anticipating entering their family businesses. These students may well seek curriculum relevant to their expected future experience. A course or two focusing on family business might be of great value to such individuals. However, while it is being contemplated by some institutions, replacing majors in liberal arts, industry-related technical specialties, business, or engineering with family-business majors probably should not be viewed as a positive direction.

RESEARCH

In 1985, John Davis reviewed the existing family-business literature and proposed an excellent research agenda. In his opinion, family-business literature's greatest shortcoming was the lack of comparative empirical studies. Family-owned businesses seldom are compared with publicly- or non-family-owned firms. He also found that the research was

- qualitative and mostly anecdotal, with little quantitative data presented;
- limited in examination of financial characteristics or business practices;
- based on case analysis of small and medium-sized family-owned and -managed firms; and
- limited in its examination of large family firms, especially publicly held firms.

To further family business research, Davis suggested an agenda including five major categories:

1. Number of family-owned and -managed businesses
2. Economics
3. Social and cultural importance
4. Business practices and business performance
5. Family influences

More than forty research topics were specified under those categories. Davis also advocated federal government involvement in building a database on family businesses (Davis, 1985).

Despite the existence of a respected journal and numerous opportunities for the presentation of research on family business at academic meetings, limited progress has been achieved in furthering the Davis agenda (Frishkoff, Davis, and Aronoff, 1988). Many reasons are behind the lack of significant research progress. Clearly, however, research efforts are hindered by the problem of defining the family business. As *Family Business Review* editors Ivan Lansberg, Edith Perrow, and Sharon Rogolsky pointed out, "Until researchers agree on what a family business is, they will find it difficult to build on each other's work and to develop a useable knowledge base." (Lansberg, Perrow, and Rogolsky, 1988, p. 2).

Much knowledge already exists, but it resides in disciplines that have seldom interacted fruitfully in the past. Thus, "new" knowledge is currently being generated not by original research, but primarily by studying literature in unfamiliar disciplines to glean theory and applications related to family businesses (Kanter, 1989). Psychologists are being forced to deal with what tax accountants know, and vice versa. Conflict resolution in family business is the intellectual domain of organizational behaviorists, family systems counselors, and lawyers (Hollander and Elman, 1988). Unified by their commitment to understanding family business, representatives of these disciplines have begun a productive exchange of knowledge and experience.

Until two years ago, no comprehensive bibliography on family business existed. Oregon State University recently developed an extensive listing of past and current literature. Its research produced a bibliography that cuts across all academic disciplines and includes a number of published and unpublished papers. While its broad scope includes popular magazine articles and books as well as academic publications and papers, the bibliography is an excellent academic resource (Frishkoff, 1987).

Some of the research interests of academicians involved with family businesses are driven by practical considerations and seem highly idiosyncratic in an intellectual context. When the University of Pennsylvania's Peter Davis was asked, for example, what research findings he would like to have in his hands at that moment, he replied, "The impact of the [owner/manager's] first heart attack on a family business." This issue is a critical one, and research on it could potentially provide significant insights into the psychosocial, managerial, and financial dimensions of family business.

To date, insights into family-business phenomena have been more often gained by experience than by structured research. Those who are interested in such phenomena frequently are confronted with lucrative consulting opportunities. Thus, their motivation can become inconsistent with the methodical investigation and reporting required by sound research.

Moreover, an institutional framework to generate support for family-business research has only recently begun to develop. Two universities, Georgia State and University of Cincinnati, recently received endowments solely for the study of family-business issues. Frank Hoy, Georgia States's Carl Zwerner Professor of Family-Owned Business, will concentrate on several research projects before moving into course development. University of Cincinnati's Sid Barton will direct the activities of the Goering Center for Family Firm Studies. While initial activities will be research-oriented, eventual curriculum development is expected.

Bernard Tennenbaum heads Fairleigh Dickenson's Rothman Institute of Entrepreneurial Studies, which includes a Family Business Center. The center will sponsor research as well as develop graduate and undergraduate courses, and will offer seminars and training programs (Aronoff and Cawley, 1989).

SERVICE

The most extensive response by academicians has come in the form of service: delivery of extracurricular programs designed to provide developmental opportunities for family businesses and their principals.

The College of Business at Oregon State University initiated a Family Business Program in 1985. Under the leadership of Patricia Frishkoff, its multifaceted approach has taken it far beyond campus boundaries. In addition to academic coursework and research, the successful program offers numerous statewide workshops, consulting services, and seminars, and an annual conference.

Baylor University's Institute for Family Business is structured along similar lines. Directed by Nancy Bowman-Upton, Baylor's Streich Lecturer in Family Business, the institute offers seminars, workshops, and an annual conference.

Washington and Lee University's Institute for Family Business differs from others in that it has a liberal arts component. Under Lawrence Lamont's guidance, the institute engages in on-going research and publication—as well as offering service to family businesses in the form of seminars and consultation (Aronoff and Cawley, 1989).

Kennesaw State College's Family Business Forum is built around quarterly seminars featuring the nation's leading family-business experts, heads of prominent local family businesses, and knowledgeable business service providers. The forum is available on a subscription basis, with yearly memberships limited to fifty firms. The forum is sponsored by a bank, a law firm, an accounting firm, and a management consulting firm. Jacksonville University, the University of Wisconsin-Milwaukee, and Arizona State University-West, among others, have used the Kennesaw model in establishing family service programs (Aronoff, 1988a).

The recognition of the importance of family businesses to U.S. society and economy has been long overdue. The application of academic resources to the understanding of family-business systems has awaited that recognition. Now, however, the fertile ground has been found, and the plowing has begun. A few seeds have been planted and have borne their first fruit. The real harvest remains before us and depends on whether academia can overcome its disciplinary strictures and institutionalized structures to respond fully to the opportunity that family business represents.

REFERENCES

Aronoff, Craig E. 1988a. "FBF is National Model." *Family Business Forum Quarterly Newsletter.* Marietta, Ga.: Kennesaw State College, Fall.

———. 1988b. "What is the Value of Family Business?" *Family Business Forum Quarterly Newsletter.* Marietta, Ga.: Kennesaw State College, Winter.

Aronoff, Craig E., and Mary Cawley. 1989. *College and University-Based Family Business Programs.* Telephone Survey, August–September.

Barach, Jeffrey A., Joseph Ganitsky, James A. Carson, and Benjamin A. Doochin. 1988. "Entry of the Next Generation: Strategic Challenge for Family Business." *Journal of Small Business Management* 26, no. 2 (April).

Bingham, Sally. 1989. *Passion and Prejudice.* New York: Knopf, pp. 49–56.

Bork, David. 1986. *Family Business, Risky Business.* New York: AMACOM.

Churchill, Neil, and Kenneth J. Hatten. 1987. "Non-Market-based Transfers of Wealth and Power: A Research Framework for Family Businesses." *American Journal of Small Business* 12, no. 2 (Winter).

Danco, Leon. 1980. *Beyond Survival.* Cleveland, Ohio: Center for Family Business University Press.

Davis, John A. 1985. "The Family-Owned Business." In *Measurement and Evaluation of the Populations of Family-Owned and Home-Based Businesses,* edited by the U.S. Small Business Administration. Washington, D.C.: Small Business Administration, pp. III, 1–III, 16.

Dyer, Gibb. 1986. *Cultural Change in Family Firms.* San Francisco: Jossey Bass.

Family Firm Institute. 1989. "FFI Activities: Transition and Growth." *Family Firm Institute Newsletter.* (January).

Frishkoff, Patricia, ed. 1987. *Family Business Bibliography.* Corvallis: Oregon State University, College of Business.

Frishkoff, Patricia, John Davis, and Craig Aronoff. 1988. "Trends in Family Business Education." Panel discussion, United States Small Business and Entrepreneurship Annual Conference, Monterey Calif., Oct.

Handler, Wendy, and Kathy E. Kram. 1988. "Succession in Family Firms: The Problem of Resistance." *Family Business Review* 4, no. 4 (Winter): 361–382.

Hollander, Barbara, and Nancy S. Elman. 1988. "Family-Owned Businesses: An Emerging Field of Inquiry." *Family Business Review* 2, no. 2 (Summer): 145–164.

Jonovic, Donald J 1981. *The Second Generation Boss.* Cleveland, Ohio: Center for Family Business University Press.

Kanter, Rosabeth Moss. 1989. "Work and Family in the United States: A Critical Review and Agenda for Research and Policy." Reprinted in *Family Business Review* 2, no. 1 (Spring): 77–114.

Lansberg, Ivan. 1983. "Managing Human Relations in the Family Firm: The Problems of Institutional Overlap." *Organizational Dynamics* (Summer): 39–46.

Lansberg, Ivan, Edith L. Perrow, and Sharon Rogolsky. 1988. "Family Business as an Emerging Field of Inquiry." *Family Business Review* 1, no. 1 (Summer): 1–7.

Lyman, Amy. 1988. "Life in the Family Circle." *Family Business Review* 1, no. 4 (Winter): 383–398.

Nelton, Sharon. 1988. "Family Business a Hot Market." *Nation's Business,* vol. 76, September, pp 2–7.

Reynolds, Patrick, and Tom Schactman. 1989. *The Gilded Leaf,* Boston: Little, Brown.

Tagiuri, Renato, and John A. Davis. 1982. "Bivalent Attributes of Family Firms." Unpublished paper.

———. 1989. "The Influence of Life Stage on Father-Son Work Relationships in Family Companies." *Family Business Review* 2, no. 1 (Spring): 47–74.

United States Association of Small Business and Entrepreneurship. 1988. "Trends in Family Business Education," Panel discussion, Annual Conference, October.

Ward, John L. 1986. "Sibblings and the Family Business." *Loyola Business Forum* 5, no. 1 (Fall): 1–27.

———. 1987. *Keeping the Family Business Healthy*. San Francisco: Jossey Bass.

———. 1988. "Growth in Family Business Education." Unpublished study.

PART THREE

Entrepreneurship in the Elementary Curriculum

9

Entrepreneurial Thinking and Behavior: What Role the Classroom?

Marilyn Kourilsky

He is fat and has beads of sweat on his forehead (the sweat is often dripping down his face); he has little or no hair on his head, no neck at all, and a big cigar stuck in his mouth. What does he do for a living? According to the drawings of youngsters in our schools, he is a successful entrepreneur. It comes as no surprise, then, that these same youngsters seldom list "starting my own business" as a career aspiration.

The decline of entrepreneurship is a real and threatening phenomenon in our society (Hundal, 1971). Not only is entrepreneurship a prerequisite for economic growth, it also is a way of reducing the power of monopoly by adding to the pool of new ideas and the exploration of new markets (McClelland, 1961).

It was the French economist R. Cantillon who coined the term entrepreneur—from *entreprendre,* to undertake. The entrepreneur was seen as an individual who obtained factors of production and combined them into products for the marketplace (Cantillon, 1755). For modern economists it was J. A. Schumpeter who brought the entrepreneurial role to the forefront. To him, the entrepreneur was a risk-taking individual who was able to seek out new markets and promote new methods of production, all of which generated economic growth (Schumpeter, 1934).

Soslow (1966) identified the true entrepreneur as someone who opens a business where none previously existed—a societal change agent capable of independent thinking. Those who start businesses solely as an alternative to wage employment are not necessarily entrepreneurial. "Entrepreneurship requires the element of growth that leads to innovation, job creation, and economic expansion" (Kent, 1984, p. 4). Most past and present experts on entrepreneurship describe the entrepreneur as an individual who is capable of and engages in divergent thinking—in lay terms, a person who may dare to think the unthinkable and sometimes believes he or she can do the undoable. Such attributes, however, are not uniquely of interest for the budding entrepreneur; they are often important traits of creative and successful people in all walks of life. Therefore, it is of significant benefit to our society to nurture in our youngsters whatever intrinsic inclinations they may have to generate divergent ideas and to integrate those divergent ideas with resources and processes to make things happen in their unique way—namely; the entrepreneurial spirit in its broadest sense. In this chapter, then, when we speak of *entrepreneurship* (either fostering or inhibiting it) our intent is to focus on the creatively divergent traits of the entrepreneurial spirit rather than on the more strict economic definition which is closely linked to the creation of new business enterprises or products.

If the traits associated with the entrepreneurial spirit are important, then organizations and societies must find ways to encourage it. It is the purpose of this chapter to discuss and analyze the effect of the typical school experience on entrepreneurship and then to suggest and describe ways in which the entrepreneurial spirit in youngsters can be fostered within the schools.

THE EFFECT OF THE TRADITIONAL SCHOOL EXPERIENCE ON ENTREPRENEURIAL SPIRIT

By its very nature and structure, the traditional K–12 experience does not foster entrepreneurially creative traits. Whereas it is not the goal of schooling to develop an abundance of business entrepreneurs, one may still be curious why 25 percent of kindergartners demonstrate important entrepreneurial characteristics (need for achievement, willingness to take risks, and so forth), whereas only 3 percent of high school youngsters manifest such talent (Kourilsky, 1977). Why are those traits cultivated in so few children? We suggest that, first, the classroom as a society is analogous to a planned economy—it is almost a simulation of a command economy; and, second, convergence and not divergence is disproportionately rewarded in the school experience.

Decisions in the Classroom

In a command or planned economy the decisions of what to produce and how to produce—the production decisions—are made by the planners; the goal is to satisfy the planners and not necessarily act in accordance with or in response to the demands of the consumers. In a market or free enterprise economy, the decisions of what and how to produce are in the end made by the consumers, and the long-term goal of production is to satisfy their demand. If consumers are dissatisfied with a product, the firm will ultimately go out of business. In the classroom, the teacher is the producer and the students (learners) are the consumers. However, by tradition, the classroom in its structure is analogous to a planned economy. The decisions of what, how, and for whom to produce are usually totally centralized and decided by the planner (in this case, the teacher). In terms of curriculum, learning opportunities, and demonstrating how learning took place, there is little autonomy given to the consumers (in this case, the students). It would probably be considered unacceptable, or odd at best, if a child were asked to show how much he or she had learned from reading a chapter by creating an annotated collage of pictures in addition to or instead of taking a teacher-generated test on the chapter's content.

Picture the classroom from the perspective of a kindergartner beginning his or her school socialization experience. The teacher is standing in front of the classroom. The kindergartner is often looking at pieces of tape on the rug and wondering, "What are those pieces of tape for?" The teacher informs the kindergartner that, "Those pieces of tape are to show you where to sit on the rug so you will not interfere with anyone else's space." Does that kindergartner feel any autonomy or control over what is going to happen in the classroom? It is not surprising that by the twelfth grade, many youngsters have lost their sense of agency—that they are waiting for and expecting someone else, the person in charge (the planner), to tell them what to learn and how to learn. College students often ask "How many pages should my term project be?" When they are told "As many as it takes you to convey your message," initially they are often dismayed, confused, and perplexed—but eventually they will be happier and more autonomous.

Convergence and Divergence in the Classroom

The student soon discovers that convergence is rewarded. The high grades go to those who have discovered what is expected, and there is often just one acceptable answer to a question, regardless of its complexity. There are "right" answers and "expected responses" to homework problems, examination questions, and sometimes even personal opinions. Even the acceptable answers are often dictated by the curriculum and the teacher's lesson plan. A student once advised her friend, "If the teacher says plant the tree with the roots in the air, you better be ready to regurgitate it back just like that." Excellent teachers reported that often when they encouraged discrepant or diverse responses they were criticized for not properly socializing the youngsters and not "preparing" them for higher education.

The unfortunate results of this imposed convergence are typified by the following incident, observed through a two-way mirror while a boy was being tested for a gifted program. As the five-year-old entered the room and interacted initially with the tester, all his observations and responses literally reeked of his intelligence. Subsequently, one of the questions given to the child was, "There is a stamped envelope on the ground right by the mailbox that is addressed and has a return address on it. What would you do with it?" The expected response is, "Pick it up and put it in the mailbox." However, the child said, "I'm going to give it back to the sender because since the sender dropped it, I think there is a chance he might not want to send it now." The tester would not accept this very rational but unexpected response, and kept on prompting him. The child kept on saying that he was going to give it back to the sender. Eventually, he got a zero on the question. Suddenly, I was painfully aware that this child's IQ score had just gone down. If that child wants to be "successful," he must give up that kind of divergent response. Sooner or later he is going to be "smart" enough to give the kind of response the teacher or tester wants.

The Terman studies on the gifted started in 1929 for children with IQs above 130. Approximately a thousand subjects were included in the research. Several were tracked for more than twenty or thirty years, some into their seventies and eighties. Terman wanted to ascertain what would happen to these exceedingly gifted people. None of them won a Nobel prize, and very few of them became entrepreneurs. A lot of them became college professors. Why did this happen? Since Terman was extremely interested in his subjects, he followed them closely and made sure they were successful in school. Perhaps by ensuring their success (in a convergent-intensive environment) he unknowingly was assisting in the loss of the divergence that they may have needed to become entrepreneurs.

The strong tendency to reward convergent academic performance is closely linked to traditional and equally restrictive notions of what qualifies as intelligence. In the typical school experience, only one type of intelligence is recognized, the analytic type, whereas there are at least three aspects of human intelligence that exist in varying degrees in every individual—the analytic, the innovative, and the practical. However, most IQ tests and intelligence models focus on the first, infrequently recognize the second, and deliberately reject the third type (Sternberg, 1982). Thus, if a parent is told, "Your child is really bright," it most likely means that your child has exhibited one particular type of intelligence—the analytic type.

Sternberg illustrates these aspects of intelligence with three idealized types. A student who excels in analytic intelligence has high test scores in school and college, ranks high on the admission acceptance lists, and is skillful in assignments calling for quantitative and critical analysis. However, this student may begin to fall behind over the years as the work begins to call for more creative and innovative thinking.

A student who excels in innovative intelligence may not necessarily have the highest test scores or perform outstandingly at analytic tasks. However, that individual excels as an innovator in coming up with new ideas and programs, is creative in writing, and is able to see an old concept in a new way.

The third type (who is technically referred to as the contextual) is the student whose test scores are only average, who is not highly proficient at analytic or innovative assignments, and who is expected to have difficulty in getting a job. However, much to the surprise of researchers, this student turns out to be quite capable of going out and earning a living (if motivated). This type of individual has practical intelligence and is "street-smart" with respect to the way the real world works and how to take creative advantage of both predictable and unpredictable environmental opportunities. It is a type of intelligence that traditional IQ tests most often fail to measure and that teachers are not trained to recognize, appreciate, or nourish. As a result, the youngster in which this type of intelligence predominates is often unsuccessful in school and may grow to use his or her street-smarts in counterproductive and even antisocial pursuits as opposed to creative pro-social entrepreneurial endeavors.

Clearly, the socialization of youth throughout today's schooling experiences tends to diminish their proclivity toward entrepreneurial thinking and behavior. However, we believe that educational experience could become a powerful influence on enhancing such propensities by implementing two strategic initiatives:

1. Throughout the schooling process, create and sustain an educational environment in which the creatively divergent traits of the entrepreneurial spirit are fostered and enhanced.
2. At strategic times in the schooling process, introduce programs that enable individuals to experience entrepreneurial thinking and behavior.

THE EDUCATIONAL ENVIRONMENT FOR FOSTERING ENTREPRENEURIAL THINKING AND BEHAVIOR

With regard to the first initiative, it is necessary, initially, to establish instructional practices that *transfer ownership* of the learning act from the planner (teacher) to the consumer (student). For example, as early as the youngsters can handle it cognitively, they should be given an assignment and allowed to choose among alternatives—for example, to select one (or more, if they like) readings to complete an assignment. In this example, they should then be encouraged to summarize the reading in their own words, express what they believed was important, and tell why. Through cooperative groups they could subsequently exchange their summaries and reviews and share with other classmates what they believed was valuable, worth emphasizing, and worth remembering. In the above scenarios the learners themselves have input into selecting primary sources and deciding what is important and significant—rather than an authority figure, the teacher, telling them exactly what to read and what to remember, and enforcing this view through examinations. Additionally, the learners could be encouraged to create a self-designed portfolio of what they have learned for Open House (back to school night for parents). These portfolios could be analogous to those produced by artists to highlight their work. In the case of the students, they might include essays, journals, scrapbook pictures, and even test results if desired. However, the important idea the teacher would communicate to the students is, *"You* are responsible for selecting and demonstrating what you have learned, and for Open House you may illustrate what you have learned in class in any way you wish." The above procedures are examples of shifting the ownership and onus of decision making from the planner to the consumer. In both subtle and blatant ways, these practices place more learning autonomy and responsibility with the student and give less control to the teacher. Learning is thus owned by the learner, and the teacher enjoys the more constructive role of expert facilitator.

In addition to transferring more ownership of learning to the student, teachers must employ classroom practices that are conducive to high levels of *achievement motivation.* Actually, the most widely cited characteristic of the entrepreneurial spirit is the desire for achievement (Mc-Clelland, 1961; DeCarlo and Lyons, 1979, Hornaday and Aboud, 1971; Timmons, 1989). However, one rarely observes classroom practices designed to enhance achievement motivation. A high achiever sets challenging goals, continuously seeks to outdo his or her own performance, and values feedback as a means of assessing goal achievement (Begley and Boyd, 1986). In general, high achievement motivation appears to result when parents or teachers encourage children to act independently, praise their performances, and provide models of achievement and aspirations for excellence (Zigler, 1973). One of the most consistent findings in research on effective teaching is that children in classrooms in which the teacher expects all children to learn achieve at a higher level than children in classrooms in which the teacher does not have uniformly high expectations (Stipek, 1988). Although this finding may not surprise most educators, its consequences are usually not reflected in common practice. This is especially true for female and minority students. Children who experience many failures adopt a life-style oriented toward the avoidance of failure rather than the achievement of success (Cromwell, 1963). They develop problem-solving abilities characterized by dependence, outer-directedness, and a willingness to be satisfied with limited accomplishments (Achenbach, 1966; Gruen and Zigler, 1968). The inability to attempt to solve problems or to affect the environment in general because of repeated experiences of unavoidable failure is called *learned helplessness;* it prevents a high level of success motivation. This learned helplessness is further aggravated by teachers with low expectation levels of their pupils (Dweck, 1975; Zigler, 1982). People who fear failure will neutralize whatever achievement motivation they may possess. They will tend to engage in very easy tasks, where there is little chance of failure, or they will pursue very difficult challenges where they cannot be held responsible if they do not succeed (Timmons, 1989).

High teacher expectations for all students could radically transform the dynamics of learning in classrooms. Youngsters who are expected to perform might indeed live up to the label of *high achiever,* and, in reality, may increase their achievement motivation and move out from under the low expectations held both by their teachers and themselves. The research pertaining to student perceptions and expectations clearly indicates that the student belief that success in school is possible is one of the most important factors related to achievement motivation (Wittrock, 1986). In addition, the teacher's creative use of strategies that focus on succeeding will serve to dissipate learners' fear of failure.

Since a high achievement motivation is an important component of entrepreneurial thinking and behavior, the school system in general as well as teachers in their daily practices should be encouraged to establish high expectation levels for all their students and to treat them as if they believe them truly capable of being successful individuals. Teachers need to be able to observe attentively and reflectively their own behavior toward students to analyze the potential effects of their behavior, and to develop strategies to overcome any negative expectations toward their students. To the extent that teachers can accomplish this, they are setting the stage for potential entrepreneurs to flourish.

Finally, teachers must encourage *tenacity* in youngsters and reward behavior in which persistence is manifested. Persistence is the proclivity of an individual to stick to a task until it is completed. If a particular strategy for solving a problem inherent in the task does not work, the persistent person will attempt another approach rather than abandon the task. For example, the entrepreneur who goes bankrupt will be more likely to say, "My business idea did not work, I need a new angle" rather than "Maybe I should give up trying to be my own boss and work for someone else." Persistence is one of the most powerful predictors of the successful application of entrepreneurial thinking and behavior; often closely tied to creativity, persistence is a manifestation of flexibility and the ability to bring divergent thinking to fruition (Torrance, 1960; Kourilsky, 1979). "More than any other single factor, total dedication and perseverance to succeed as an entrepreneur can overcome incredible obstacles and setbacks" (Timmons, 1989, p. 32). Entrepreneurs who successfully build new enterprises possess an intense desire to overcome hurdles, solve problems, and complete the job. They are not intimidated by difficult situations. In fact, their self-confidence and general optimism seems to translate into a view that the impossible just "takes a little longer." (Timmons, 1989).

In a typical classroom there is often a tacit time limit on the learners' propensity for persistence. The attitude that "if you don't get it now, you never will," is pervasive in classrooms and should be discarded. The successful implementation of *mastery learning* in a classroom would be an important step toward creating an environment where persistence would be rewarded and enhanced. According to D. R. Krathwohl, B. S. Bloom, and B. B. Masia (1956), mastery learning is based primarily on the premise that most members of society are capable of acquiring each type of competence needed and that personal qualities and environmental factors (including the school) determine which individuals will finally acquire each type of competence. In this approach, teachers (in cooperation with the learners) may set the goals, objectives, and standards for learning, which they expect all students to achieve or master. Teachers instruct, guide, and reteach, if necessary. Although in the final analysis each learner owns and is responsible for his or her learning, mastery on the part of all students becomes the ultimate goal and the one for which the effective teacher is willing to be held accountable. Thus, if a child fails the midterm and is able and willing to invoke persistent behavior to ultimately master the materials, it is his or her final performance with respect to the material that is weighted and counted. The notion that you only have one chance to learn the chapter and will get an "F" if you fail is eliminated in favor of the notion that you can learn the chapter through persistence, and that learning, even though it takes a little longer, will be recognized, valued and rewarded.

If teachers in training (and in-service teachers as well) could be exposed to the importance and practice of transferring ownership of the learning act to the learner, manifesting high expectation levels for all learners, and, finally, utilizing mastery learning techniques, they would be more likely to create such an educational environment in their own classrooms. One way to achieve these goals would be to have multiple experiences of these concepts as part of their teacher training. Thus, teachers themselves would experience a learning environment conducive to nurturing the entrepreneurial spirit—one in which they would feel autonomous, have a high achievement motivation, and persist in the ultimate achievement of their endeavors. As alluded to earlier, these qualities—which are certainly important for creating new business products—are fundamentally linked to improving the quality of life for the individual and building a society in which productive members thrive.

In addition to creating an environment that in general is conducive to the entrepreneurial spirit, it is also desirable at strategic times in the school process to introduce programs in which individuals can experience entrepreneurial thinking and behavior. Previous business experiences (of a variety of types) rather than formal schooling have been shown to provide the most significant training for entrepreneurship (Mayer and Goldstein, 1961; Lamont, 1972).

PROGRAMS TO HELP INDIVIDUALS TO EXPERIENCE ENTREPRENEURIAL THINKING AND BEHAVIOR

One of the best ways to acquire knowledge and know-how is to learn by doing. There are numerous curriculum guides available that provide the foundations for entrepreneurship (e.g., give suggestions and procedural knowledge for starting one's own business) but do not give the youngsters actual experience in entrepreneurial thinking and behavior. They do not emphasize the second and third types of intelligence by encouraging innovative thinking and practical behavior. As C. A. Kent observes, most of the widely available entrepreneurship curriculums and materials are narrow in their focus and are primarily oriented toward teaching students survival skills (Kent, 1989).

In the course of researching, investigating, and analyzing numerous projects and curriculums on entrepreneurship (which have potential for rewarding the innovative and practical forms of intelligence) we have found several key characteristics that often mitigate significantly either in favor of or against the potential success of an entrepreneurial program. Some of the features that are predictors of a successful entrepreneurial program for youngsters include the following:

- They are predominantly experience-based, with follow-up guidance provided by an expert.
- The participants *perceive* that they are bearing the risks and experiencing the consequences of their decisions.
- The teachers perceive the program is doable in their classroom.

Those entrepreneurship programs that should raise warning signals in the minds of a potential user are predominated by the following features:

- The success of the program is inordinately dependent on the individual characteristics of the teacher or implementer.
- There is excessive logistical resistance to the implementation of the program (e.g., planning for the program is too time-consuming, preparation materials are too costly, or the teachers do not believe the benefits of the program are worth the administrative hassles of implementing it).

- There is serious cognitive resistance to the program (e.g., the teacher is afraid he or she does not understand the program well enough to teach it effectively).

The guidance we offer the potential implementer of an entrepreneurship program is to select as models those that rank high with regard to the above positive characteristics and be cautious of programs that may suffer in the minus column. Although most programs will exhibit some aspect of the negative characteristics cited, the teacher should be encouraged by the fact that most minuses can be compensated for if the pluses are sufficiently solid, as in the case of the three programs on which we have chosen to focus.

REAL ENTERPRISES: RURAL EDUCATION THROUGH ACTION LEARNING

REAL Enterprises are school-based development enterprises designed for high school students in rural communities to research, plan, set up, operate, and own an economically viable, long-term small business in cooperation with local schools (De Largy, 1988).

The program encompasses educational, economic, institutional, and individual goals. In terms of its educational objectives the program strives to help teachers and students develop interest, understanding, and competence with respect to entrepreneurship and small business ownership. Its economic goals include improving, expanding, and diversifying the economic base of a community as well as creating a positive attitude toward the local economy. The major institutional objective of REAL is to help rural schools become small business incubators, and its aim for individual participants is to increase their employability both within and beyond the local community and to generate income and work experience in ways that are compatible with being a good student.

School-based REAL Enterprises are established real businesses, open and accessible to all students, with the students as the actual owners and operators of businesses. (The businesses are integrated into the school's curriculum.) These businesses are guaranteed access to start-up capital and supported with appropriate outside assistance.

The organization of REAL Enterprises partnerships between communities and local school systems requires administrative support and a person responsible for the program. One full planning year is necessary to develop feasibility, explore the local community and economy, create a list of possible businesses, and develop a formal business plan. A second year is also required to continue training and to implement and run the chosen businesses.

There are various kinds of businesses set up in REAL Enterprises. They include businesses in which all the money involved circulates in the local community, businesses providing a product or service that is exported, and businesses where money goes out of the community for outshopping. They are often funded by various foundations to facilitate their initial operation.

Frequently, the programs have been focused on students who are either economically disadvantaged, slow learners, single-parent children, or special education students—some of whom would otherwise be potential dropouts. The actual businesses initiated have varied and include swine production, day-care centers, construction agencies, and bookkeeping services. A university export trading company has been incorporated as well.

REAL Enterprises in its conceptualization exemplifies many of the features of a successful entrepreneurial program. It is predominantly experienced-based, with follow-up guidance provided by an expert, and to a major extent the participants bear the risks and consequences of their decisions. In this way, the students can utilize practical intelligence and receive the type of recognition that is usually reserved for the analytics.

The major challenge of REAL Enterprises is to improve the logistics of implementation so that teachers (and administrators) will perceive the program as doable in the classroom. It suffers the malady common to so many innovative ideas: It is extremely difficult to obtain the type of leadership necessary to insure project success and gain community support. Many of the local firms may fear the potential competition of these student-generated businesses, and administrators unfamiliar with the concept may be reluctant to adopt it. It is also difficult to tailor each school-based business to local needs. Some of these difficulties could be overcome by collaborative workshops in which leaders from the communities, the developers of the project, professional economic educators, teachers, and administrators meet to share ideas, to receive training in their areas of weakness, and to plan specific implementation strategies—blueprints for action in their communities.

JUNIOR ACHIEVEMENT INSTRUCTIONAL MODEL: APPLIED ECONOMICS

The Applied Economics (AE) program designed for high school students is a combination of a textbook approach to teaching economics and a student company designed to put the economic lessons to practical use. Specifically, the AE curriculum includes a text illustrated with graphs and charts, workbook exercises, a computer-based management and economic simulation, a business consultant from the community, and a student company activity. The major goal of AE is to provide young people with practical economic education programs and experiences in the competitive private enterprise system through a partnership with the business and education communities.

The textbook includes such concepts and principles as opportunity costs, aggregate demand and supply, market failures, markets and prices, business organizations, internal and external finance, division of labor and productivity, competition, role of government, monetary theory, balance of payments, and comparative economic systems.

The student workbook contains a variety of knowledge-level questions to answer, charts and graphs to interpret, issues to analyze, and problems to solve. Students are asked to make economic and business-related decisions; in some cases they must relate learned principles to new situations, while in others they are asked to evaluate alternatives and make value judgments.

In the management and economic simulation exercise, the students participate in a simulation in which a group of businesses comprising an industry produces and prices a product. To improve business, the companies decide how much to invest in marketing, capital equipment, and research and development. The teacher may manage the economic environment by altering such factors as the interest rate on borrowing, the availability of credit, the corporate tax rate, and industry demand.

A business consultant from the community, in cooperation with the teacher, works with the class one day a week throughout the semester. In the student company activity, the youngsters take out a company charter, elect officers, issue stock, and conduct other activities over a six-week period. As a company, students choose, produce, and market a product. Eventually, the company closes the books, prepares an annual report, and liquidates the business.

Applied Economics includes many of the features that are predictors of a successful entrepreneurship program. It has a large experiential component in which the youngsters learn by doing and have a constructive outlet for their practical intelligence. Because of the network support, most teachers perceive that the program is doable. However, because the program is one semester in duration, teachers often find themselves compromising either the concept-acquisition component or the entrepreneurial segment in order to meet the time constraints. The program, especially the segment that addresses entrepreneurship, could be significantly enhanced if the curriculum were spread over a one-year period.

The major challenge to the program is to create experiences, perhaps warm-up activities, prior to creating the student company, in which individuals perceive they are bearing the risks and experiencing the consequences of their business decisions. Real life entrepreneurs engage in new enterprises that try to satisfy consumer demand, make production decisions, and attempt to earn a profit instead of experiencing a loss. In AE, the product is selected by the whole class with the help of the teacher and sometimes a business consultant, the production decision is made by the same group, and the risk is taken by the seller of the resources that the class uses to produce the product. Since the entire class works on the same production project, the risks and consequences of decision making experienced by the individual are fairly diluted. The process, then, is more akin to participating in a simulated product-development task force at a corporation rather than participating in a more exposed and unpredictable entrepreneurial situation.

The Mini-Society Instructional System

The Mini-Society Instructional System is a self-organizing, experience-based approach for teaching economics and other social sciences to elementary school children. A major emphasis of the Mini-Society is on entrepreneurial education and exploration. In the Mini-Society, students actually experience and then resolve economic and social problems through the creation and development of their own classroom society. Teachers in Mini-Society classrooms do not teach in the ordinary sense. Instead, they create learning situations and debrief students after each session.

The Mini-Society starts, as all economies do, with a scarcity situation. For example, the teacher brings a number of felt-tip pens to class, deliberately supplying fewer than the number of students. Since all the students want pens, they are motivated to resolve the dilemma. Should the pens be allocated on a first-come, first-served basis? Should there be a lottery, or a free-for-all?

Students discover that they can use a price mechanism to allocate scarce resources, provided there is some sort of currency and distribution of income. The class agrees, for example, that students receive three *quiblings* for punctuality, five for completing homework, and two for not disturbing others. Those willing to pay the market price in quiblings get the pens.

The incentive system exists primarily to introduce money into the Mini-Society. Wealth is created in the next stage. With the money they earn, children buy and sell goods and services such as pencils, erasers, and their time. Some start businesses, such as tutorial services, accounting and insurance companies, banks, wallet factories, and food concessions. The list is limited only by the children's imaginations. Mini-Societies differ from each other—unlike ordinary simulation exercises—because the number and type of businesses depend exclusively on student entrepreneurship.

Teachers offer their services as paid consultants and perform the executive functions of government. The students, meeting in a discussion group, enact laws. To pay for government services, such as cleaning the cage of a class pet rabbit, taxes are levied. Once the money supply is in circulation, children often decide to put an end to "government payments" for attendance and other matters, and to reduce taxes.

The teacher's most important role is that of a debriefer at discussions held after Mini-Society activities. For example, a child starts to produce wallets—an item much in demand because of the introduction of money. Another notices the high price received by the wallet producer and starts a competing wallet business. The price of wallets decreases and both now find the production of wallets less profitable. At this time, the teacher debriefs the children and leads a formal discussion on the effect of the increased supply on prices. The children understand and retain the lesson because they have just experienced the supply effect in action.

The Mini-Society served as a prototype for two other programs. The Kinder-Economy (grades K–2) is the most structured because five-year-olds require teachers to lead them through many situations that older children can create for themselves. The Max-Economy (grades 7–12) is the least structured, permitting any economic activity within the law. Research shows that youngsters in these programs increase their self-esteem and assertiveness, acquire a greater sense of control over their lives, and have a greater awareness and more positive attitude toward entrepreneurship (Cassuto, 1980; Kourilsky and Campbell, 1981; Kourilsky, 1977, 1980, 1983, 1985).

Mini-Society contains most of the features that are predictors of a successful entrepreneurial program. It is experience-based, with systematic follow-up guidance provided through debriefings. The youngsters perceive they are bearing the risks and experiencing the consequences of their decisions. Its major challenge is to increase the confidence of the teachers who are implementing the system in the classrooms. They must perceive that the program is doable and that they can make it happen in their individual and unique classrooms. Through in-service training and extensive networking, this problem has been addressed, and Mini-Society has been implemented in over one hundred thousand classrooms throughout the United States.

CONCLUSION

The school experience can be restructured to foster the entrepreneurial spirit in its broadest sense, and in so doing will enhance our youngsters' inclinations to generate divergent ideas. Specifically, teachers can be trained to recognize and reward the entrepreneurial spirit in their day-to-day classroom activities, and programs in which youngsters have an opportunity to try out entrepreneurial behavior can be implemented at strategic times in the school experience. Perhaps in the near future, when youngsters are asked to draw a picture of a successful entrepreneur, they will sketch a self-portrait.

REFERENCES

Achenbach, T. M. 1966. "Cue-Learning and Problem-Learning Strategies in Children." Ph.D. diss., University of Minnesota.

Begley, T. M., and D. P. Boyd 1986. "Psychological Characteristics Associated with Entrepreneurial Performance." Proceedings of the Sixth Annual Babson College Entrepreneurship Research Conference, pp. 146–163.

Cantillon, R. 1755. *Essai sur la nature du commerce en general.* London: F. Gyles.

Cassuto, A. 1980. "The Effectiveness of the Elementary School Mini-Society Program." *The Journal of Economic Education* 11, no. 2 (Spring): 59–61.

Cromwell, R. L. 1963. "A Social Learning Approach To Mental Retardation." In *Handbook of Mental Deficiency,* edited by N. R. Ellis. New York: McGraw-Hill, pp. 41–91.

DeCarlo, J. F., and P. R. Lyons 1979. "A Comparison of Selected Personal Characteristics of Minority and Non-Minority Female Entrepreneurs." *Journal of Small Business Management* 17 (October): 22–29.

De Largy, P. 1988. "REAL Enterprises." Unpublished manuscript.

Dweck, C. S., and D. Gilliard 1975. "Expectancy Statements as Determinants of Reactions to Failure: Sex Differences in Persistence and Expectancy Change." *Journal of Personality and Social Psychology* 32, no. 6 (December): 1007–1084.

Gruen, G., and Zigler, E. 1968. "Expectancy of Success and the Probability Learning of Middle-Class, Lower-Class and Retarded Children." *Journal of Abnormal Psychology* 73, no. 4: 343–352.

Hornaday, J. A., and J. Aboud 1971. "Characteristics of Successful Entrepreneurs." *Personnel Psychology* 24, no. 2: 141–153.

Hundal, P. S. 1971. "A Study of Entrepreneurial Motivation: Comparison of Fast and Slow Procession Small Scale Industrial Entrepreneurs in Punjab, India." *Journal of Applied Psychology* 55, no. 4: 317–323.

Junior Achievement, Inc. 1987. *Applied Economics.* Colorado Springs, Colo.: Junior Achievement, Inc.

Kent, C. A. 1984. "The Rediscovery of the Entrepreneur." In *The Environment for Entrepreneurship,* edited by C. A. Kent. Lexington, Mass.: D. C. Heath.

————. 1989. "Awareness: Cornerstone of Entrepreneurship Education." *Business Education Forum* 43, no. 7 (April): 35.

Kourilsky, M. 1977. "The Kinder-Economy: A Case Study of Kindergarten Pupils' Acquisition of Economic Concepts." *The Elementary School Journal* 77, no. 3 (January): 182–191.

————. 1979. "Optimal Intervention: An Empirical Investigation of the Role of the Teacher in Experience-Based Instruction." *The Journal of Experimental Education* 47, no. 4 (Summer): 339–345.

————. 1980. "Predictors of Entrepreneurship in a Simulated Economy." *Journal of Creative Behavior* 14, no. 3 (3d quarter): 175–198.

————. 1983. "The Effect of the Success-Oriented Teacher on Pupil's Perceived Personal Control and Attitude Toward Learning." *Contemporary Education Psychology* 8, no. 2 (April): 158–167.

————. 1985. "Economic Reasoning and Decision-Making of High School Students: An Empirical Investigation." *The Social Studies* 76, no. 2 (March-April): 69–75.

Kourilsky, M., and M. Campbell 1981. "The Influence of Instructional Intervention in Entrepreneurial Attitudes of Elementary School Children." In *Entrepre-*

neurship Education, edited by D. L. Sexton and P. M. Van Auken. Waco, Tex.: Baylor University Press, pp. 42–50.

Krathwohl, D. R., B. S. Bloom, and B. B. Masia. 1956. *Taxonomy of Educational Objectives: Handbook I, Cognitive Domain.* New York: Longman, Green.

Lamont, L. M. 1972. "The Role of Marketing in Technical Entrepreneurship." In *Technical Entrepreneurship: A Symposium,* edited by Arnold C. Cooper and John L. Komives. Milwaukee, Wis.: Center for Venture Management.

McClelland, D. C. 1961. *The Achieving Society.* Princeton, N.J.: Van Nostrand.

Mayer, K. B., and S. Goldstein, 1961. *The First Two Years: Problems of Small Firm Growth and Survival.* Washington, D.C.: Small Business Administration.

Schumpeter, J. A. 1934. *The Theory of Economic Development.* Cambridge, Mass.: Harvard University Press.

Soslow, N. G. 1966. "A Comparison of the Origins and Orientations of True Entre- preneurs, Other Owners and Business Hierarchies." *Dissertations Interna- tional,* p. 27.

Sternberg, R. J. 1982. "The Nature of Intelligence." *New York University Education Quarterly* 12, no. 3, pp. 10–17.

Stipek, D. 1988. *Motivation to Learn: From Theory to Practice.* Englewood Cliffs, N.J.: Prentice-Hall.

Terman, L. M., and M. H. Oden. 1949. *The Gifted Child Grows Up.* Stanford, Calif.: Stanford University Press.

———. 1959. *The Gifted Group at Mid-Life.* Stanford, Calif.: Stanford University Press.

Timmons, J. A. 1989. *The Entrepreneurial Mind.* Andover, Mass.: Brook House.

Torrance, E. P. 1960. "Exploration in Creative Thinking." *Education* 81: 216–220.

Wittrock, Merlin. 1986. "Students' Thought Processes." In *Handbook of Research on Teaching,* edited by M. Wittrock. 3d ed. New York: Macmillan, pp. 247– 314.

Zigler, E. F. 1973. *Socialization and Personality Development,* Reading, Mass.: Addison-Wesley.

Zigler, E. F., M. E. Lamb, and I. L. Child, 1982. *Socialization and Personality De- velopment.* New York: Oxford University Press.

10

Economics and Entrepreneurship Education in the Elementary Grades

Francis W. Rushing

Entrepreneurship is now the focus of discussion, and sometimes debate, among academics, practitioners, and public policymakers. Some describe entrepreneurship as *the* emerging academic field of the 1980s and 1990s. Others remark that it is only the rediscovery of an old notion looking for a contemporary treatment within existing disciplines (i.e., economics and management). All who enter the discussion generally conclude that entrepreneurship is important in the context of modern societies and that it warrants attention by scholars and educators.

The literature on entrepreneurship has exploded over the past twenty years. Researchers have explored the definition of the entrepreneur and entrepreneurship. They have identified many personal characteristics or attributes of entrepreneurs and discussed at great length (in thousands of pages) the roles and functions of the entrepreneurs within the economic environment. The stage is now set to shift the focus of the discussion to entrepreneurship education. First, is entrepreneurship education desirable? If undertaken, will it result in outcomes that will contribute positively to the well-being of a society? Second, if desirable, when should the education programs begin and how should they be designed to most effectively achieve the broad goal of increasing the entrepreneurial talent within a society and more successfully employing that talent for the economic well-being of the citizens?

When this topic first reemerged in the 1970s, some college professors became advocates of the development and teaching of entrepreneurial courses at colleges and universities. As the acknowledged importance of entrepreneurship increased, some educators advocated teaching entrepreneurship in secondary schools, since many potential entrepreneurs may not go to college.

In recent years, national organizations as well as local educators have been exploring entrepreneurship curriculums. Most of the secondary entrepreneurship curriculums, like the collegiate ones, emphasized the formation and management of a business after offering entrepreneurship as an alternative career opportunity.

There is another set of fundamental questions to be asked: Can entrepreneurial talents or attributes be developed, and if so, can this be done in a formal educational environment? I believe the answer to both questions is "yes."

To develop the support for these responses, this chapter is broken down into three additional sections. The second section reviews the literature on the development of attributes associated (and positively correlated) with entrepreneurial behavior. The third section discusses current materials or programs that are used in economic and entrepreneurial education. The last section describes what more might be done to increase the effectiveness of enhancing entrepreneurial attributes.

REVIEW OF LITERATURE

Many scholars have attempted to determine the attribute that best predicts entrepreneurial behavior. The discussion by educators of entrepreneurship generally stumbles over the fact that in the past we have not been able to identify potential entrepreneurs. We recognize entrepreneurs through their behavior. If we can identify potential entrepreneurs, then we can teach them the requisite skills for successful entrepreneuring. In addition, if we know the critical attributes of successful entrepreneurs, educational programming may be able to increase the total amount of entrepreneurial talent and thereby increase the future number of entrepreneurs.

In this section four studies from the literature have been selected to sample the discussion about attributes and the prediction of entrepreneurship.

1. Ron Lachman, in the article, "Toward Measurement of Entrepreneurial Tendencies," attempted to help establish the connection between personality characteristics and entrepreneurial behavior (Lachman, 1980). The author, after considering previous research, singled out one sociological variable, achievement values, and two psychological variables, achievement motivation and dependency, as the most important characteristics to

test concerning their relationship with entrepreneurial activity. That is, the author hypothesized that individuals with high achievement motivation and values and low dependency needs would have a greater potential for entrepreneurial behavior than those without these characteristics.

In order to test this hypothesis, Professor Lachman contrasted two similar groups of managers in Israel according to whether they were associated with entrepreneurial behavior. A questionnaire was then used to measure the three characteristics for each member of the two groups. The author's findings provided evidence that an individual could be reliably placed in either group according to both the sociological characteristic, achievement values, and one of the psychological variables, achievement motivation. Dependency, however, was found not indicative of an individual being an entrepreur or a non-entrepreneur. My conclusion is that entrepreneurs can be identified by personality characteristics as opposed to a functional identification; in other words, they are entrepreneurs because they have acted like entrepreneurs.

2. Michael Palmer's "The Application of Psychological Testing to Entrepreneurial Potential" is a thought piece rather than an empirical study (Palmer, 1971). He takes up the problem of functional or ex post as opposed to ex ante identification of entrepreneurs. The author's concern is with the difficulties of measuring entrepreneurial potential, which would be highly useful in providing entrepreneurial talent to areas which need economic development but lack a pool of entrepreneurial individuals capable of taking advantage of opportunities in the environment.

After reviewing the literature regarding the definition and role of the entrepreneur, Palmer concluded that the use of attitudinal and motivational tests provides the opportunity to identify potential entrepreneurs. Furthermore, he singles out decision making under conditions of uncertainty as the key variable in testing for entrepreneurial talent. Thus, the author concluded that some measure of an individual's perception of risk and ability to handle it would be extremely useful in making an ex ante identification of potential entrepreneurs.

3. David C. McClelland's "Achievement Motivation Can Be Developed" is an important article which makes an argument for the need for motivational training to accompany programs geared toward increasing the environmental opportunities of individuals and groups (McClelland, 1965). In his view, there is little point in providing additional opportunities for those without the achievement motivation or need which are requisite for taking advantage of such opportunities. Abundant evidence has been gathered concerning the failure of programs that are intended to better the circumstances of individuals yet have neglected to develop in them the psychological characteristics necessary to successfully utilize the program. The author took the view that training in achievement motivation is pos-

sible, and proposed the use of training programs in conjunction with the expansion of opportunities. McClelland suggested four elements to be included in such a program:

- Goal setting;
- Language of achievement;
- Cognitive supports; and
- Group supports.

Having conducted a program of this type in India, McClelland observed a doubling of entrepreneurial activity. Thus, he concludes that it is not enough to merely improve the available opportunities for people. There must also be present the achievement motivation that will enable individuals to take advantage of those opportunities. Fortunately (at least if we are convinced by McClelland) motivation can be taught and developed in the individual regardless of age.

4. Marilyn Kourilsky, in a *Journal of Creative Behavior* article, "Predictors of Entrepreneurship in a Simulated Economy," is also concerned with the ex ante identification of entrepreneurs (Kourilsky, 1980). The author reviews the literature and points out that learning theory suggests that the cognitive element of the individual—that is, the ability to use information and education, is much more amenable to change than is the motivational element—an observation that challenges, but does not refute, McClelland's findings. During the course of her study utilizing the children in her Mini-Society, Kourilsky concludes that risk taking is not a good entrepreneurial indicator. This conclusion contradicts Palmer's findings.

What Kourilsky found through her study was that persistence was the most significant predictor of entrepreneurial success. Further results were that academic ability and initiative were the next two important indicators for boys, while maturity and perception of success were the next two for girls. She then emphasized the need for further research to determine whether the predictors of entrepreneurial success would be the same for adults, her point being that if it is possible to determine the relevant characteristics related to entrepreneurial behavior, it will then be possible to make a concerted effort to develop and enhance them at an early age, thus increasing the pool of entrepreneurial talent in society.

To summarize the four articles, McClelland and Lachman view motivation as being the key indicator of entrepreneurial potential, Palmer suggests decision making and risk handling as appropriate measures, and Kourilsky identifies persistence as most significant.

From these and other studies, a short list of entrepreneurial attributes can be derived:

1. need for achievement;
2. creativity and initiative;
3. risk taking and setting of objectives;
4. self-confidence and internal focus of control;
5. need for independence and autonomy;
6. motivation, energy, and commitment (Gasse, 1985); and
7. persistence.

Although no consensus has formed around one attribute being the most important, it seems all these attributes can be developed or reinforced in an educational environment, and are not mutually exclusive. One or more can be enhanced without diminishing or adversely affecting others. How can this be put into practice?

REVIEW OF EXISTING PROGRAMS

If we accept as an educational objective the need to increase entrepreneurial activities within our economy through use of curriculum materials that discover and develop entrepreneurial attributes, thereby increasing the pool of entrepreneurial talent, we must build a framework in which these curriculums will reside. I will advocate that entrepreneurship education be part of the economics education instruction. The child must be exposed to economics concepts that form a cognitive domain in which entrepreneurs and entrepreneurship can be developed. It is the economic environment in which the entrepreneur has relevance and, some would argue, critical importance.

One possible schema describes five periods during which entrepreneurial attributes and skills can be developed:

1. Preschool
2. Grades K–7 and middle school grades, 6–8
3. Grades 8–12
4. College
5. Adult education

Preschool: This period extends from birth to the child's entry into a formal educational system such as kindergarten. Parents are a strong influence on personality development, but increasing numbers of children are placed in day-care facilities which will also influence their cognitive and personality development.

K–7: These are the elementary grades. During these years the child becomes more aware of family members as role models as well as being influenced by formal education. These formative years, in which the child's personality is still flexible and receptive to new ideas, seem to be optimal for the development of entrepreneurial attributes. During the whole period the child could be exposed to economic and entrepreneurial concepts. Toward the end of the period and in the first years of high school (the middle school years, 6, 7, 8), the student could study the role of entrepreneurs in the economy and learn of entrepreneurial opportunities that exist within the economic and social structures.

Grades 8–12: This period would consist of continuing enhancement of attributes and further development of awareness of entrepreneurial opportunities, and would mainly focus on the skills necessary to plan, form, and manage an entrepreneurial venture.

College: Education in this period would provide more formal and in-depth entrepreneurial, economics, and management courses. Knowledge will also be increased by work experience.

Adult: Education would consist of taking advantage of special instruction in business formation and management through national, state, and local networks like the Small Business Administration and its Small Business Development Centers, and local groups like SCORE (Service Corporation of Retired Executives), which is made up of consultants who are retired business managers.

Throughout these periods, people will learn through their personal job experiences and by observing others like their parents, cohorts, and former associates.

The focus of this chapter, however, is on the second item in the above schema, K–7. If educators are to effectively incorporate entrepreneurship into the curriculum, it is necessary, first, to establish a justification for its inclusion and, second, to identify a vehicle or vehicles by which to do it. This author would argue that the justification has been made above and can further be reinforced by the argument that economics education is appropriate at all grades and ages. Finally, if we accept the premise that entrepreneurship education is, in part, a subset of economics education (it might also be considered a partial subset of management education), then we must look at economics and entrepreneurship materials to see how broad and effective they are at the elementary level.

1. *Master Curriculum Guide in Economics: A Framework for Teaching the Basic Concepts,* by the Joint Council on Economic Education (Saunders et al., 1984).

The *Framework* is a classic document among economics educators which effectively identifies most of the key concepts that constitute economics and economic understanding. The *Framework* identifies entrepreneurs in its discussion of productive resources (human capital), but fails to identify the role of entrepreneurs in generating new businesses and, consequently, economic growth. The *Master Curriculum Guide* is used, as its title suggests, as a framework for teaching basic economic concepts. Entrepreneurs and entrepreneurship are an integral aspect not only of economic theory, but also of economic practice. The omission of giving an important role to entrepreneurs and entrepreneurship by the *Master Curriculum Guide* leaves a gap in the framework that must be filled if entrepreneurship is to assume its appropriate place in economics education.

Calvin Kent, in a working paper entitled "What Economic Educators Should Teach About Entrepreneurship," identified five essential economic understandings associated with entrepreneurship which should be emphasized (and in this case incorporated into) the economics curriculum (Kent, 1986). According to Kent, entrepreneurship

- is a productive resource;
- requires profits;
- creates technological change;
- generates jobs; and
- causes economic growth.

Each understanding leads from the identification of what an entrepreneur is and what roles and functions he or she plays within the economic processes. The *Framework* should incorporate the broader concept of the entrepreneur in its next edition and should explain the five understandings that Kent has identified.

The *Master Curriculum Guide* does place emphasis on one critical function of the entrepreneur: decision making. It helps develop a decision-making grid and various quantitative tools for economic analysis. The materials for grades K–12 published by the Joint Council on Economic Education contain a wealth of useful, imaginative, and effective strategies for teaching economics. The *Framework* and its associated strategies can build economic understanding of great benefit to producers, consumers, and citizens, but it does not place sufficient emphasis on the various roles entrepreneurs play within economics.

The *Framework* is an important document because it identifies the key economic concepts. A logical extension of the *Framework* is a K–12 scope and sequence for economic education. The National Specialized Center for Learning Theory and Economic Education at Georgia State University has published an Economic Education K–12 scope and sequence. Although the scope and sequence are the culmination of the efforts and views of teachers, professors, curriculum coordinators, and administrators, it reflects the *Framework*'s outline of economic concepts. It, like the *Framework*, is deficient with respect to the infusion of entrepreneurial concepts into the scope and sequence. It has no reference to the development of entrepreneurial attributes.

The deficiencies of the *Framework* and, hopefully, future scope and sequences, will be partially remedied by the Pew Foundation's support of curriculum development in entrepreneurship through the design of new curriculum materials. These materials are for the secondary grades, but they do incorporate many entrepreneurial concepts, and can serve as a point of departure for curriculum development in the elementary grades. None of these documents addresses the idea of entrepreneurial attribute development or enhancement, however. They implicitly assume that entrepreneurial talent is fixed and that the task of the educator is to help these individuals identify entrepreneurial opportunities and train them to take advantage of them. This reflects a necessary, but not sufficient, condition for maximizing entrepreneurial behavior in the economy.

2. *Mini-Society: Experiencing Real-World Economics in the Elementary School Classroom* by Marilyn L. Kourilsky. Menlo Park, Calif.: Addison-Wesley Publishing Company, 1983.

The Mini-Society is perhaps the best of the strategies currently used in the lower grades in teaching economics and the characteristics of entrepreneurship. Kourilsky has demonstrated that not only does Mini-Society effectively teach economics, it also enhances reading and math skills. Mini-Society is developed from the realization of scarcity, an economic problem. This reality forces the participants to grapple with many real-world problems including decision making, innovation, imagination, dealing with failure, and learning the dynamics of the marketplace and the importance of information and business skills. Student participants must form and manage businesses within the economic system they organize.

The Mini-Society does foster learning of the basic economic concepts, principally through learning by doing. Experiencing the realities of doing business is a great teacher. Success motivates and failure forces adaptation, thought, and increased efforts. Mini-Society and its newer offshoot, Kinder-Economy, foster the characteristics that entrepreneurs require. Perhaps the best feature is that it fosters those difficult-to-teach attributes of imagination and foresight. The materials reinforce the positive traits of entrepreneurship and help build strategies for dealing with failure to achieve objectives.

3. *Case Studies.* The Georgia State University (Atlanta) Center for Business and Economic Education.

Case Studies provides the opportunity to substitute printed matter for personal visits or video presentations by or about entrepreneurs. The Georgia State University Center for Business and Economic Education has over the past five years put together a series of case studies for students at all grade levels including the elementary grades.

All the elementary-level cases present basic economic concepts and create activities to reinforce them. The cases generally help to develop decision-making skills and basic concepts of entrepreneurship, markets, prices, supply and demand, competition, and so forth. Two cases struck me as providing something more—*Chick-fil-A* and *Keeping up with the Jones's Kids: A Case Study of the Little People.* In these cases, the entrepreneurs—the founders of the two businesses studied—are presented in such a way as to emphasize a broad range of entrepreneurship skills: imagination, dealing with uncertainty, taking risks, changing the organization and management of the firm as economic conditions change, and hard work over a long period of time. The presentations are a good blend of facts and exercises. The exercises are designed to permit a wide latitude of responses to questions and situations. There are no prescribed right or wrong solutions, and there is room for individual responses that can be shared with everyone.

These two cases are clear demonstrations of the ways that case studies can be effectively used for entrepreneurial education within economics education. *Chick-fil-A* was designed for grades 2 through 5, while *The Little People* spans grades 4 through 6.

4. *I Can Do It,* The American Entrepreneur Series by the National Federation of Independent Business. San Mateo, Calif.: National Federation of Independent Business, 1986.

I Can Do It is a series of three films or videos featuring three entrepreneurs. The stories of these three entrepreneurs is a valuable aid for anyone teaching entrepreneurship. Each case is a unique and interesting presentation. In different ways, each conveys to the viewer (and learner) how each entrepreneur got started; the hard work required; the necessity for concern about sound business principles of management, finance, and marketing; the importance of the customer; and the importance of teaching your children about the business and providing opportunities for development of employees' abilities. Each film provides positive reinforcement ("You *can* do it"), yet it does so with the realism of meeting payrolls and sweating out decision outcomes.

The films feature a black male, a white female, and a white male in very interesting businesses: printing, adventure travel guides, and an expanding dairy/food business. These presentations are visually appealing and, even more important, are educationally sound and a real resource for students in all but the lower grades. Packaged with a guide, these materials will find a positive reception by those teaching entrepreneurship.

New videos need to be developed for grades K–4, particularly. Audiovisual materials should highlight positive role models, focusing on personal attributes of the entrepreneur and encouraging student activities that reinforce the concepts taught and help the students identify with the entrepreneurs.

WHERE DO WE GO FROM HERE?

Children in elementary grades can learn economics. This has been researched and demonstrated (Kourilsky, 1987). Economics can be taught

Figure 10.1
Focus of Entrepreneurship Education, by Grade Level

Grades K-5	Grades 6-8	Grades 9-12
Basic Economics	Economic Concepts	Economic Concepts
ENTREPRENEURSHIP ATTRIBUTES	Entrepreneurship Attributes	Entrepreneurship Attributes
	BUSINESS OPPORTUNITIES	Business Opportunities
		BUSINESS MANAGEMENT

to young children by a number of methods (Armento, 1987). The new challenge for economics educators is to introduce entrepreneurship education into the elementary grades while continuing to emphasize economic concepts. In the K–7 programs, the focus should be first on economic principles, and then on the development and enhancement of entrepreneurial attributes. During the later elementary (or first middle) grades, the entrepreneurship content should have students looking at the economy for entrepreneurial opportunities. This can be done by exploring new ways of doing old things or by examining new inventions, products, or services—while continuing to learn new economic concepts and enhancing entrepreneurship attributes.

These objectives at the elementary level are part of a spiraling curriculum. Figure 10.1 shows where the emphasis in entrepreneurial education should be placed by grade level. At all grade levels, economics is being taught. The capitalization reflects the focus of the entrepreneurship education.

In the review of the literature, I listed the characteristics of entrepreneurs. Each characteristic is desirable from the societal as well as the individual perspective. Certainly, curriculums that help to develop these attributes will have positive outcomes. Creativity and inventiveness will apply equally to future inventors, scientists, and artists. Motivation, self-confidence, and persistence instilled in future members of the work force will undoubtedly please employers and enhance efficiency and productivity.

What methods are available or might be developed to accomplish this objective of entrepreneurial attribute development and enhancement? The

Kinder-Economy and Mini-Society proved to be effective at teaching economic concepts, developing entrepreneurial attributes, and providing insights into business opportunities. These programs do require some blocks of time and teachers who have had training in the programs. They also require a supportive principal and fellow teachers who understand the process as well as the learning outcomes.

Case Studies also achieve multiple objectives: reading, decision making, recognition of role models, insightfulness, and learning from past successes and failures. The cases should be drawn from the local business community so that young students have some familiarity with the product or service involved or recognize by name or reputation the individual business owners and operators.

A third set of materials needs to be developed. These are materials that are attribute-enhancing: brief units that stretch the students' minds, influence their personalities, challenge their creativity, and develop their problem-solving and decision-making skills. These materials could be based on the experiences that D. McClelland has had in increasing the achievement factor in people. From a curriculum perspective, there might be less resistance to their use than to, say, the Mini-Society because of the time factor. However, teachers will need training to use these materials if only to convince them of the desirability of their inclusion in the curriculum at all.

Another approach might be for school systems to have trained specialists (like the visiting art teacher or reading specialist) whose responsibility is to conduct attribute enhancement training. These special teachers could develop or adapt programming that could help develop entrepreneurial attributes without requiring large blocks of classroom time.

Economics education has been finding its way into the elementary curriculum. What needs to be done is to infuse the economics education process with entrepreneurship education and attribute development. To effectively do the latter requires additional research to serve as a foundation for new classroom materials. To teach those materials requires teachers with cognitive skills and imagination. In addition, the effort requires supportive administrators and parents. It will undoubtedly require that educators determine the opportunity costs of these actions.

American education is suffering from schizophrenia. Demands are for more structure, large numbers of tests, and lockstep-like education. However, entrepreneurial education requires the antithesis: individual development, fewer "right" and "wrong" answers, and greater tolerance for deviation from norms.

Entrepreneurial children frequently come from entrepreneurial family environments. If schools are to reinforce or influence the development of entrepreneurs, then the environment must be more entrepreneurial. I am not sure American education can meet this challenge, but it must try!

REFERENCES

Armento, Beverly. 1987. "Ideas for Teaching Economics Derived from Learning Theory." *Theory into Practice* 26, no. 3 (Summer): 176–182.

Gasse, Yvon. 1985. "A Strategy for the Promotion and Identification of Potential Entrepreneurs at the Secondary School Level." In *Frontiers of Entrepreneurship Research, 1985,* edited by J. A. Hornaday, E. B. Shils, J. A. Timmons, and K. H. Vesper. Wellesley, Mass.: Babson College, Center for Entrepreneurial Studies, pp. 538–550.

Kent, Calvin A. 1986. *What Economic Educators Should Teach about Entrepreneurship.* Waco, Tex.: Baylor University, National Center for Entrepreneurship in Economics Education, pp. 12–13.

Kourilsky, Marilyn L. 1980. "Predictors of Entrepreneurship in a Simulated Economy." *Journal of Creative Behavior* 14, no. 3 (3d quarter): 175–98.

———. 1987. "Children's Learning of Economics: The Imperative and the Hurdles." *Theory into Practice* 26, no. 3 (Summer): 198–205.

Lachman, Ron. 1980. "Toward Measurement of Entrepreneurial Tendencies." *Management International Review* 20, pp. 108–116.

McClelland, D. 1965. "Achievement Motivation Can Be Developed." *Harvard Business Review* 43, no. 6: 6–24, 178.

Palmer, M. 1971. "The Application of Psychological Testing to Entrepreneurial Potential." *California Management Review* 13, no. 3: pp. 32–38.

Saunders, Phillip, G. L. Bach, James D. Calderwood, and W. Lee Hanson. 1984. *Master Curriculum Guide in Economics: A Framework for Teaching the Basic Concepts.* 2d ed. New York: Joint Council on Economic Education, 71 pp.

11

Economics and Entrepreneurship Education for Young Adolescents

Ronald A. Banaszak

I know of no safe depository of the ultimate powers of the society but the people themselves; and if we think them not enlightened enough to exercise their control with a wholesome discretion, the remedy is not to take it from them, but to inform their discretion
—*Thomas Jefferson* (Beck, 1980, p. 389)

Democracy demands well-informed citizens. Today, citizens cannot be considered well-informed or function effectively without being literate about the economy and entrepreneurship. Of all the literacies citizens need, these are especially important, for they are a body of knowledge and a way of thinking about complex choices that citizens have to make on both societal and personal levels.

True understanding of the economy and entrepreneurship is not casually acquired by merely surviving in our economy. It requires formal instruction that should be part of the education of all citizens. Young adolescents, those students twelve to sixteen years old, are not now receiving adequate formal instruction about our economy and entrepreneurship. The following uninformed answers to simple economics questions were given by twenty-seven randomly selected eighth grade students interviewed by the author (Banaszak, 1984).

"Who benefits from the economic system? Just the rich and wealthy, I think."

"The Federal Reserve is the extra soldiers the government has in case of an emergency."

"Gross National Product? Sounds like something somebody chewed up and spit out!"

"Government is more important to the economy because it's government that starts businesses, keeps them up and running."

The last response is one of the most disturbing. The majority of the students expressed the belief that government was more important in our economy than business. Only three believed that business was more important. This result is even more startling because the interviews were conducted in three Utah schools, in a community that is usually described as pro-business. Those students who expressed a reason for choosing government always referred to its rule-making powers. Perhaps they thought government was more important because they had studied so much about government and so little about business.

Young Americans, taught so little about our economy, are unprepared to function as capable economic decision makers. This is unfortunate and potentially dangerous, because today Americans are being asked to make critical decisions on a vast array of sophisticated issues relating to personal finance, business (including entrepreneurship issues), and public policy. Our future promises only greater complexity. Misunderstanding of how our economy functions weakens our children's potential to lead happy, successful lives, and undermines the very foundation of our democratic society. Policies adopted by economically uninformed citizens are likely to be harmful to the efficient functioning of our economy and hinder the entrepreneurial activities our economy so desperately needs.

ECONOMICS AND ENTREPRENEURSHIP FOR YOUNG ADOLESCENT LEARNERS

Economics and entrepreneurship are subjects well-suited for study in grades 6 through 9. They allow students to examine their personal development, study role models, and explore the larger society they are entering. Young adolescents are experiencing dramatic physical, emotional, social, and psychological changes. These youngsters are just emerging from the safety of their homes into the larger society, developing biologically and intellectually, and becoming more adult but not yet mature. Inquiring, willing to explore, yet needing the security of a peer group, they are becoming participants in the outside world, developing attitudes and values that will remain with them for the rest of their lives. At the same time, they are beginning to be held responsible for their actions. Young adolescents face an enormous range of alternatives, requiring that they make choices and deal with resulting consequences. Dealing with the newfound variety of alternatives, choices, and consequences requires new skills and is quite risky. Learning about entrepreneurs, individuals who have creatively responded to their environment and seized control of the situations they are in, can help young adolescents take charge of their own lives.

Economics is the study of decision making. Usually the decisions deal with the allocation of resources. Economics can assist students in understanding such questions as: What employable skills do I have? Why should I work? What determines wages and prices? How does one gain food, clothing, and shelter? Why do people work together for their material well-being? Economic reasoning is not and should not be restricted to material matters, however. Economic reasoning can also help young adolescents as they make decisions regarding human relationships, such as selecting friends, dating behavior, and whether to use drugs.

Entrepreneurship includes the study of entrepreneurs, what they do to organize resources in new businesses for the purpose of producing goods and services, and their common personality characteristics. Not everyone desires to start a new business, and certainly most young adolescents do not, but everyone should be aware of the problems and struggles, the risks and rewards, and the joy and defeat entrepreneurs experience. More important, everyone would benefit from studying entrepreneurs as role models, learning about the value of self-confidence, a positive attitude, perseverance, innovativeness, willingness to take risks, personal control, and other entrepreneurial personality traits.

There are additional reasons why the study of economics and entrepreneurship is especially appropriate for young adolescents. The following four reasons seem most important.

1. During their early teens, young people are increasingly aware of and involved with our economic system. They begin to recognize that they are part of a world larger and more complex than their immediate family and community. Their part in the labor force and their spending powers are increasingly significant. Further, they are beginning to think seriously about their future occupations. They wonder about the role of business, hearing both good and bad comments about entrepreneurs. Furthermore, through the media they learn much about the business hero and the business villain.

2. These students are developing new cognitive abilities, permitting them more sophisticated ways of reasoning. They are moving from concrete to abstract reasoning. This change helps them reason about physical and social events that are unobserved and unobservable. They are able to consider economics not as made of isolated concepts, but as an integrated system, and to picture themselves in the positions held by others, such as business owners, politicians, bankers, and so forth.

3. Young adolescents are forming their attitudes. The study of economics and entrepreneurship provides an opportunity to present students with factual information they can use to build their own attitudes, whatever those attitudes are. This is especially true with regard to business and business leaders. Without factual instruction, students will be left to form their opinions based on casual conversation and powerful media portrayals of entrepreneurs such as the ruthless J. R. on "Dallas."

4. Since most young adolescents are still enrolled in grades 7 through 10, regardless of their intelligence, socioeconomic background, or career goals, economics and entrepreneurship education aimed at these grades has the potential of reaching almost every student. Further, instruction in economics and entrepreneurship may encourage students to remain in school and not drop out.

GOALS FOR YOUNG ADOLESCENT ECONOMICS AND ENTREPRENEURSHIP EDUCATION

Generally a middle or junior high school economics and entrepreneurship education program should help students gain the knowledge, values, and reasoning abilities necessary for them to become successful participants in our economic system. Davis (1987, p. 60) identified six subgoals for economic education:

1. Develop a commitment to the basic values of the American economic system.
2. Recognize the basic features to the U.S. economy that distinguish it from other economic systems.
3. Become aware of the strengths and problems in our mixed market economy.
4. Actively construct new meanings about the nature of their own economic behavior (what students choose to do) and the economic behavior of the people in the world.
5. Apply an economic reasoning framework and thinking skills to fundamental human issues, dilemmas, and moral questions.
6. Develop a healthy skepticism toward such matters as issues stated too simply, issue options defined too narrowly, solutions that imply little or no cost, or solutions that are devoid of humane considerations (e.g., people's feelings, values, and preferences).

Additional goals for young adolescents' entrepreneurship education include

- know the role and function of entrepreneurs in our market-driven economy and
- understand and practice entrepreneurial characteristics such as high self-esteem, willingness to take risks, innovativeness, accepting responsibility for personal actions, and persistence.

DEFINING ECONOMICS AND ENTREPRENEURSHIP EDUCATION FOR YOUNG ADOLESCENTS

Designing an effective economics and entrepreneurship education program for young adolescents requires clarity in the use of the terms *economics, economic literacy, economic reasoning,* and *entrepreneurship.*

Defining Economics

Economics is the discipline concerned with the allocation of limited resources among unlimited wants. The economy, composed of economic institutions, is the organized way we transform resources into desired goods and services. Economics is the study of how this process works.

Both a body of knowledge and a way of thinking about certain phenomena, economics includes a variety of related concepts, generalizations, theories, and models that describe the ways limited resources are allocated. Economists have stated that economics depends on a "body of theory to provide a kit of tools with which to analyze the complexities of the real world" (National Task Force on Economic Education, 1961, p. 17). Economics also is a methodology for investigating and better understanding how the economy works. For many professional economists, economics is an apparatus and a technique for learning about the operation of the economy. John Maynard Keynes expressed this view well when he defined economics as "a method rather than a doctrine, an apparatus of the mind, a technique of thinking, which helps its possessor to draw correct conclusion" (Keynes, 1930, p. 6). Keynes's "technique of thinking" is the scientific method that economists use in their search for generalizations that have broad applications and predictive power. The scientific method teaches that the acquisition of knowledge must be independent of the economist's personal values. Like other scientists, economists must be objective or positive, that is unprejudiced, following truth wherever it leads, focusing on what is, not what should be. Friedman (1953) declared that "positive economics is, or can be, an 'objective' science, in precisely the same sense as any of the physical sciences" (1953, pp. 4–5). Economics does not involve providing practical advice about which economic policies should be adopted, but rather concerns how to predict the consequences of those policies. Making economic policy requires economic literacy.

Defining Entrepreneurship

Scholars do not agree as to the precise meaning of the term *entrepreneurship. Webster's* defines an entrepreneur as "one who organizes, owns, manages and assumes the risks of a business (Webster's Third New International Dictionary). Interpreted broadly, it seems clear that entrepreneurs are enterprising individuals who on their personal initiative decide to take an action that involves risk for the sake of reward, for them or their community. The action can involve any part of their lives, and the reward may be monetary or nonmonetary. Some entrepreneurs are better than others, of course, and some play with higher stakes, but an entrepreneurial spirit and entrepreneurial skills are of great benefit both to society and to the individuals that possess them.

Entrepreneurship is taking calculated action. It is recognizing that a free market system offers significant personal rewards for intelligent action. It is the knowledge that each individual is responsible for his or her own destiny and that success is both possible and worth the effort. If the individual is the elementary particle of our economy, entrepreneurship is the elementary force. This force can be seen in the following examples, in which each individual in his or her own unique way is expressing entrepreneurial behavior:

- A youngster in the ghetto determines to study hard in school to escape his environment.
- An employee puts his idea in the company suggestion box.
- A teacher quits a secure teaching position to return to college to earn a doctorate.
- A group of students start an anti-drug campaign on their high school campus.
- A teacher agrees to teach economics for the first time.
- A secretary goes to night school to learn additional skills to qualify for a promotion.
- An inventor creates a new machine.
- A group of mothers organize an anti-drunk driving organization.
- An author writes a book and submits it to publishers for review.

Entrepreneurship education for young adolescents should use the stories of entrepreneurs to teach students the personal characteristics or attributes of entrepreneurs. These attributes include all the following:

1. willingness to act on ideas;
2. willingness to take responsibility for one's own future (accepting personal responsibility and being self-reliant);
3. belief that success is possible and worth the effort;
4. self-confidence (believing in one's own ideas and having a positive self-image);
5. desire to do the best possible job with one's talents;
6. goal-oriented;
7. creative, innovative, and flexible;
8. approaches problems with an attitude that they can be solved;

9. recognizes that the production process involves the combined efforts of many individuals, each of whom must be efficient and productive in their roles; and

10. knows that the free market economic system offers significant personal rewards for intelligent action.

Defined in such a manner, entrepreneurship becomes critical for young adolescents.

Defining Economic Literacy

Through our everyday experiences, we learn about the economy and about entrepreneurs. While some of what we learn is correct, much is incorrect and incomplete. Kenneth Boulding has suggested that the goal of economics education is to move the ordinary citizen from a "folk" knowledge of the economy to the more comprehensive knowledge of professional economists (Hansen, 1982). Thus, becoming economically literate can be viewed as the process of gaining a more complete and accurate knowledge of the economy.

Economic literacy involves more, however. It is not synonymous with the discipline of economics, but rather is different in several ways. The discipline of economics seeks to discover new knowledge. Economic literacy involves individuals knowing and applying fundamental economic ideas to make rational decisions about the use of limited resources. An economically literate individual understands basic economics, the institutions that comprise our economic system, and the role of entrepreneurs, and can use that knowledge to conduct an objective, reasoned analysis of economic issues. Economic reasoning, a highly transferable skill, is the central benefit of education for economic literacy. Thus, economically literate citizens enjoy a more complete understanding of their world, are better able to make reasoned decisions, and are more fully in control of their economic futures.

Economic literacy also differs from the discipline of economics in its normative, or values, dimension. Through economic reasoning, individuals try to manage the use of their limited resources in ways that will lead to the most complete fulfillment of their goals. In general, a resource should be diverted from less important to more important uses. Doing so requires an understanding of what one personally values in order to determine which choice is most likely to further those values. While the discipline of economics can be descriptive and value-free, the application of economic knowledge cannot be separated from the values of those using it. The choices entrepreneurs make, for example, reveal what they consider to be important. The discipline of economics provides information about the probable consequences of various policy alternatives. Economic reasoning gives individuals the tools to choose the alternatives that will best further personal and societal goals. Thus, being economically literate must include a knowledge of what we value, both individually and as a society.

Defining Economic Reasoning

Economic reasoning refers to a system for making decisions. Since economics deals with choices about the use of limited resources for unlimited wants, decision making is the central skill of economics. Economic decision making is a skill that can be learned and needs to be widely used by workers as well as entrepreneurs. It is a logical, reasoned approach using economic concepts and generalizations. This method of analysis is thought by many, both in and out of the economics profession, to constitute the unique and most productive contribution of the discipline to social scientific thought. Economic decisions involve these six steps:

1. Clearly identify the details of the decision situation. What choice is involved?
2. Determine what personal or social goals are to be attained. What are you trying to achieve by the decision? Which goals are of highest priority?
3. Identify all the alternative choices.
4. Consider each alternative choice and its costs, benefits, and consequences.
5. Decide on the best alternative for reaching the desired goals. Which alternatives are most feasible? Which have the least undesirable effects?
6. Review and evaluate the decision. Did it help attain the desired goal? Did predicted consequences occur? Did it maximize benefits that could be obtained from the resources used?

An economics and entrepreneurship education program would be deficient if it did not include instruction about the following economic relationships that are useful as we make economic decisions: trade-offs, laws of supply and demand, marginal analysis, cost-benefit analysis, and short-term and long-term effects.

Trade-Offs. Decisions about the use of productive resources seldom become mutually exclusive. We do not choose between guns or butter, but rather between relative amounts of guns and butter or various production possibilities. In making decisions, it is imperative to consider the trade-offs, or choices, being made between alternative uses of the resources.

Laws of Supply and Demand. The laws of supply and demand state relationships between quantities demanded by consumers and quantities producers are willing to supply at a given time, assuming all other conditions remain constant. The law of demand states that as price increases, the quantity demanded decreases, and, conversely, as price decreases, the quantity demanded increases. The law of supply states that as price rises, producers are willing to increase the quantity supplied. As price falls, the quantity producers are willing to supply also falls. The tendency in the economy is for the quantity demanded and the quantity supplied to move toward an equilibrium price at which the quantity producers are willing to produce is identical with the quantity consumers are willing to buy.

Marginal Analysis. Economics decision makers attempt to make choices that maximize output and satisfaction. Marginal analysis is used to determine the value of producing or consuming an additional unit of the same good or service. The law of diminishing marginal utility teaches that additional quantities of goods yield successively smaller increments of satisfaction. Marginal productivity shows us the additional output received by adding an additional unit of resources as input.

Cost-Benefit Analysis. Every decision involves costs and benefits. By examining the costs associated with each decision in relation to the expected benefits, we attempt to make choices that maximize benefits for the least cost.

Short Run and Long Run. When examining the consequences of a decision it is important to consider the long term, as well as the immediate effect. A choice that has a less desirable short-term effect may be the better choice if it has a much more desirable long-term effect.

SELECTING ECONOMICS AND ENTREPRENEURSHIP CONTENT FOR YOUNG ADOLESCENTS

Of critical importance to the success of an economics and entrepreneurship education program for young adolescents are the economic concepts or generalizations taught. In time, research may identify which concepts are most important, but for now, only advanced mathematical concepts can be excluded. Two scope and sequence projects provide some guidance. The Joint Council on Economic Education published a report that suggests appropriate economics content for grade-level spans (Gilliard, 1988), and B. J. Armento (1987) suggests economics content by grade level span. Actually, most economics and entrepreneurship content can be taught to young adolescents if presented in an appropriate manner; still, some concepts are more pertinent than others.

The concept of *economic landscape,* those parts of the economy encountered by students aged twelve to sixteen, provides help in determining and presenting appropriate economic and entrepreneurship content. Their economic landscape consists mostly of businesses such as banks, retail stores, farms, factories, service shops, and products, and also includes churches, schools, and government agencies. Students should learn how these institutions and those who own and work in them help society meet its material needs.

By consciously building on their economic landscape, economics and entrepreneurship educators can link new knowledge to the student's existing information base and, at the same time, give new insights into familiar institutions and events. The local factory is seen as more than a place where people work. At the factory, human, natural, and capital resources are combined to produce goods desired by consumers, whose purchases produce income for workers and profits for investors. The clothing store at the shopping mall is part of a complex distribution network that serves producers as much as customers. Scarce products are efficiently rationed in a convenient manner among millions of customers all across the country. Banks can be seen not just as impressive buildings, but as institutions that mutually benefit both savers and borrowers.

Focusing on products and services of interest to students provides a second way to investigate their economic landscape. There is no shortage of products and services directed at young people. By examining the consumer choices they and their peers make, students can better understand economic reasoning. They also realize that their choices affect what products are produced.

A third way to view students' economic landscape is through the social roles they play and observe. Family member, member of social groups, friend, worker, consumer, entrepreneur, and citizen are among these roles. By examining the economic dimensions of each role and how the roles relate to one another, students will gain a more sophisticated understanding of the economy. In addition, it provides opportunities to examine societal values, moral dilemmas, and value conflicts. Further, since examples can be found locally, examining social roles provides another effective way to understand the local community.

TEACHING ECONOMICS AND ENTREPRENEURSHIP TO YOUNG ADOLESCENTS

"Complexity and unreality—these are the two great barriers to vitalizing economic education" declared Harold Clark, an economics education reformer, in 1940 (Clark, 1940a, p. 399). His comment, referring to both the selection of economics content and the manner of its instruction, is almost as true today as then, and his comment describes most entrepreneurship education as well. In many classrooms, instruction is little more than memorization and regurgitation of facts and terminology with minimal student understanding. Such teachers are prone to adopt the professional jargon without the understanding, resulting in a tyranny of terminology in which the labeling of phenomenon is believed to be equivalent to comprehension.

Instead, the methods of teaching about the economy and entrepreneurship should capitalize on the special characteristics and abilities of young adolescents. On the college level, economics and entrepreneurship are appropriately taught in an abstract manner. Unfortunately, that method of presentation has dominated the way economics and entrepreneurship are taught at all grade levels. If economics could only be presented as an abstract subject, it would be most inappropriate for young adolescents. If entrepreneurship is just learning about how to start a business, it is inappropriate as well. However, economics does not have to be abstract. Entrepreneurship can have real meaning for students. Economics is a discipline we use whenever we decide how to use any scarce resource, whether it be our income, our time, or some other commodity, and entrepreneurship tells us to be persistent and decisive in our decisions. College-level abstract economics is distilled from real-world events. To teach young adolescents, we need to get closer to those real-world events, largely avoiding mathematical models and advanced analytical tools. We need to stress the role of entrepreneurs in our economy and bring economics back to the level of people working together, in an orderly fashion, to supply the goods and services we need.

The appropriate presentation of economics and entrepreneurship content to young adolescents should be concrete, show the many ways people are involved in the economy, involve the students actively in the learning process, and relate new knowledge to existing student knowledge.

Concrete Presentation

Young adolescents will benefit most from a concrete presentation about our economy and entrepreneurship. These students are in (or approaching) a transition in their thinking ability from concrete operational to formal operational thinking. To understand the importance of this change in thinking ability for economics and entrepreneurship education, we need to briefly distinguish between concrete and formal operational thinkers.

Concrete operational thinkers are able to classify and order objects, hold two or more variables in their mind simultaneously, and reconcile apparently contradictory data. Their ability to reason about physical and social events, however, is limited to those they have observed or participated in. In contrast, formal operational thinkers are able to reason about economics and entrepreneurial events that they have not directly observed or participated in. They can manipulate information in new ways, evaluate their own thinking, consider verbal statements and propositions, and comprehend abstract ideals like justice and freedom. It is important to remember that these are not discrete, static stages that appear overnight, but rather overlapping stages of continuous development.

Even though young adolescents are only beginning to become formal thinkers, and even though some are further in the transition than others, all adolescents will benefit from a concrete approach. Concrete experience will help them learn abstract ideas, for it is the building material from which abstract ideas can be constructed (Ausubel, 1964). By manipulating empirical data gained from concrete experience, students are able to develop abstract concepts. Even those students who are already thinking in a formal manner will benefit (Cantu and Herron, 1978). Actually, formal thinkers may learn better from concrete experiences than concrete thinkers (Sheehan, 1970). Thus, students might reflect on the role scarcity plays in their own lives. What recent decisions about scarce family resources have they or their families been forced to make? How did they finally choose between various alternatives? Likewise, they can consider how they have behaved entrepreneurially in their lives. Building on such concrete experiences is the most effective way for young adolescents to develop an understanding of abstract ideas (McKinnon and Renner, 1971).

People-Oriented Approach

For young adolescents, it is important to stress that the economy is made up of people who make decisions. These youngsters, newly conscious of their peer group, are developing new relationships and self-images, and are beginning to think seriously of their own career choices. Putting the emphasis on people who are active in the economy builds on these emerging interests and new relationships. The study of entrepreneurship provides role models for students and shows how they can influence their own futures by the decisions they make today.

Active Involvement in Learning

Fortunately, economics and entrepreneurship provides many opportunities to simulate economic activities within the classroom. Students can, for instance, operate a class store or establish a budget for their own classroom. Simulations and games reflect economic and entrepreneurial reality. Further, because students are more totally involved in the learning experience, listening, speaking, and using information, they are more likely to learn. Active involvement seems to improve both the immediate and the delayed recall of factual information. As a result of actively using economics and entrepreneurship concepts, students develop an understanding of the concepts' symbolic representations. This process gives the student the opportunity to gradually learn a principle from its concrete representations (Wollman and Lawson, 1978). A market simulation in which students buy and sell goods at different prices, record and analyze their transactions, and create their own supply and demand graphs is superior to presenting young adolescents with arbitrary supply and demand graphs and then analyzing them.

Experiences also provide concrete input from which to develop an understanding of the economy and entrepreneurship. Students can act on the content being learned and use it in new situations, thereby learning how to manipulate information. This leads to a deeper understanding (Nucci and Gordon, 1979). Just knowing the terms of economics and entrepreneurship, the technical jargon, does not guarantee understanding. Often students can learn the correct definitions or the right answers without understanding what they are saying. For example, many eighth grade students recently interviewed by the author commented that the major difference between our economic system and that of the Soviet Union is that we have freedom of choice and the Soviets do not. Later in the questioning, however, the same students often said that economic decisions in our system were made by the government. The contradiction was not clear to the students, who had memorized the right answer to why our system is different from the Soviets', but did not understand what that distinction means.

Linkages

New knowledge must always be linked to what is already known. Economics and entrepreneurship information taught to young adolescents must relate to their personal body of knowledge, yet be sufficiently novel to capture their interest (Kolodiz, 1977). We all have contextual frameworks that we have acquired over time. New knowledge is more powerfully learned if it hooks into our framework in a meaningful way. New knowledge also may cause our framework to be adjusted (Torney-Purta, 1990). However, if the new knowledge is unrelated to previous knowledge or to our conceptual framework, then it will be memorized and forgotten, or not learned at all.

ECONOMICS AND ENTREPRENEURSHIP IN THE CURRICULUM

Economics and entrepreneurship content can be added either by infusing it into courses or by establishing a separate course. There are advantages and disadvantages to both methods.

Infusion of economics and entrepreneurship into another course such as American history, civics, or geography can take one of several forms. First, the lesson may be unrelated to the content of the course. Like a current events day, the economics or entrepreneurship lesson fills a period but is not connected to other topics being studied, as it is outside the normal content flow of the course. Second, the normal content of an existing course can be used to provide examples of specific economics and entrepreneurship terms. For example, students could be taught the term *scarcity,* and then, during the study of colonial America, be asked to find examples of scarcity and the decisions people made because of it. Other concepts such as incentives, opportunity costs, and so on, similarly can be explained with examples from the courses. Third, an economics or entrepreneurial aspect of a topic already present in the course may be taught. For instance, the Industrial Revolution, the rise of corporations, the Great Depression, the panics of the 1800s, the establishment of the national bank and its ending under Andrew Jackson, and the impact of economic growth on society are economics and entrepreneurial topics that could be taught in an American history course. Infusion into existing courses may be as short as a few lessons that are taught in one or a few periods, or as long as an entire unit, which may take several weeks to complete.

There are some serious problems with the infusion strategy. Taught in the context of a course, economics and entrepreneurship ideas have a content framework to which they can be related, but that framework frequently is ignored and lessons are just dropped into a course. Further, separate infusion lessons are likely to result in a disjointed coverage of economics and entrepreneurship content rather than an organized, sequential one. When the economics and entrepreneurship content is taught with the normal content of another course, it is difficult to know how much is actually being taught about economics and entrepreneurship. Were one or two lessons taught, or many? An additional complication is that history, geography, or civics books do not adequately explain economics and entrepreneurship terms. Their purpose is not to teach economics and entrepreneurship, but to teach history, civics, and geography. Often, these textbooks, written by individuals not knowledgeable about economics, contain factual errors and important omissions. To compensate for these shortcomings, teachers using the infusion strategy must purchase and use supplemental materials, which is both expensive and awkward. Also, it often leads those promoting economics and entrepreneurship education to focus on individual teachers purchasing the materials instead of district- or school-wide curriculum change.

Despite these problems, infusion has been the primary means for presenting economics and entrepreneurship content to young adolescents. The power of infusion is its potential to teach all students, not just those enrolled in economics or entrepreneurship classes, with content that can be repeated year after year. Perhaps most important, the infusion of economics and entrepreneurship is usually easier to achieve than curriculum change that involves substituting a new course for an existing one. Changing the status quo is difficult. The dominant social studies course sequence was originally recommended by a National Education Association committee in 1916 (National Education Association, 1916). Once established, this sequence has been resistant to change. Teachers are trained to teach those courses, and textbooks are published for them. Needless to say, economics and entrepreneurship courses are not often part of the curriculum for young adolescents.

Nevertheless, economics especially is making inroads into the curriculum. A growing new trend is the establishment of a semester or quarter course in economics. In a few school districts such courses have been offered for years, but they are the exception. Part of the new interest in economics for young adolescents is due to the activities of the Foundation for Teaching Economics (FTE), which has selected young adolescents as its target audience. The FTE's statement of purpose declares it was established to "foster understanding of the American economic system and the role of the individual within the system" (Foundation for Teaching Economics, 1988, p. 2). It achieves this mission primarily by funding the creation of student materials designed to make it easier for teachers to give instruction about economics and entrepreneurship. The FTE funded the creation of the first textbook specifically designed with a fresh approach for young adolescents (Clawson, 1988). Using case studies of the production processes of common products, the text shows economic ideas being used by individuals. Numerous activities provide many opportunities for students to use newly learned information. The text can be used as the basic book for a one-semester economics course.

The Foundation for Teaching Economics also funds the development of other print material, filmstrips, and videos. Some, like *Famous Amos: The Business Behind the Cookie* (1985) and *Ice Cream and Economics: Ben & Jerry's Homemade,* (1988) are specifically designed to teach about entrepreneurship. All these student materials are especially designed for young adolescents and provide teachers with materials or tools with which to teach economics content to young adolescents. The FTE's materials are in use in all fifty states.

The Foundation for Teaching Economics is not alone in its efforts to promote economics and entrepreneurship education for young adolescents. The National Council for Social Studies' statement, *In Search of a Scope and Sequence for Social Studies* (1984) recommends a one-semester course in economics for young adolescents in eighth or ninth grade. The NCSS report suggests that the economics course be paired with a one-semester law-related education course to create a full year of social studies instruction. Further, Junior Achievement offers a semester-long program called Project Business, which is taught by a local businessperson who instructs a class for one period a week. The program utilizes the businessperson's experience, but has a standard topical structure.

As the importance of economics and entrepreneurship for young adolescents becomes better known, it is expected that the number of separate courses as well as the amount of infusion into existing courses will considerably increase.

CONCLUSION

Young adolescents are confronted with dramatic emotional, psychological, social, and physical changes. These students are beginning to confront economics in many aspects of their lives. Economic choices are a daily event for them. They are aware of business and hear much, in general, about entrepreneurs. Therefore, the introduction of economics and entrepreneurship understanding for the young adolescents is both reasonable and important.

Sound economics and entrepreneurship instruction needs to present challenging learning tasks that actively involve the learner and that recognize young adolescents' emerging capacity for abstract thought. Economic reasoning has been stressed. The economic landscape of young adolescents has been examined and three aspects detailed: institutions in the economy encountered by them; products and services of interest to them; and social roles played by and observed by them. The use of entrepreneurs as desirable role-models has been described.

Economic and entrepreneurship instruction for the young adolescent can be accomplished without teaching the full range of ideas and vocabulary from the economics discipline. This chapter rests on the assumption that for students to become effective, participating citizens and for the U.S. economic system to remain viable and dynamic, education must provide a basic understanding about how our economy works, a method of analysis to examine the economy, and a pragmatic view of the entrepreneural role.

REFERENCES

Armento, B. J., ed. 1987. *Scope and Sequence for Economic Education K-12: A Proposed Framework.* Atlanta: Georgia State University, National Specialized Center for Learning Theory and Economic Education.

Ausubel, D. 1964. "The Transition from Concrete to Abstract Cognitive Functioning: Theoretical Issues and Implications for Education." *Journal of Research in Science Teaching* 2: 261–266.

Banaszak, Ronald A. 1984. *Speaking about Economics.* Videotape. San Francisco: Foundation for Teaching Economics.

Beck, E. M., ed. 1980. *Barlett's Familiar Quotations.* 15th ed. Letter from Thomas Jefferson to William Charles Jarvis, September 28, 1820. Boston: Little, Brown.

Brockhaus, R. H. 1982. "The Psychology of the Entrepreneur." In *Encyclopedia of Entrepreneurship,* edited by C. A. Kent, D. L. Sexton, and K. H. Vesper. Englewood Cliffs, N.J.: Prentice-Hall, pp. 39–55.

Cantu, L., and J. Herron. 1978. "Concrete and Formal Piagetian Stages and Science Concept Attainment." *Journal of Research in Science Teaching* 15: 135–143.

Clark, H. F. 1940a. "Vitalizing Economic Education." *Social* 4: 397–403.

———, ed. (1940b) *Economic Education.* 11th yearbook. Washington, D. C.: National Council for Social Studies.

Clawson, E. U. 1988. *Our Economy: How It Works.* 3d ed. Menlo Park, Calif.: Addison-Wesley.

Clow, J. E. 1984. "Economic Facts of Life Needed by Entrepreneurs." *Business Education Forum* 38: 9–13.

Davis, James E. 1987. *Teaching Economics to Young Adolescents: A Research-Based Rationale.* San Francisco: Foundation for Teaching Economics.

Foundation for Teaching Economics. 1988. *Annual Report.* San Francisco: Foundation for Teaching Economics.

Foundation for Teaching Economics and KQED. 1988. *Ice Cream and Economics: Ben & Jerry's Homemade.* Videotape.

Foundation for Teaching Economics and MTI Teleprograms, Inc. 1985. *Famous Amos: The Business Behind the Cookie.* Videotape.

Friedman, Milton. 1953. "The Methodology of Positive Economics." In *Essays in Positive Economics,* edited by M. Friedman. Chicago: University of Chicago Press, pp. 3–43.

Gilliard, J., J. Caldwell, B. Dalgaard, R. Highsmith, R. Reinke, and M. Watts. 1988. *Economics: What and When.* New York: Joint Council on Economic Education.

Hansen, W. L. 1982. "Are Americans Economically Literate?" In *Economic Education: Investing in the Future,* edited by William H. Peterson. Knoxville: University of Tennessee Press, 22–37.

Kent, C. A. 1985. "Entrepreneurship." *The Elementary Economist* 7: 1, 12.

Keynes, J. M. 1930. *The Scope and Method of Political Economy.* New York: Macmillan.

Kolodiz, G. 1977. "Cognitive Development and Science Teaching." *Journal of Research in Science Teaching* 14: 21–26.

McKinnon, J., and J. Renner. 1971. "Are Colleges Concerned with Intellectual Development?" *American Journal of Psychology* 39: 1047–1052.

National Council for Social Studies. 1984. "In Search of a Scope and Sequence for Social Studies." *Social Education* 48: 249–262.

National Education Association, Committee on Social Studies. 1916. *The Social Studies in Secondary Education.* Bulletin 28. Washington, D.C.: National Education Association.

National Task Force on Economic Education. 1961. *Economic Education in the School.* New York: The Committee for Economic Development.

Nucci, L., and N. Gordon. 1979. "Educating Adolescents from a Piagetian Perspective." *Journal of Education* 161: 87–101.

Saunders, P., G. L. Bach, J. D., Calderwood, and W. L. Hansen. 1984. *Master Curriculum Guide in Economics: A Framework for Teaching the Basic Concepts.* New York: Joint Council on Economic Education.

Sheehan, D. 1970. "The Effectiveness of Concrete and Formal Instructional Procedures." *Dissertation Abstracts* 31, p. 274A.

Torney-Purta, Judith. 1990. "Political Socializtiton." In *Citizenship in the 21st Century,* edited by William Callahan and Ronald A. Banaszak. Bloomington, Ind.: ERIC Clearinghouse for Social Studies/Social Science Education.

Wollman, W., and A. Lawson. 1978. "The Influence of Instruction on Proportional Reasoning in Seventh Graders." *Journal of Research in Science Teaching* 15: 227–232.

PART FOUR

Entrepreneurship Education at the Secondary Level

12

Integrating Entrepreneurship in the Secondary Curriculum: Economics and Other Courses

Calvin A. Kent

The purpose of this chapter is to suggest where entrepreneurship can be appropriately integrated into the curriculum of the secondary schools. Entrepreneurship has become one of the clearly recognized trends sweeping not only this nation, but also the world (Kent, 1984a; Brinks and Coyne, 1983; Heilbroner, 1986). Recent years have seen a phenomenal growth at the college level in courses designed to teach the skills necessary for entrpreneuring (U.S. Small Business Administration, 1986). In addition, entrepreneurship curriculums designed to meet teaching objectives at the secondary level are beginning to appear. Since the majority of high school students do not go on to college, if there is indeed value in training for entrepreneurship, the subject should be introduced in the high schools. How that can be accomplished is the topic of this chapter.

WHAT IS ENTREPRENEURSHIP?

It is necessary to understand what is being discussed when reference is made to entrepreneurship. Entrepreneurship is incorrectly equated only with starting a small business. While new venture creation is the most prevalent form of entrepreneurship, it is not the only form. To limit the definition of entrepreneurship to just new venture creation unnecessarily limits the study of entrepreneurial activity. Entrepreneurship may be the result of a team effort in an existing organization such as a large corporation or even within a government bureaucracy (Schollhammer, 1982; Drucker, 1984; Naisbit, 1985).

Furthermore, there is a tendency to lump entrepreneurs and managers together. While out of necessity entrepreneurs often manage their own enterprises, to equate entrepreneurship with management is misleading. The literature demonstrates that the essential difference between entrepreneurs and managers is perception (Kirzner, 1983). Entrepreneurs do more than just combine the other factors of production; they perceive a need in the marketplace for goods and services or for new technologies. Entrepreneurs are willing to act on these perceptions and, in so doing, to take a risk that the new product or technology will succeed in the market. It is this quality of perception, and the subsequent action on the perception, that distinguish entrepreneurs from managers. Entrepreneurs should be considered a separate economic resource, whereas managers should be viewed as a specialized form of labor.

There is a lack of consensus among writers as to precisely what is meant by the term *entrepreneurship*. Schumpeter (1979) equated entrepreneurship with innovation in the broadest sense of the term. To him, innovation went beyond discovery and included implementation and/or commercialization. The entrepreneur sees an unexploited niche, and fills it by developing a new product, devising a new service, discovering a new technology, or formulating a new organization. Invention is not innovation. Invention involves seeing the niche and developing a way to satisfy the perceived need. Innovation goes further, however, requiring that the idea be actually implemented or at least tried in the market. This involves the risk that the introduction of new ideas always entails.

Harwood (1982) defined the characteristics of entrepreneurs as

1. taking initiative;

2. assuming considerable autonomy in the organization of resources;

3. sharing risks;

4. participating in uncertain rewards; and

5. innovating in more than an incremental or marginal way

It may be even more illuminating to follow Martin's (1982) lead by delineating who are not entrepreneurs:

1. Persons who would give only orders (they are managers)

2. Persons who risk only their capital (they are investors)

3. Persons who create in a literary, artistic, or dramatic sense, unless that creation is innovative and exploited for gain by their own efforts

It is easier to define entrepreneurship by its results than by its characteristics. There are five things that entrepreneurs do. They

1. introduce a new product or service in the market or implement a new approach to a social problem;
2. develop and implement a new technology that lowers costs and improves efficiency;
3. open a new market by introducing products, services, or technology not previously available;
4. discover a new source of supply for a scarce resource or methods of increasing the supply from existing resources by more efficient exploitation; and
5. reorganize an existing enterprise, either private or public, by innovative management.

Under these definitions entrepreneurship is much broader than just starting a new business. It can include innovative activities in large corporations, nonprofit organizations, and even government agencies or socialist enterprises. Programs in entrepreneurship education must recognize the full scope of entrepreneurial activity and not confine themselves to how to start and manage a small business.

DIMENSIONS OF ENTREPRENEURSHIP EDUCATION

In teaching the next generation of entrepreneurs it is important to note that entrepreneurship education has at least two broad dimensions. The first dimension is awareness, and the second is skills. Each of these can be further broken down. A program that focuses only on the skills entrepreneurs need to run a business omits vital understandings and will exclude those students who are not aware of the possibility that they could be entrepreneurs.

Awareness

Education for entrepreneurship awareness takes two forms. The first concerns the student becoming aware of the past, present, and future roles that entrepreneurs play in society. It is important that as part of the process of education students become aware of the importance of entrepreneurs in the growth and development of the American economy and the economies of other nations.

It has been suggested that one of the reasons why the supply of potential entrepreneurs has been limited is because entrepreneurship is rarely portrayed in a favorable light (DiBacco, 1987). While this problem may be less significant now than it was a few years ago, it is still fair to say that the impression most students have of entrepreneurs is, to a degree, unfavorable. The caricature of entrepreneurs that prevails in the media as well as in the curriculum materials students use in schools is not positive. Entrepreneurs are rarely portrayed as heroes. They are often viewed as villains, buffoons, or both. When asked to identify entrepreneurs from the media, students almost invariably recall J. R. Ewing from the television show "Dallas"—hardly a desirable role model for students to wish to emulate.

Allowing students to experience positive entrepreneurial role models, either by class contact or through curriculum materials, becomes the first step in entrepreneurship education, and should begin well before the secondary grades. This can be accomplished by in-class speakers, by viewing videos, or by reading case studies. The direct approach of "elbow rubbing" is very effective. By far the best method is an internship that leads to a mentor relationship between the student and the entrepreneur (Murphy, 1988).

A second form of awareness comes through allowing the students to see that entrepreneurship may be a career possibility for them. It is a rare school where the career counselor has any idea of how to present entrepreneurship as a possible vocation. There are folders, films, and reference materials of all sorts regarding various trades and professions, but relatively little has been done to supply vocational counselors with the materials that they need for students who might wish to explore the possibility of entrepreneurship. Some materials that do exist may tend to overglamorize the entrepreneur. The students need to understand that while there are rewards to the entrepreneurial life, entrepreneurs live with risk and constantly face the possibility of failure. Although many varieties of psychological tests have been developed to determine the aptitude of students for various other occupations, no such battery has yet been forthcoming to do the same for venture initiators.

Skills

As was the case with awareness, the skills in entrepreneurship also consist of two components (Scanlan et al., 1980). First are the technical insights that students must possess if they are to be successful entrepreneurs. While it should be obvious, it is worth reiterating that successful entrepreneurs must possess a high degree of technical knowledge in the field of their entrepreneurial activity. It is unlikely that someone knowing nothing about auto mechanics would be successful if they open their own garage. The first prerequisite for entrepreneurship education is to make sure that students have the vocational skills necessary to successfully compete in the marketplace.

The second skills component covers certain managerial skills that entrepreneurs need to learn. While entrepreneurs often are poor managers, this does not need to be the case. Entrepreneurs must have the necessary financial management skills to at least understand the information arrayed before them by their accountant or banker as well as sufficient savvy to keep the necessary records for their own use and for tax purposes.

Entrepreneurs also need to understand that to be successful they must work with other people. Human relations does not seem to be a long suit for most entrepreneurs, who often fail to understand the needs and wants of those with whom they work. They may often become annoyed when their employees fail to share either their vision or their dedication. As is always the case, communication is the key to human relations, and is a skill that most potential entrepreneurs need to acquire.

There is also another set of skills entrepreneurs must possess that are more introspective. There are psychological factors that separate entrepreneurs from others. Entrepreneurs are those individuals who possess a great deal of inner control. They recognize that their successes or failures are their responsibility and not something that can be attributed to others. They are self-starters and are goal-oriented. As a result they view failure in a different context. They do not see failure as rejection, but rather as a building block that they may use as the foundation for their future success. The very word *entrepreneur* conjures up the idea of risk taking. Students with poor self-images are unlikely to take the risk that entrepreneurship requires. If they do, they may be devastated if the risk results in defeat. Since entrepreneurs possess these traits, some have questioned whether entrepreneurs can be taught these instincts and personal qualities or whether they are born with them. This question is addressed in the latter part of this chapter.

ENTREPRENEURSHIP IN SPECIFIC COURSES

Where should entrepreneurship be introduced and taught in the high school curriculum? As could be suspected, there are several courses and levels at which entrepreneurship can be integrated. While a full unit on entrepreneurship could be taught as a self-standing, independent course of study, this is not the only approach, nor necessarily the most effective. Even if a freestanding entrepreneurship course is provided in the curriculum, its effectiveness will be enhanced if entrepreneurial insights are provided throughout the curriculum. If entrepreneurship education is isolated in a single course, it will be missed by many students who could profit from exposure.

Economics

The first course where the infusion of entrepreneurship should occur is in the high school economics course. There are certain basic concepts regarding entrepreneurship that should be integrated into the economics curriculum if the economics students are to have a complete and accurate idea of how the market system functions and how the process of economic growth begins and is sustained (Kent, 1989). Fundamental economic literacy is essential for entrepreneurs, but most economics curriculums today ignore the vital position of entrepreneurs in the economy.

There are four micro- and three macroeconomic concepts regarding entrepreneurship that should be included. First, in microeconomics, entrepreneurs should be presented as a factor of production. The students, when first introduced to the scarce factors of production, should realize that entrepreneurship is a separate and distinct factor from labor, land, or capital. In fact, entrepreneurs discover or create the other three factors as well as organizing them to turn those inputs into more highly valued outputs.

Second, students should know that entrepreneurs create disequilibrium. Traditional economics shows how markets move toward equilibrium in reconciling the forces of supply and demand. Entrepreneurs create disequilibrium by the introduction of new products or processes into the marketplace and, thus, create entirely new markets while destroying old ones (Baumol, 1968). Entrepreneurs do more than respond to price signals; they introduce new products and technologies that create new demand curves when consumers become aware of the availability of new products. New technologies also effect costs and create entirely new relationships between price and the amount producers will supply.

The role of profits, a third microeconomic concept, needs to be more fully developed. While the desire to earn a profit is a motivating force for entrepreneurs, it is not the only one. Certainly the desire for autonomy and the need for achievement are equally as important, yet they are rarely included in economists' models (Brockhaus, 1982). Traditional economic analysis views profits as a residual that measures the difference between costs and revenues. The sterile cost and revenue curves of most microeconomic chapters leave the students without a full understanding of the dynamics of the profit motive.

In addition, the absence or presence of profit does not necessarily indicate whether entrepreneurship is taking place. Many successful ventures are not profitable during their formative years. In addition, the existence of profits may reflect nothing more than a monopoly position achieved by a firm and not an entrepreneurial innovation.

The final microeconomic concept is the role of entrepreneurs in innovation. Schumpeter (Schumpeter, 1979; Martin, 1984) saw innovation as what distinguished the entrepreneurs from others. Entrepreneurs are constantly developing new ideas and new technologies and introducing them into the marketplace. It is a very useful insight for economics students to understand that the process of innovation is not mysterious. There is a person behind it who has the idea and who perfects and commercializes it as well.

On the macroeconomic side, students first need to recognize the pivotal position of entrepreneurs in economic growth, both for the developed and the underdeveloped world. Entrepreneurs provide the new technologies that improve the material welfare of humankind (Seldone, 1980). As these new technologies are developed and introduced, new jobs are created. This is a mixed blessing, as some jobs may be destroyed as old products and technologies are made obsolete. While it was often felt in the underdeveloped world that government would have to assume the role of the entrepreneur because there was not sufficient indigenous entrepreneurial talent, this idea has been disproved by the recent explosion of entrepreneurial activity in the less developed lands (Bauer, 1981). Given both economic freedom and adequate incentives, entrepreneurship can be a universal phenomena propelling economic growth.

Second, students discussing macroeconomic policy should be aware that creating an environment conducive to entrepreneurship is an effective policy for job generation. The statistics show that new and growing ventures generate a disproportionately large amount of the jobs in the economy, particularly jobs at the entry level (U.S. Small Business Association, 1983). Traditional macroeconomic theory assumes that if aggregate demand and aggregate supply are appropriately manipulated by fiscal and monetary policy, investment opportunities will be created and jobs will be automatically forthcoming. A better understanding of the entrepreneurial process will show the obvious shortcomings in that approach.

Third, macroeconomic analysis focuses on the mechanical relationship between aggregate supply and demand. Variables that are subject to quantification such as interest rates and money supply, receive attention. However, as Keynes (1936) himself emphasized, behind all these relationships there are entrepreneurs who must make the decision whether to invest. An understanding of entrepreneurs and entrepreneurial motivation should be included in the discussion of macroeconomic equilibrium.

Placing entrepreneurs in the pivotal position that is rightfully theirs in the study of economics would do much not only to improve student comprehension, but also to aid in the enjoyment of their high school economics course.

Business Education

Perhaps the next most obvious place where entrepreneurship should be included is in the high school business education curriculum. This is the appropriate place for the financial and human management skills to be introduced, developed, and practiced by potential entrepreneurs. The most appealing approach to business education is to have the students view themselves as employers rather than employees. In such a role the student then asks, "What is it that I want out of those who work for me? What sort of behaviors and attitudes would I find desirable?" This role reversal from the way business education is often taught may be the most effective way of inculcating the necessary work virtues.

While there is some disagreement, most business education programs in entrepreneurship include twelve specific managerial skills that entrepreneurs need to possess and that should be covered in the business education curriculum (Ashmore and Pritz, 1983). These include the following:

1. Selecting the form of business ownership
2. Doing market research
3. Locating the business
4. Financing the business
5. Identifying legal issues
6. Complying with government regulation
7. Acquiring skills in decision making
8. Managing people
9. Promoting the product
10. Keeping business records
11. Managing finances and credit
12. Protecting the enterprise

It is not necessary that students master each of these skills in the high school business course. What is essential is that prospective entrepreneurs recognize that they will need to develop these skills should they entrepreneur or that they will need to have on their entrepreneurial team either as employees or consultants those who do possess these skills. At a minimum, entrepreneurs must know enough to understand what their employees or consultants will tell them.

Government

The action of government in creating and limiting the environment for entrepreneurship should be included in high school courses on government. Those portions of these courses that deal with government taxes and regulation should be careful to demonstrate that these policies may not have a neutral effect on the entrepreneurial environment (Vesper, 1983). By reducing the rewards to entrepreneurial activity, taxes also reduce the likelihood of the entrepreneurial event (Kent, 1984b; Stoll and Walter, 1980). Regulation is a burden to all businesses, but more especially to small entrepreneurial ones that generally have less ability to bear the costs of compliance (Chilton, 1984). Whole industries have been destroyed by government regulation, while new industries have been created by the same force. It would be good if government students could identify *paper entrepreneurs*, the new breed of business persons who make profits for their firms, not by innovating new products or introducing new technologies, but by discovering the loopholes in the tax code and the means to skate around the labyrinth of government regulations (Reich, 1980; Hughes, 1980).

Comparative studies should be undertaken concerning the role of entrepreneurs under alternative political structures. Why has there been a movement toward the free market in command societies? Is there a relationship between political and entrepreneurial liberty? To what extent is the existence of one type of liberty essential for the presence of the other? These are fundamental questions that students need to explore in the high school government course. Other questions to consider include the following: Can government bureaucrats be made entrepreneurial? To what extent can privatization of governmental functions reduce costs and improve services by substituting entrepreneurial for bureaucratic provisions (Kent, 1986)?

Psychology

The course of psychology is an excellent place for students to learn about the psychological characteristics of entrepreneurship and to determine if those characteristics describe them (Brockhaus, 1982). The high school psychology course that goes beyond description and has students evaluate their own personalities and motivations is a means of both identifying and motivating potential entrepreneurs. An answer to the question, "Can the psychological characteristics of entrepreneurs be taught?" can be attempted. A course that allows students to develop their own concepts of self-worth and inner control would be an outstanding addition to the process of entrepreneurship education. Psychology courses that are largely descriptive and theoretical will probably contribute little to the understanding of entrepreneurship or to the creation of the next generation of entrepreneurs.

Sociology

As with courses in psychology, courses in sociology can also be important in the total entrepreneurship curriculum. The study of the sociology of entrepreneurship is in its infancy, but there are several ideas that are consistent with the thrust in entrepreneurship education (Harwood, 1982; Shapero and Sokol, 1982). Students should recognize that entrepreneurs both shape and are shaped by the culture in which they live. They should consider the following: Why do some ethnic groups seem to be more entrepreneurial than others? What is the impact of displacement (immigration, unemployment, divorce, etc.) on the tendency to entrepreneur? Is there a "culture" pertaining to entrepreneurship that can be developed or destroyed? Is entrepreneurship a way of integrating "outsiders" (minorities, women, etc.)? While current high school sociology courses generally do not raise these questions, raising them would be profitable for students with an active or latent interest in entrepreneurship.

History

The importance of the entrepreneur as a historical figure should not be overlooked. History teachers can do a great deal toward expanding the horizons of their students by focusing on case studies of entrepreneurs who have contributed to the betterment of humankind at all times and in all places (DiBacco, 1987). Case studies are particularly valuable if a variety of alternative stories are included that allow the students to relate to entrepreneurs of the different races and genders.

As long as history courses inaccurately portray entrepreneurs as robber barons, it is unlikely that students will view entrepreneruship as a desirable vocation (Folson, 1987). History courses often focus on politicians and generals and their contributions. Entrepreneurial history is equally as important for students to understand their heritage. The "mega innovations" that have forever changed the course and direction of history should be included, with emphasis on the individuals who introduced them and the struggle that their entrepreneurial effort involved. To understand who we are and how we got to our present position, students must comprehend the role of the entrepreneur. History can contribute to entrepreneurial alertness by allowing students to see how niches were found in the past so that they may be better equipped to find their own niches in the future.

One last contribution that the study of entrepreneurial history can make is to allow students to understand that most progress is made through small steps. While the mega innovations are important, progress really occurs as ideas are adapted and refined. The cumulative process of improving and changing old ideas in an incremental way to better satisfy consumer or producer needs is the form most entrepreneurial activity takes. The evolution of new processes and technologies is an essential ingredient in entrepreneurial history.

Science

Entrepreneurship can also be a thread woven into the fabric of science courses. Since technological advance often begins with scientific insight and continues because of entrepreneurial persistence, students should understand the relation between scientific discovery and entrepreneurship (Martin, 1984). Many of the great scientists were also entrepreneurs, who not only invented but also innovated in the most complete sense of bringing their product or technology into the marketplace. Thomas Edison was not only a scientist, he was also an entrepreneur who demonstrated how science can be commercialized and brought from the laboratory to the marketplace.

The computer industry is filled with stories of entrepreneurs whose ideas were both developed and commercialized. Learning these stories may be as important as studying the scientific rules, theorems, and laws. The scientific genius who is a potential inventor may receive additional inspiration and motivation by understanding the relationship between science and the process of entrepreneurship. Science students need to know that having a good idea is not enough; the process must be completed by bringing that idea to the market and having it accepted.

CONCLUSION

Those who design secondary curriculum should make sure that entrepreneurship is not neglected. As this chapter has demonstrated, entrepreneurship is neither a separate nor an alien concept, but rather one that can enrich the students' understanding of a variety of secondary subjects. At the same time there is a societal benefit. As knowledge about entrepreneurship is more widely dispersed throughout the high school curriculum, the likelihood of individuals becoming entrepreneurs will be enhanced and the benefits to the economy from expanded entrepreneurial activity will be insured.

REFERENCES

Ashmore, M. Catherine, and Sandra G. Pritz. 1983. "Program for Acquired Competency in Entrepreneurship [PACE]." Rev. ed. Columbus: The Ohio State University, National Center for Research and Vocational Education.

Bauer, P. T. 1981. *Equality: The Third World and Economic Delusion.* Cambridge, Mass.: Harvard University Press.

Baumol, William J. 1968. "Entrepreneurship in Economic Theory." *American Economic Review* 58, no. 2 (May): 64–71.

Brinks, Martin, and John Coyne. 1983. *The Birth of Enterprise.* London: Institute for Economic Affairs.

Brockhaus, Robert H., Sr. 1982. "The Psychology of the Entrepreneur." In *The Encyclopedia of Entrepreneurship,* edited by C. A. Kent, D. L. Sexton, and K. H. Vesper. Englewood Cliffs, N.J: Prentice-Hall, pp. 38–56.

Chilton, Kenneth. 1984. "Regulation in the Entrepreneurial Environment." In *The*

Environment for Entrepreneurship, edited by C. A. Kent. Lexington, Mass:
Lexington Books, pp. 91–116.

DiBacco, Thomas B. 1987. *Made in the U.S.A.: A History of American Business.*
New York: Harper and Row.

Drucker, Peter F. 1984. *Innovation and Entrepreneurship.* New York: Harper and
Row.

Folson, Burton W. 1987. *Entrepreneurs vs. the State.* Reston, Va.: Young America's
Foundation.

Harwood, Edwin, 1982. "The Sociology of Entrepreneurship." In *Encyclopedia of
Entrepreneurship,* edited by C. A. Kent, D. L. Sexton, and K. H. Vesper.
Englewood Cliffs, N.J.: Prentice-Hall, pp. 1–98.

Heilbroner, Robert. 1986. *The Worldly Philosophers.* 6th ed. New York: Simon and
Schuster.

Hughes, Jonathan R. T. 1980. "Entrepreneurship." In *The Encyclopedia of American Economic History,* edited by G. Porter. New York: Scribner, pp. 214–
228.

Kent, Calvin A. 1984a. "The Rediscovery of the Entrepreneur." In *The Environment for Entrepreneurship,* edited by C. A. Kent. Lexington, Mass.: Lexington Books, pp. 1–20.

———. 1984b. "Taxation and the Entrepreneurial Environment." In *The Environment for Entrepreneurship,* edited by C. A. Kent. Lexington, Mass.: Lexington Books, pp. 69–91.

———. 1986. *Entrepreneurship and the Privatizing of Government.* Westport,
Conn.: Quorum Books.

———. 1989. "Entrepreneurship as a Concept in Collegiate Principles of Economics Texts." *Journal of Economic Education* 20 (Spring): 153–164.

Keynes, J. M. 1936. *The General Theory of Employment, Interest and Money.* New
York: Harcourt, Brace.

Kirzner, I. M. 1983. "Entrepreneurship and the Future of Capitalism." In *Entrepreneurship and the Outlook for America,* edited by J. Bachman. New York:
The Free Press, pp. 149–173.

Martin, Albro. 1982. "Additional Aspects of Entrepreneurial History." In *The Encyclopedia of Entrepreneurship,* edited by C. A. Kent, D. L. Sexton, and K. H.
Vesper. Englewood Cliffs, N.J.: Prentice-Hall, pp. 13–18.

Martin, Michael J. C. 1984. *Managing Technological Innovation in Entrepreneurship.* Reston, Va.: Reston Publishing.

Murphy, Margaret, M. 1988. "Interns and Mentorships in Entrepreneurship Education Programs." Paper delivered at the conference on Entrepreneurship in
Economic Education, Widener University, March 11.

Naisbitt, John. 1985. *Reinventing the Corporation.* New York: McGraw-Hill.

Reich, Robert B. 1980. "Pie Slicers vs. Pie Enlargers." *The Washington Monthly*
(September): 20–25.

Scanlon, Thomas J., et al. 1980. *Entrepreneurship Education.* Springfield: Illinois
State Board of Education, Department of Adult Vocational and Technical
Education.

Schollhammer, Hans. 1982. "Internal Corporate Entrepreneurship." In *The Encyclopedia of Entrepreneurship,* edited by C. A. Kent, D. L. Sexton, and K. H.
Vesper. Englewood Cliffs, N.J.: Prentice-Hall, pp. 209–226.

Schumpeter, Joseph A. 1979. *The Theory of Economic Development.* London: Transaction Books (originally published 1934).

Seldone, Arthur. 1980. *Prime Mover of Progress: The Entrepreneurs in Capitalism and Socialism.* London: The Institute for Economic Affairs.

Shapero, Albert, and Lisa Sokol. 1982. "The Social Dimensions of Entrepreneurship." In *The Encyclopedia of Entrepreneurship,* edited by C. A. Kent, D. L. Sexton, and K. H. Vesper. Englewood Cliffs, N.J.: Prentice-Hall, pp. 72–88.

Stoll, Hans, and James Walter. 1980. *Tax Incentives for Small Business,* Chicago: Heller Small Business Institute, 1980.

United States Small Business Administration. 1983. *The State of Small Business: A Report of the President.* Washington, D.C.: Government Printing Office.

———. 1986. *National Survey of Entrepreneurial Education.* Vols. 1–6, 3d ed. Washington, D.C.: Government Printing Office.

Vesper, Karl H. 1983. *Entrepreneurship and National Policy.* Chicago: Heller Institute for Small Business.

13

What Entrepreneurship Education Should Teach About Economics

John E. Clow

The age of entrepreneurship education in the schools has certainly arrived. Collegiate courses and programs flourished during the 1980s. A number of new or reactivated programs at the high school level focusing on entrepreneurship and small business development were initiated, among them this particular project.

It is interesting to speculate how and why this recent movement started. It probably gained momentum when an increasing number of business leaders in the late 1960s and 1970s fulfilled Maslow's Hierarchy of Needs by leaving secure positions and starting their own businesses. These people were probably seeking the highest rung of Maslow's hierarchical ladder—self-fulfillment—since they had achieved the lower needs such as economic security and social esteem. They defined self-fulfillment as being their own boss and using their skills and knowledge to create something new on their own. As increasingly more small businesses were created, an interest in educating college-level students in small business development was spawned, which created the interest in the college-level courses.

Then along came the oil crisis and an increased buffeting of corporate America in the 1980s by foreign competition. New products, services, and work procedures were deemed important to keep jobs and create new ones in order to maintain or improve our standard of living. It was then recognized that the creative, innovative energies of all Americans, not just a few, should be harnessed, and that there should be a better understanding by the populace of how and why new business development is important and good, rather than something to be frowned upon. Consequently, we now see increased activity at the below-college level in order to reach more of the populace.

A brief perusal of the entrepreneurial education movement shows that it should be multidisciplinary in nature. The positive contributions that can and should be made from different disciplines such as business administration, communications arts, economics, history, mathematics, psychology, and sociology are necessary understandings for being an entrepreneur, working for an entrepreneur, or understanding how the entrepreneur relates to the total economic and social system.

THE PURPOSE OF ECONOMICS IN AN ENTREPRENEURIAL PROGRAM

Economics should play an integral part in the entrepreneurship program because the entrepreneur has played and continues to play an important economic role in our society. The four primary objectives for economic education in an entrepreneurial education program are to develop a general understanding of

1. economic principles that operate in our economic system;
2. the way that businesses of all sizes operate in our economic system;
3. the role of the entrepreneur or intrapreneur in our economic system; and
4. the ways a budding entrepreneur can implement a successful business venture.

Given that the first three of the four objectives are general in nature, a primary focus of economics in a entrepreneurship program should be to develop generic economic understandings. These general understandings are not only important for the aspiring entrepreneur but also essential for the person who does not become an entrepreneur. Understanding our economic system, how businesses operate in the system, and the role of the entrepreneur are necessary for all students in the assumption of their roles as citizens, consumers, and wage earners.

In other words, entrepreneurial education is a natural vehicle to develop economic literacy. The generalizations that follow show that economic concepts provide an important backdrop and stage direction for the entrepreneurial function.

SELECTED ECONOMIC UNDERSTANDINGS TO EMPHASIZE IN ENTREPRENEURIAL EDUCATION

There are many economic generalizations that could be delineated. The following are twelve that the author considers most important. Most of them are microeconomic in nature, primarily because the focus is on the entrepreneur, an individual, operating in our economic system.

1. *Our economic and political system encourages private enterprise.* The freedoms to own property and to start a new business are characteristic of our economic and political system. Laws are enforced that protect both these freedoms. Various types of help are provided by government to the small business person, including tax advantages and assistance from the Small Business Administration. The thousands of small businesses that are formed each year (some estimate more than sixty thousand a year) indicate that our economic system provides an environment where small business enterprises are encouraged. The market concept on which our economic system is based provides an economic incentive (the profit motive) to start one's own business.

The system does not guarantee success. In fact, many small business ventures fail each year. The market basically provides a medium whereby the entrepreneur has the freedom to either succeed and earn a profit or fail and take a loss. In other words, risk is involved in starting a new business enterprise. Generally, our various levels of government do not step in to save a small business that has failed because such an action negates one of the goals of a market system, economic efficiency.[1] For instance, why save a firm that is producing something that the consumer does not want or will not be purchased at the market price? Why save a firm that is poorly managed? If government did save such firms, society would be pumping resources into enterprises that the market had indicated were not needed or wanted by the consumer or that were not using resources efficiently.

2. *Entrepreneurs are the idea people and the organizers of other factors of production.* Entrepreneurs are individuals who come up with ideas that will hopefully result in profitable ventures. They are opportunity seekers who implement ideas that have not been pursued by others. These ideas could be new products or services to be sold or new ways to make or improve on the production of existing products or services. Entrepreneurs are also people who are responsible for putting together the other factors of production—the natural resources, labor, and capital goods—in order to make the item. Granted, some entrepreneurs hire managers to implement organizational process, but the entrepreneur is ultimately responsible for this function.

3. *Entrepreneurs create jobs in our economy and have created new types of positions.* In the 1980s, newly formed small businesses and existing small businesses were the major creators of new jobs in our economy. During the 1980s, large corporations streamlined operations which included the elimination of many jobs. For example, it is estimated that the *Fortune* 500 companies lost two million jobs from 1980 to 1985. Without small businesses, America currently would not be the envy of the world

for its ability to create new jobs for its labor force. Over six million jobs, for example, have been added to the United States economy since 1980, due primarily to small businesses.

This, in turn, means that after graduation from high school or college, a greater portion of students will procure their initial position in a small business than was true of their counterparts in the 1960s and 1970s. There is a need for the graduates to understand that the job descriptions for many positions in a small business are quite different than those found in larger ones. Large corporations, for example, generally call for considerable specialization of function, whereas small businesses require employees who can handle a greater breadth of duties. This holds true for both lower- and higher-level positions.

Another difference relates to flexibility. Change in procedures, items to be produced, and staff generally takes more time in a larger firm than a smaller one, the phrase "small is beautiful" certainly holds true if a primary goal is flexibility. It is much simpler to move a relatively small amount of capital goods, natural resources, and labor to the production of a new item than making such changes in a large business. Thus, the ability to be flexible and to be more of a generalist are the keys to success in being an entrepreneur and working in a small business venture.

4. *Every decision of the entrepreneur has an opportunity cost.* The entrepreneur is faced with the scarcity of resources, having only so much labor, capital equipment, and natural resources with which to operate. He or she also has only so much financial resources to work with, including what can be gained from credit lines. Choices have to be made as to how to use these resources to optimize the return, considering both short- and long-term effects.

The entrepreneur must realize that if resources are used for one purpose they cannot be used for another. An entrepreneur's time spent on planning marketing strategies cannot be used to analyze financial statements. Similarly, the money used to buy a piece of equipment cannot be used to pay salaries. With every decision, there is an opportunity cost, which is what is given up when choosing one alternative over the next best choice.

An understanding of opportunity cost enables the entrepreneur to realize that there are no perfect choices. Sacrifices must be made if resources are used in one way instead of another. The key to informed economic decision making is to select the best imperfect choice.

5. *Most decisions involve small or marginal changes.* Most decisions of the entrepreneur do not involve an "all or nothing" or "yes or no" type of proposition. Instead, they focus on small changes—a little more of this or a little less of that. How much more or less of goods or services should be produced at a given time? Should a few more additional workers be hired, or should some be let go? The key to wise decision making, even

with these marginal changes, is to carefully compare what is gained and what is given up or traded-off in making each marginal change. Obviously, the principles of opportunity cost again come into play here. A lot of poorly made marginal changes can lead to future difficulty for the business venture.

6. *Prices act as signals to buyers and sellers.* Entrepreneurs should understand the general principle that prices act as a rationing and allocating device for both buyers and sellers. At any given price for a good or service, some consumers will be able and willing to buy, while others will not. Those who are not able to buy the item at the market price are rationed out and thus do not obtain the item.

On the seller side, the market price for an item determines whether individual producers will change their level of production. If the market price is viewed as high relative to costs, producers will be encouraged to increase production, thus using more resources to produce the item. If the market price is viewed as low relative to costs, producers will be encouraged to decrease production, thus using fewer resources to produce the item.

The economic laws of demand and supply demonstrate the way in which prices act as signals. The law of demand indicates that generally, as prices increase, the quantity demanded decreases, and as prices decrease, the quantity demanded increases. The law of supply, in turn, indicates that as prices increase, the quantity supplied increases, and as prices decrease, the quantity supplied decreases.

A knowledge of the working of the price mechanism can help students understand the rationale behind different pricing strategies. For example, putting goods on sale in order to deplete one's inventory certainly is consistent with the law of demand. A firm that uses a policy of low prices with low profit margins per unit is expecting a high volume of demand for its goods to achieve a favorable profit picture. Another firm can successfully offer the same goods at much higher prices with a higher profit margin, knowing that it cannot rely as much on volume because of the higher price. In their price structures, both firms show an understanding of how prices act as signaling devices. As marketing experts tell us, pricing is a part of the marketing mix.

7. *Ways in which the price of goods and services are established and changed.* There are many dimensions to supply and demand that the entrepreneur should understand. In too many cases, we focus only on how the equilibrium price at any point in time is reached through the interaction of buyers and sellers in the marketplace. If that is the extent to which supply and demand are covered, the student of entrepreneurship does not become acquainted with the dimensions of why prices can and do change, which is important to both buyer and seller. Students should recognize that the prices for many goods and services are not static. Causes for change

on the demand side include changes in the tastes and preferences of buyers, in the price of substitute and complementary goods and services, and
in the income level of the consumer. Causes of change on the supply side
include changes in costs of productive resources, new technology, natural
causes (such as weather), and the opportunity cost of other types of productive enterprises.

Many entrepreneurs in their new ventures create a disequilibrium in the
product or service area in which they are involved. For example, if an
entrepreneur starts producing a new product at a lower price than what
is currently offered in the marketplace, the new product could create disequilibrium in the existing market since the market price may change as
well as the amount supplied. Similarly, if an entrepreneur starts producing
an entirely new product, disequilibrium could very well occur in the market for substitute goods since consumers might switch to the new product
from the substitute product.

Thus, teaching about equilibrium price is a starting point, but disequilibrium is very important as well. An understanding of factors contributing
to price changes enables the entrepreneur to gain a better grasp of timing
the purchase of needed productive resources and of understanding the
effects of price increases and decreases on his or her customers.

8. *Profits play an important role in our economy.* An important motivating force behind economic behavior is individual self-interest. Profits
are an important motivator for individuals to start a new business. Producers seek to maximize their profits and are encouraged by the profit motive
to combine productive resources in the most efficient way to produce the
goods and services consumers want to buy.

Entrepreneurs need to understand both the definition and the functions
of profit. The profit from a business is commonly thought of as what remains after the costs have been deducted from the revenue derived from
the sale of goods and services. It is important for entrepreneurs to understand that the return to the entrepreneur from the business venture could
well include profit and a return on labor for managing the business. As an
example, an individual running a business full time with an annual return
of $25,000 from the firm is getting a return on both his or her investments,
money and labor. An important consideration here is how well this return
compares to the next best alternative use of one's resources. Taking a look
at whether the return is a good one given the alternative choices is wise
from an economic point of view. This should be done on both a short-
and long-term basis.

On an initial short-term basis, many small businesses will not show very
high profits when comparing the return to an alternative use of resources.
Most successful new ventures have a minimal profit or even a loss during
the first few years of operation because of the costs of getting started and
gaining acceptance. Even with a business that turns a profit year after year,

the average return may not be as good as if the money were invested in certificates of deposit and the entrepreneur worked for someone else. Still, many entrepreneurs in such situations would not liquidate their business because of the freedoms they enjoy in operating it and the possibility that the enterprise may garner a much better return in succeeding years. Such thinking is common among many entrepreneurs. Analysis of comparative return, however, is still important in that it fosters clearer thinking about reasons why a business should be continued, expanded, sold, or discontinued.

Profits are to be used for two purposes. Some profits of a firm are given to individuals or groups to save or spend as they please. Some profits are maintained by the firm to use for such purposes as updating the productive facilities and equipment so as to promote growth. Certainly, this function of profit is important for the firm to stay competitive. This is an essential understanding for an entrepreneur.

9. *Productivity can be increased in a number of ways.* Entrepreneurs should be concerned about increasing productivity in order for their businesses to remain competitive in the marketplace and to achieve satisfactory profit levels. Productivity is the amount of output per unit of input. Productivity can be increased by producing more goods or services (output) with the same amount of resources (input) or by producing the same amount of goods and services (output) with less resources (input).

Mass production strategies involving specialization of labor, improved technology, or better trained workers are common ways to increase productivity. Better organized work flow and improved health care for workers also contribute to increased productivity.

Students should be shown through realistic examples how these principles are indeed true in the world of the entrepreneur. A study of the beginnings of the Ford Motor Company shows how Henry Ford used the assembly line for mass production procedures to decrease costs and increase productivity. This, in turn, led to lower prices for the Ford automobiles compared to much of the competition. The computer revolution has shown how new machines can increase the productivity of offices and factories. Many businesses, including small ones, provide in-service training in order to improve the productivity of their workers.

As pointed out previously, small businesses generally do not have the level of specialization, capital equipment, and extensive training programs that are found in large ones. Nonetheless, these sample principles can still be applied to a small business for increasing productivity.

10. *There are different types and forms of competition.* The entrepreneur should have some basic understandings of competition and the types of competition found in various market areas, particularly the area in which he or she wants to open a business.

First of all, students should understand that there are both price and non-price competitive factors. Some firms traditionally charge higher prices for the same item than other firms in the same area. Such firms are often quite successful because of such factors as good location, easy return policy in case of dissatisfaction, excellent personal service, a higher-income clientele, proven reliability, or a more pleasant environment in which to shop. Examples of the principle of non-price competition can generally be found in your own community.

It is also important for students to be able to identify market structure. Market structure refers to the degree of competition prevailing in a particular market area and the extent to which the government, under various laws, intervenes in the market to influence the pricing process and the rate of profit. Some markets are quite competitive, with many sellers, none of whom can affect the market price, and entry into and exit from the industry are therefore relatively easy. Other markets are dominated by a small number of sellers whose individual actions can affect and sometimes control prices. Entry is more difficult, and as a consequence substantial market power may rest with a few producers.

The principle of monopolistic competition should be a major focus. Many firms set their products or services apart from those of the competitors through product differentiation. There are many examples of this in our present world. For example, a McDonald's hamburger is perceived by many in our society as quite different from the hamburger sold at the local mom and pop restaurant. When many people want a hamburger, they automatically think of McDonald's and do not even think of other sources for hamburgers. Certainly, one of the factors that assists in this differentiation process is promotion, which includes advertising.

Future entrepreneurs should develop an intuitive understanding of these different kinds of competition and be able to apply them to real-life situations that they encounter. Furthermore, the successful entrepreneur needs to keep constantly abreast of what the competition is doing and might plan to do and be alert to new opportunities that have not been pursued by competitors. These understandings can be applied in several ways—including making decisions regarding what business to start; what goods and services should be carried, added, or deleted to an operating business; and the pricing policies to be pursued. Otherwise, a successful venture may go awry.

11. *Government regulations and intervention affect the marketplace.* In our economy, there are some goods and services that are produced by both private and public entities. Examples include schools and recreational programs. Starting a business in a product or service area where there are a number of competitors that are subsidized or run by the government poses special problems. A major problem relates to price competition. For example, a new golf course run by a governmental unit may charge lower user fees than one run by a private concern because some

or many of the direct costs are covered by direct taxes. In such a case, the private golf course must seek out ways other than price to compete.

The effect of governmental regulation in the marketplace must also be understood by the entrepreneur. Some kinds of government regulation, such as antitrust actions and antifraud activities, promote fair competition in market areas, while others are primarily geared toward standards for goods and services offered for sale, and environmental issues in the workplace and the community. Generally, these types of activities increase the cost of the good or service to be produced because business must assume additional costs.

Another type of government regulation is to control prices for various goods and services; for example, price supports in various agricultural areas, or price controls for various forms of energy, housing in some major cities, and public transportation systems. The ramifications of various types of government intervention and regulation should be understood by students as they affect their decisions as entrepreneurs.

Other forms of government intervention are in the form of direct incentives to the entrepreneur. Loan assistance from the Small Business Administration and tax abatements by the local government are examples. Deductions provided by federal tax laws to the small business owner is another.

Still other governmental actions, such as fiscal and monetary policies, are used to promote the economic health of the total economy. Such policies, however, certainly affect the individual entrepreneur. For example, if government dramatically increased taxes, a local shopkeeper could well feel an impact from that action through somewhat lower sales resulting from decreased disposable income of the consumer. Similarly, if the Federal Reserve System implements a tighter monetary policy because of inflation, a small business person will have to pay more interest on a loan to gain the new equipment, which may mean changes in profits and/or prices charged the consumer. Knowing how fiscal and monetary policies work in our economy can better enable the entrepreneur to make more informed decisions.

12. *Our economic life is a series of interdependencies.* The entrepreneur should well understand that a small business is certainly not an island unto itself. It affects other institutions and individuals and is in turn affected by them. A small business depends on consumers to buy goods and services, and it relies on other businesses and individuals to provide the needed resources. Small businesses also depend on government to provide some basic goods and services so that economic activities can take place. These interrelationships between and among households, businesses, and government can be shown through the circular flow mechanism.[2]

The entrepreneur should also be aware of other interdependencies, such as depending on foreign business as customers or as providers of goods to be sold. In the production function, interdependency is an important concept that is apparent in mass production strategies. Our society has been moving toward increased interdependency throughout its history. Many examples in the local community can exemplify the principle of interdependency.

PREDICTED FUTURE OF ENTREPRENEURIAL EDUCATION

Entrepreneurial education could well become a main focus or educational theme of the 1990s. It will probably not be called entrepreneurship education, but it *will* include much of the flavor with an emphasis on private initiative, the creative genius of the individual, innovation, and the ways our economic system rewards these qualities. It can and will envelop the Back to Basics approach with its emphasis on general skills and understanding since those are necessary for implementing innovative changes in both the private and public sectors.

There are two reasons for this opinion. One is the groundswell of interest for innovation in both sectors of our economy. In the private sector, without new goods and services and new ways of producing them, America will continue to lose markets and jobs and experience a lower standard of living. Thus it is imperative to educate more students in the process of creative innovation and how the economic system provides rewards for successful ideas.

In the public sector, there is a growing awareness that many of our public institutions are outmoded and ineffective. Innovative changes must enable the public institutions to provide services consistent with what society needs for the 1990s. A good case in point is the current attack on the school reform movement which many feel is beneficial for some but detrimental to a majority of students, especially at the high school level. Requiring more courses at the secondary level for all students is viewed by many as being a "quick fix" approach that will not deal with the multiplicity of learning problems that exist. A need exists for some creative energies from intrapreneurs to institute effective change.

Another reason for the entrepreneurial focus pertains to education cycles which generally alternate between traditional and nontraditional emphases. The 1980s Back to Basics approach has obviously focused on a traditional one. In the 1990s the public will turn its attention to other serious problems, which will probably be nontraditional in nature. One such problem could well be innovation, which obviously ties in with entrepreneurship.

Innovation education can be easily integrated into the various disciplines found in the high school. Entrepreneurial activities abound. History and literature could cover entrepreneurs of an earlier era. Science courses could replicate experiments that were revolutionary in their day and brought forth new products or a new orientation for looking at scientific theory.

Occupational education could focus on the specific skills needed for being a successful entrepreneur. The ways in which entrepreneurs use and need basic skills could also be implemented.

Even if innovation education does not become pervasive, entrepreneurial topics and courses will probably become more popular in the schools. As compared to the 1960s, there is a more positive attitude toward business and more particularly small business on the part of the general public and school personnel. This will probably continue to improve during the 1990s because small business development is seen as an important means of saving jobs and promoting economic security. Thus, entrepreneurial programs at the secondary level will flourish.

Economic educators should play an important role in shaping these programs. Entrepreneurship education, just like career education, consumer education, and citizen education is an important vehicle in teaching economic concepts and the economic way of thinking.

SUMMARY

The application of economic principles through entrepreneurial experiences is not only possible but also worthwhile for students. First of all, all students can gain an understanding of the role of the entrepreneur in a market-oriented system, which is important at this time when increasing innovation seems to be a national priority. Also, students will learn the nature of our economic system and how it works. A third benefit is that students can gain a better understanding of how economic concepts can be used in making practical decisions. Certainly, the focus in an entrepreneurial course will primarily be oriented toward applying the concepts from the perspective of the entrepreneur or the business person. Hopefully, however, students will visualize how these same economic concepts can be helpful in making decisions as wage earners, consumers, and citizens. A final benefit at the high school level is that the budding entrepreneur can be provided with basic economic principles that will help in initiating and operating a small business.

To understand the entrepreneurship role and how to fulfill it, some basic economic concepts must be understood. Entrepreneurship education is an excellent vehicle to teach these economic principles.

NOTES

Some of the ideas and the format for presenting ideas in this chapter were spawned from "Economics Within the Marketing and Distributive Education Program," by William A. Stull and H. Craig Petersen found in *Economics in the Business Education Curriculum* (New York: Joint Council on Economic Education, 1985), pp. 50–54.

1. There have been instances where the government *has* stepped in to save a business. Guaranteed loan assistance, for example, was extended to the Chrysler Corporation in the 1970s by the federal government. Such action is occasionally offered to large businesses that have major government contracts and are perceived as having a major impact on the economy.

2. For an explanation of the circular flow mechanism see Phillip Saunders and others, *Master Curriculum Guide in Economics: A Frame for Teaching the Basic Concepts,* 2d ed. (New York: Joint Council on Economic Education, 1984), p. 23.

14

Entrepreneurship in Vocational Education

M. Catherine Ashmore

Entrepreneurs are not *born* . . . they *become* through the experiences of their lives.

—Albert Shapero, 1982

Personal initiative and diverse special skills are the ingredients for an entrepreneurial economy. Vocational educators are recognizing that these same ingredients are the purpose of vocational programs in the high schools and two-year colleges. The missing link has been education for entrepreneurship as part of vocational program priorities.

Entrepreneurs come from every level of education, and many have emerged from poverty or lack of so-called educational success. Vocational educators have recognized that starting a business is a natural outcome of vocational skills training, and they are moving ahead to encourage the entrepreneurial spirit in all kinds of young people.

It is significant that the Congressional Commission on Jobs and Small Business identified vocational education as an important opportunity for mobilizing our people to create a needed ten million new jobs for the next decade.

Those who dream of creating a business need the skills to run one. Every state should review the educational offerings of its schools—in particular, its vocational

programs in secondary schools and community colleges—to make available training in business creation including business and financial planning, cash flow management, employee development, and managing and consolidating growth. Efforts
should be made to involve small business owners in developing these curricula as
well as in teaching. (National Commission on Jobs and Small Business, 1987), p.
29.

Vocational education offers an educational opportunity for young people who need a choice of routes to success and personal self-esteem. A
student may have had problems with Latin or chemistry but may handle a
computer like a whiz, and can make a business of it. Students may be
better at creating marketing strategies and advertising slogans than understanding Shakespeare or advanced algebra. They may be highly skilled at
working with their hands to create electronic systems, but unable to write
a term paper about the history of electronics. Fortunately, it takes a great
variety of skills to meet the needs of one economy. Fortunately as well,
vocational education offers students a way to find their own specialties
and make the most of them. Finally, and equally fortunate, vocational educators are recognizing economic development opportunities by adding
entrepreneurship education to the skills taught in many programs.

Today's business owners also recognize that education is an important
partner in the success of America's entrepreneurs—both current and future. It is significant that eighteen hundred business owners, delegates to
the 1986 White House Conference on Small Business, voted for entrepreneurship education as their sixth priority. This is particularly important
when you consider all the government tax and regulation issues that might
have taken precedence. The delegates asked the nation to move forward
in this way:

The federal government should encourage the advancement of entrepreneurial education and the study of the free enterprise system by promoting an early awareness of the free enterprise system, beginning with primary education and continuing through all levels of education. This would include the teaching of foreign
language and intercultural practices, thereby increasing our national awareness of
global economies and their interaction, and encouraging a greater competitiveness
by small business in international markets. This training should be taught by small
business people or teachers with hands-on entrepreneurial experience and must
include curriculum input from small business people. (U.S. Small Business Administration, 1987, p. 6)

Business owners are already closely connected to vocational education
programs. They serve on advisory boards, curriculum committees, as classroom speakers and co-op employers. Many vocational teachers are also
part-time business owners. This existing partnership makes vocational education unusually qualified to continue to nurture the business creation

concepts that have made this nation grow and recover quickly in times of recession.

WHAT IS ENTREPRENEURSHIP EDUCATION?

Vocational education leaders recognize that all young people should be exposed to entrepreneurship education, and that they, the leaders, are not the only actors in the game. It is important for educators to recognize the opportunities for entrepreneurship and include concepts about small business creation in all levels of education. Lest educators accept this idea and get into turf battles over entrepreneurship education, we suggest that it is a lifelong learning process where everyone can have a role.

The National Center for Research in Vocational Education developed the Lifelong Entrepreneurship Education Model (Figure 14.1) to explain what entrepreneurship education means to different audiences at different stages of educational development. It assumes that everyone in our educational system should have opportunities to learn at the beginning stages, but the later stages are targeted specifically to those who really wish to start a business. Further, it is appropriate to address different facets of entrepreneurship education as they relate to the particular purpose of each educational area.

BASICS (STAGE ONE)

In primary grades, junior high school, and high school we hope that young people have learning experiences that allow them to see business ownership as real opportunity for everyone. We call this stage the Basics. In addition, they need to learn about our economy and the benefits of the free enterprise system. Small business is an essential ingredient because it represents over 90 percent of all businesses, creates most of the new jobs, and is credited with most of the inventions in this country. Knowledge of our economy enables young people to make career decisions and be capable voters in their future.

Most important, the first, or Basics, level can provide all young people with the vision that anyone can be a business owner in America. However, without achieving the basic education and learning all they can, they will find it much tougher to succeed.

Motivation to learn and a sense of individual opportunity are the special outcomes at this level. Entrepreneurs come from all kinds of backgrounds and educational levels. To learn that anyone can succeed if he or she has the skills and the courage is an important way to help all young people understand the American economy.

Figure 14.1
Lifelong Entrepreneurship Educational Model

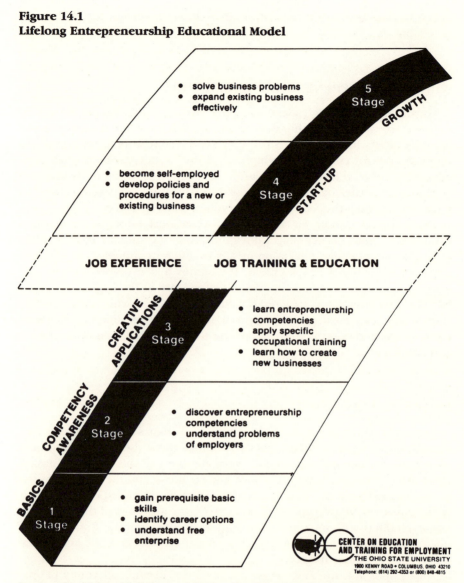

Source: Adapted from M. Catherine Ashmore. *New Directions for Vocational Education.* Columbus, Ohio: National Center for Research in Vocational Education, 1986.

COMPETENCY AWARENESS (STAGE TWO)

This stage may begin anywhere in the educational system where we can teach some of the skills of business ownership through Competency Awareness. In math classes we can use cash flow projections to teach addition and subtraction. In English classes we can use sales demonstrations as a communications activity. In social studies we can focus on the way exports and imports with various countries link us economically. Finally, in vocational education we can learn how to start a business using the technical skills of a particular vocational program.

In these and thousands of other examples, it is important to remember that the focus is on business ownership awareness, and it is not appropriate to try to teach everything a person might need to know to really start a business. Instead, by infusing different concepts in many classes we will begin to develop more awareness of what a business owner needs to know.

The special outcomes at this level deal with speaking the language of business and seeing the problems of business from the small business owner's viewpoint. To walk in the entrepreneur's shoes is, perhaps, to learn about what really causes businesses to succeed or fail, and about the importance of employee productivity, loyalty, and competence.

CREATIVE APPLICATIONS (STAGE THREE)

The idea of learning how to start a business while still in school is relatively new to most educators. There is much to know about starting a successful business. Unfortunately, most adults will not take the time to learn all about business when they are ready to start their own. Studying entrepreneurship in school allows each student to develop a unique business idea and carry out the decision-making process through a complete business plan.

Although it still is only an educational experience, the Creative Applications level requires a much greater depth and breadth of knowledge than either of the previous stages. Students will gain a conceptual framework for all the tasks a business owner must know how to handle—much as we teach future doctors, teachers, and airline pilots before we send them out to practice on real people. They will learn how to analyze the business community and study community demographics to target their marketing strategy. They will learn that markets go beyond a single community—and possibly include other countries—as they analyze global business opportunities.

This stage takes place in advanced high school vocational programs, some special courses for any high school student, some two-year colleges where there are special courses and/or degrees for small business and entrepreneurship, and some colleges and universities. However, it should not be assumed that because you major in business in college you will learn how to start a new business. This has not traditionally been the purpose of these courses.

The major outcome at this stage is greater creativity; in finding business opportunities and close-to-real experience through putting a plan together to really start a business long before students are ready to really become entrepreneurs.

EXPERIENCE AND ADVANCED EDUCATION AND TRAINING

There is a break in the Lifelong Entrepreneurship Education Model at this point to emphasize the need for other experiences and forms of education that contribute to the ability to start a business. Work experience can be planned to round out expertise in a particular field before starting your own business, or job experience of any kind can give insight into the right way to run your own business.

Education, too, helps develop confidence and skills that contribute to the success of business operation. Most students are not ready to begin a business immediately after graduation from high school or even after college. However, it is useful to note that a recent National Federation of Independent Business (NFIB) study of five thousand entrepreneurs across the country showed that most entrepreneurs do not have a college degree. The percentages were as follows:

High school degree or less	40%
Some additional college coursework	26%
Various college degrees	34%

Many entrepreneurs decide to open a business at a time of crisis in their lives. They carry the option with them because of their experiences in stages one through three, but do not actually decide to open a business until they find a great business opportunity or until their economic security is threatened. Situations such as the loss of a job, a plant closing, divorce, the death of a spouse, lack of a job promotion, or an employer's decision to move to another location often prompt potential entrepreneurs to try to launch a business of their dreams. Whatever the cause, this time in a person's life aids in developing expertise, contacts, and a sense of the way a business should be run.

BUSINESS START-UP (STAGE FOUR)

Community education programs are widely available to help adults make decisions about starting a business. They may be found in vocational school adult programs, two- and four-year college continuing education programs, and a growing variety of privately owned training programs. The U.S. Small Business Administration sponsors many of these programs as well as running trainings of their own through the Service Corporation of Retired Executives (SCORE) and Small Business Development Centers (SBDCs).

All these programs seek to help the inexperienced person make decisions about a potential new business. They use various delivery strategies, from one-day seminars, and twenty-week programs to one-on-one counseling. New programs are emerging to help special groups of people start a business—notably women, minorities, Native Americans, the handicapped, single parents, the elderly, the unemployed, welfare mothers, and so forth. Each of these groups has special problems to address.

The major outcome of such programs is that business start-ups have much more extensive planning and their owners know the realities as well as the opportunities for success. Another outcome is that some people decide that business ownership is not for them before they invest their personal savings and fail. Programs at this stage apply knowledge of all previous stages to the real world. Unfortunately, in the past many people started businesses without any knowledge of the requirements for the job. It is the belief of educators at all these stages that appropriate education and training will successfully reduce the well-known failure rate of American small business.

BUSINESS GROWTH (STAGE FIVE)

Assistance to existing small businesses is available from most of the institutions that provide help in Business Start-Up (Stage 4). This last level of learning is important for keeping up with new information such as tax changes, or just to add general business knowledge not gained earlier. Business owners value their time so much that it is difficult to attract them to such programs unless they serve a real need.

Often business owners do not seek help until they are so far into trouble that it is almost impossible to turn the situation around. Educators are recognizing that continuing seminars or support groups following Stage four can keep business owners in touch with an adviser who knows their business and in whom they have trust.

This stage may consist of a series of seminars and workshops that change constantly to meet the demands of the community, or there may be a regularly established program designed to help with the major problems we anticipate from all small businesses, such as financial planning, inventory control, improving sales, managing cash flow, and so forth.

Whatever topics are chosen for providing assistance to small business owners, it is evident that there is a great need for continuing support for our small business economy. It is estimated that we currently have eighteen million small businesses in the United States and that we will have twenty-five million by the year 2000 (U.S. Small Business Administration, 1986). It is appropriate that more than three thousand colleges and universities, more than twelve hundred two-year colleges, and more than seventeen thousand local school districts provide the resources these businesses will need to be successful.

WHAT DOES RESEARCH ON ENTREPRENEURS TELL US?

In thinking about teaching potential entrepreneurs about business, it is useful to consider the research on entrepreneurs. Researchers have tried to find some common elements that will help educators know how to nurture this important element of our economy.

Some educators argue that all business owners are not entrepreneurs (Drucker, 1985). They feel that a true entrepreneur is an illusive type who somehow successfully makes businesses grow large and constantly change; all the rest are merely small business managers.

For purposes of economic development and job creation, we prefer to call entrepreneurs all people who have the courage to invest their time and resources in a business in hopes of making a profit. If the definition alludes to creativity, we believe it may take as much creativity to survive as a small business or be successfully self-employed as to develop a huge business. We prefer Karl Vesper's (1980) description of the various types of entrepreneurs as follows:

Solo self-employed individuals: Those professionals, repair personnel, tradespeople, sales agents, and others who operate alone

Team builders: Those individuals who plan to grow large if the business succeeds—to expand rapidly because of one or more advantages that arise

Independent innovators: Traditional inventors who are only interested in making an idea work. They generally allow investors to take over, and often sell out when the business grows

Pattern multipliers: Those who spot an effective business pattern, quite possibly originated by someone else, and multiply it to realize profits on additional similar ventures

Economy of scale exploiters: Entrepreneurs who use the fact that unit costs tend to shrink as volume expands to develop discount businesses of many types

Capital aggregators: Those who pool a substantial financial stake to imitate financial institutions

Acquirers: Entrepreneurs who enter a business by taking over or buying a going concern

Buy/sell artists: Those who concentrate on buying a company, improving it, and then selling it for a profit

Conglomerators: Entrepreneurs who make corporate acquisitions, often using stock to purchase other companies

Speculators: Those who purchase and resell such items as commodities, art and antiques, leases, crops, and so forth, for the purpose of making a profit

Apparent value manipulators: Those who repackage or remarket a product or asset in a new way that adds considerable value to the item

In research conducted for the National Federation of Independent Business (NFIB), Arnold Cooper suggested that half of our entrepreneurs have owned a business (Cooper, 1983). This suggests that a great number of people, who have no such role models at home, could benefit from learning about business start-up opportunities as part of their educational system.

Entrepreneurs often start their first business at a very young age. In a national survey, one out of three entrepreneurs had started a business before age thirty (Cooper, 1983). In a similar study in Ohio, entrepreneurs who had been in high school vocational programs were significantly more likely to start a business before age twenty-eight than the balance of the business owners surveyed (Ashmore and Guzman, 1988).

Entrepreneurs generally believe they can control their own future (Brockhaus, 1980). They do not believe in luck or the influence of others; rather, they have a confidence in themselves and their ideas that can often be attributed to their educational experiences and role models. Although others will caution them against risk, entrepreneurs moved forward believing in their own abilities to accomplish things. Vocational education is providing experiences to build positive self-esteem and confidence in young people—supplying the building blocks of an internal locus of control.

More than 50 percent of entrepreneurs start businesses in areas in which they already have job experience (Cooper, 1980). Vocational education provides such job experience much earlier, and in a setting where the experience can be analyzed to improve business skills. Vocational students use such job experience as an incubator, to learn realistically how businesses are run and to prepare to branch out on their own. What better way is there to learn how to start a restaurant than to study the profitable systems of McDonald's, Wendy's, or Pizza Hut as an employee?

Finally, we find that personal savings are the most important source of funds to the beginning entrepreneur (Ashmore and Guzman, 1988). Vocational programs provide work experience opportunities that get young people into the mode of earning, saving, and investing money long before their peers. This is a special opportunity for vocational education to encourage entrepreneurship, particularly for those who do not have easy access to finances from their families.

In fact, entrepreneurship education may be an equity issue for all kinds of individuals who cannot see other ways out of poverty. Certainly it has provided opportunities for creating wealth among the very poor immigrants who have come to America from all parts of the world in this decade and throughout our history.

WHAT IS VOCATIONAL EDUCATION?

It is not fair to assume that the reader understands what vocational education is. This is particularly true because vocational education is quite different in every state and has changed throughout the century as economies have also changed.

Vocational programs are funded jointly by the U.S. Department of Education through the Carl D. Perkins Act; through state funds, which vary greatly by state; and through local education funding priorities. Because educational decisions are primarily made at the local level, vocational program options can be extremely diverse. Basically, vocational program options in high schools and vocational centers can be grouped into six major service areas as follows:

1. *Agriculture:* This includes various programs related to agriculture in both urban and rural areas. Agriculture education programs help students explore farm-related businesses they can start in addition to basic farming. Furthermore, horticulture and small-animal care skills can lead to business start-ups in both urban and rural areas.

2. *Business education:* This subsumes various programs, starting as early as seventh grade in some states, that teach all the skills of business operation and management. Business programs teach about many opportunities for small business start-ups in providing business services needed by other businesses or in providing the management skills needed by an investor or technical entrepreneur.

3. *Health care:* This includes a variety of programs available in some states to introduce students to occupations in medical technology, nursing, dental care, and so on. This is a rapidly growing career area and a rapidly growing area for new businesses as well.

4. *Home economics:* These programs address both consumer homemaking skills and occupational areas such as food service, clothing and textiles, and child care. They may start as early as seventh grade and progress through the senior year. Entrepreneurship is a logical application of home-based skills for people who find they must be employed or choose to use these skills for their careers. Often home-based businesses are suggested for those who need to combine employment and family care needs.

5. *Marketing education:* Various programs exist for developing general marketing expertise or specialized skills in a number of areas such as fashion merchandising, retailing, wholesaling, tourism, or food marketing. Students may use their marketing competencies to create business ideas that meet all kinds of consumer needs or business services. The technology is broadly applicable to many types of businesses and new business start-ups.

6. *Trade and industrial education:* The largest variety of specialized programs offer students skills in such trades as carpentry, electronics, cosmetology, auto-mechanics, building trades, welding, computer-automated drafting and manufacturing (CAD/CAM), and many other technical and apprentice-type occupations. Young people learn to be self-employed and to work as subcontractors and small business owners in relation to all these programs. They are truly the backbone of the economy in many rural areas.

Although the notion that improving the quality and quantity of education is related to our economic competitiveness may have been a revelation to some people in the 1980s, it did not come as a surprise to the vocational education community. According to Stuart Rosenfeld of the Southern Policies Growth Board,

Economic growth has been a basic goal and an expected outcome of vocational education for three-quarters of a century. The current groundswell of public and private support for nonvocational education for similar economic goals and the new "conventional wisdom" that education is an investment rather than an expenditure, are in part a consequence of vocational education's long and happy marriage to economic growth. (Rosenfeld, 1986, p. 7)

Vocational education was seen in the early part of this century as the way to prepare people for supervisory positions in nonprofessional occupations. Over time it has changed to meet the needs of the work force: first from agricultural priority to industrial priority, and then to today's emphasis on an information and service economy. As vocational education grew and vocational career centers were built across rural America, vocational education became part of the local infrastructure. As such, economic developers encouraged vocational education to assume the role of training an entire work force to meet the needs of any major corporation willing to move to that area.

In addition to recruitment and training, vocational educators and schools began to provide technical assistance including management courses, to businesses. Vocational education designed to meet the particular needs of specific large companies currently is viewed as the most direct, most demonstrable, and most successful way that vocational education has to economic growth (Rosenfeld, 1986).

It was not until the early 1980s that vocational educators began to see a new opportunity for human capital development through entrepreneurship education, as they began to recognize the great number of small businesses in our economy. Over 85 percent of the businesses in this nation employ fewer than 20 people, and these businesses tend to create the new jobs in our economy and employ young, inexperienced workers (U.S. Small Business Administration, 1986).

NATIONAL LEADERSHIP INITIATIVES

The first indications of interest in entrepreneurship as part of vocational education came from the funding of teaching materials by the U.S. Office of Education in the 1970s. A number of new products were offered to the vocational education community, including ETC (Entrepreneurship Training Components) and PACE (Program for Acquiring Competence in Entrepreneurship).

By the early 1980s, the new U.S. Department of Education was funding a major project in cooperation with the U.S. Department of Commerce to run entrepreneurship education and training workshops in twenty major cities. At this time, Terrence Bell, U.S. secretary of education, issued a policy paper recommending entrepreneurship education as a part of vocational education. The policy suggested that this new initiative would provide leadership for other educators to follow in the public schools.

Leadership for entrepreneurship education in vocational education has developed to different extents in various states. In 1983, ten states formed state-level task forces to determine their priorities for entrepreneurship education. Many of their activities to bring state agencies together on this subject are still in operation. Vocational education assumed the leadership in forming these state task forces and gained visibility among other agencies for the interest vocational educators are taking in entrepreneurship education.

The National Entrepreneurship Education Consortium was formed in 1984 to encourage state leaders in vocational education to support the infusion of entrepreneurship education in vocational programs. Now numbering over thirty states, the consortium operates to create new strategies for entrepreneurship education and to share the ideas of each state. The organization shares a common mission and supports activities by its central office staff at The Ohio State University to keep up-to-date on entrepreneurship education. The consortium provides primary leadership for vocational education's thrust to add entrepreneurship education to its many program areas.

STATE LEADERSHIP APPROACHES

Each state educational agency has chosen different routes to infuse entrepreneurship education into its vocational programs. They recognize the differences in their state systems and try to implement the most effective means to encourage new programs.

HIGH SCHOOLS AND AREA TECHNICAL SCHOOLS

The choice to infuse entrepreneurship education still rests with each individual teacher. Infusion means including units and activities on entrepreneurship along with the regular curriculums. For most teachers this is not easy because they are not familiar with the content. They have had little training to teach entrepreneurship and they have little time to learn about it on their own. Unless teachers believe that entrepreneurship is important for their students, it is not likely to become part of their teaching plans.

A major strategy for encouraging infusion is to conduct teacher in-service workshops. These workshops often are part of teacher conferences. Many states have tried to reach teachers through their common groups (Marketing, Agriculture, Home Economics, Trade and Industrial, Business, and Health), where teachers have traditionally worked together on new educational concepts. These teachers know each other and have a common perspective on their area of vocational education.

Other states have recognized that all high school vocational students should have opportunities to explore entrepreneurship and have conducted workshops for all their vocational teachers at the same time. Such teacher training approaches are more difficult because different programs have greatly varying opportunities to infuse entrepreneurship. Some programs teach ninth-graders, some all grades, and some only seniors. Some programs are in rural areas or the inner city where it is not easy to find role models. The teachers who come to these workshops, by nature of their choice to be there, are the most likely to be interested in creative ways to help their students find new career opportunities and skills. These workshops can be offered in various regions of the state, allowing for economy of time and travel for the teachers and school system.

Teacher in-service training is a major expense to states and local systems, and is not undertaken without significant commitment from education leaders. One approach to developing such support has been to conduct special meetings for school administrators on the importance of entrepreneurship education. High school principals, superintendents, and vocational directors greatly influence what happens in the schools. Those who believe that entrepreneurship is a logical outcome of vocational training will provide their teachers with the necessary support for this new component of vocational education.

Another major strategy to support the teaching of entrepreneurship is for a state to develop its own entrepreneurship curriculum materials. The state's materials will draw heavily on materials developed for national adoption, but they will also include the state's specific needs and examples. Often these materials are designed to be used as a supplement to currently published materials, and both products become the subject of teacher in-service workshops.

In some states the legislature has acted to support entrepreneurship education. Thus, new money has become available to support teacher education in entrepreneurship at all levels of the five-stage model.

Some students learn about entrepreneurship as the topic of a summer leadership camp. This option is only open to young people selected for such a camp but has been found to be a very exciting experience for the students who are selected.

Vocational student organizations provide another avenue for entrepreneurship education. These are nationally sponsored clubs such as the Distributive Education Clubs of America (DECA) for marketing students, Business Professionals of America (BPA) or Future Business Leaders of America (FBLA) for business students, Vocational Industrial Clubs of America (VICA) for trade and industrial program students, Future Farmers of America (FFA) for agriculture program students, Future Homemakers of America (FHA) for home economics students, and Health Education and Related Occupations (HERO) for health-based training program students. Each organization has state and national competition that teaches leadership development, business understanding, and entrepreneurship competencies. DECA, FBLA, BPA, and FFA have specific competitions in entrepreneurship and free enterprise.

At the local level, activities of the vocational student organizations focus on competencies of entrepreneurship. These include running school stores and other fund-raising businesses connected to the skill training program. In entrepreneurship training opportunities the teacher allows the students to plan, organize, operate, and evaluate the fund-raising project. The purpose is not to see how much money the teacher can make; rather, it is an experience in business that can lead to a broader understanding of business decisions for all students.

The vocational student organizations also have a great number of activities that connect them to local businesses. This is an excellent way for high school students to learn civic pride as well as an understanding of local businesses. Vocational educators are beginning to focus field trips and class speakers on the creative small businesses in an effort to understand the phenomenon of job creation and economic development of which vocational students are a major part.

An alternative to the infusion of entrepreneurship education into existing vocational programs is to offer it to high school students as a separate class. In some states this is considered a capstone-type option after other vocational programs have been completed. There are some vocational schools that have added an extra class period per day so that all students can be exposed to employability skills and entrepreneurship. Furthermore, there are some states that have approved entrepreneurship education for high school economics education credits. In this case it is taught as applied economics and used as a way to demonstrate how the free enterprise system works.

When entrepreneurship can be offered as a special course, many more of the competencies can be taught at a high school level. There is then plenty of time to develop a real business plan or even to run a real business. In a number of states a rural development activity is being tested. Using the school as an incubator, teachers are assisting students in starting real businesses. If successful, these businesses might be bought out by the student at graduation and provide ongoing self-employment opportunities for such rural area graduates.

At the secondary level, entrepreneurship education's major focus is to open this career option to all young people and to let them know what is needed to make a successful business. It does not matter how much skill students develop in business management as long as they have experiences that encourage the idea and learn where they can go to learn more when they are really ready.

POSTSECONDARY TECHNICAL SCHOOLS AND COMMUNITY COLLEGES

Once students decide to go further with technical skill preparation they may also decide to pursue further entrepreneurship education. Programs to teach entrepreneurship are quite new to most postsecondary occupational training areas. Even when available, entrepreneurship education has rarely been offered to all occupational programs. Instead, it generally takes the form of a course or a degree program for business majors. We still have a long way to go with instructors in programs such as food service, computer technology, or fashion merchandising to see these students as business owners rather than only as employees.

However, the postsecondary schools have been particularly responsive to the needs of adults in their communities who wish to start a business. Creative approaches to helping adults start all kinds of businesses are available through the continuing education programs. Many of these programs have targeted the needs of specific populations such as displaced workers, minorities, or women in business.

Special projects have been funded by state education agencies, the Job Training Partnership Act (JTPA), or the Small Business Administration (SBA) to encourage the proliferation of these adult training programs in all sizes of communities throughout the states. Materials have been developed to assist educators and business owners to teach these classes in a practical and realistic way. Unfortunately, many of these programs have been used for trying to prepare adults who wish to start a business when they have absolutely no business education background. It is a real challenge to prepare business owners with such limited experience, but it is certainly far better that they seek such help than trying to learn it all on their own.

The Small Business Administration, through its Small Business Development Center (SBDC) network has linked up with these postsecondary programs in many states. The established adult training programs throughout many communities in each state are a natural delivery system for the SBA's small business development program. In addition to business start-up programs, they also offer training for existing small business owners who recognize a need for improving their business competencies and getting help with newly emerging problems.

The Small Business Management (SBM) program exists through vocational schools and community colleges in many states. Its mission is to help existing businesses solve their problems, and thus encourage growth and success in the community. Occasionally these programs are connected to the SBDCs, but more often they operate separately with more emphasis on training than in the traditional SBDC. The SBM program establishes a long-term relationship with business owners. It follows an established program that provides continuity with special emphasis on understanding financial issues.

Further details on the many types of entrepreneurship education being sponsored by vocational education can be obtained from state consortium representatives or the consortium management at the Ohio State University. A database of both state and local programs is being developed as a major project of the National Entrepreneurship Education Consortium. Contacts are available for each level of the lifelong learning model, and new programs are constantly being sought for the database.

BENEFITS TO VOCATIONAL STUDENTS

Developing human capital potential through entrepreneurship education has far more outcomes than merely preparing some students for eventual self-employment. In addition, we believe that there is an equity option in this program that can empower groups of Americans who have until now been excluded from commercial ventures. By learning about the process of business formation, the necessary linkages, and the leveraging of resources, it seems possible that more people can move into creative business ownership than ever before. Even for those who choose not to start a business, the mysteries of the job market can be significantly reduced.

Entrepreneurship education can provide many different types of benefits to different students as they move through the educational process. They include the following:

Career planning: Students should understand the unlimited options of starting a business or some day becoming self-employed. Generally, most of them are not ready for this at graduation; however, they should know about such options.

Basic economic awareness: A view of the free enterprise system as it exists today is the most critical economic knowledge for American youth. The global competition of tomorrow requires a broad understanding of the opportunities and responsibilities of our economy.

Business understanding: Whether a person owns a business or is an employee, it is helpful to the operation of this business for the person to understand all business functions. Entrepreneurship education in the public schools will give all students a stronger business base.

Application of skills: Entrepreneurship education may serve as a vehicle for students to see ways to become employed with the skills they are acquiring in a vocational program. It provides a method to explore all the ways these job skills may be applied to community business needs.

Community understanding: Students may use the entrepreneurship education program to study entrepreneurs in the community, to discover opportunities for new businesses in the area, to gain an understanding of the suppliers available, and to analyze the demographics that will affect the success of selected small business ventures.

Self-understanding: Experience with the life story of successful entrepreneurs can help students think about their personal attributes and life-style choices. It is important to look at both the positive and negative factors in one's own make-up before choosing entrepreneurship as a career.

Orientation to change: Students will learn to look for changes that may lead to business opportunities of the future. Entrepreneurs seem to have a single-minded drive to try the new and stay ahead of the competition.

Creativity: Entrepreneurship education encourages all kinds of innovative thinking related to new products, new services, changes in demographics, new technology, societal change, and community needs. Creating a business on paper that might be started in your community is an excellent exercise in business creativity.

Business decision making: Successful business owners and their employees need a strong business management background if they are to know how to successfully make everyday business decisions.

YOUNG ENTREPRENEURS

The proof of the claims for entrepreneurship education can be found in the stories of vocational graduates who have started their own businesses. Generally, they choose to develop businesses that are logical outcomes of their vocational training. Sixty young entrepreneurs are described in the case studies in a new curriculum product designed for high school vocational students. Entitled *Risks and Rewards of Entrepreneurship,* this product was developed by the National Center for Research in Vocational Education as a result of an Ohio project sponsored by the Ohio Department of Education, Division of Vocational and Career Education. These case studies will be used to provide role models for other vocational students.

More should be known about vocational graduates as we move to improve education. The success stories of a great variety of vocationally trained entrepreneurs paint an exciting picture:

1. *Michael Calderone* of Calcom, Inc. says, "I pride myself with designing unique, one-of-a-kind systems (i.e., intercoms, fire alarms) that fulfill special needs. We create cost effective solutions to our customers' requirements." In high school Calderone studied electronics because he did not expect to have the money to go to college. Since then he has earned about half his college engineering degree.

2. *Pamela Sue Myers* of CurlyCue Beauty Salon says that her business is "highly competitive so it is essential to stay in tune with current fashion trends and adapt them to clients' needs." A high school cosmetology course got her started in the field.

3. *Lane Craig* says his affinity for selling and his love of animals naturally made him interested in starting his pet shop in Kansas City, Missouri.

4. *John Smith* took a variety of vocational classes, all of which combined to give him the skills to start his Appalachian Chair Company in Talbott, Tennessee.

5. *Julie Bourdo* started Toledo River Cruise Lines in Ohio when she was 21 years old and today grosses $2.5 million annually. She values her high school training in sales and marketing, and being "out in the field to learn."

6. *Andrew De-Vito's* training as a jeweler started with his sales training in marketing education in high school in Rockaway, New Jersey. He gives his marketing education teachers much of the credit for his business success today. He says the training he received in DECA was more beneficial than the college degree he got later.

7. *Brett Gibson* of Terra Haute, Indiana, is the youngest role model of the lot. Although still a marketing education high school senior, he has been in his own successful business since age ten.

This group of young entrepreneurs are contributing to the beginning of a national study to determine what makes these young vocational graduates choose entrepreneurship as a career. This may be one of the most exciting new messages to emerge about the outcomes of our public education system and the impact of vocational education on this nation's human resource development.

ATTITUDES ARE EVERYTHING

If vocational education is to make a significant impact on the entrepreneurial attitudes of millions of high school and two-year college students each year, it will depend on the attitudes of our teachers. Vocational teachers often have been business owners, or may even run a business and teach at the same time. This real experience makes them particularly competent to teach about entrepreneurship. It also provides them with many connections in the community who can help their students.

America's most valuable economic resource lies in the knowledge, skills, and attitudes of our work force—present and future. Entrepreneurship education is a vehicle for vocational education that brings new prospects and challenges as we compete for our global economic position in the twenty-first century. Whether vocational graduates become entrepreneurs or merely more knowledgeable employees does not matter; both outcomes are important to the future economic success of this nation.

REFERENCES

American Institutes for Research in Behavioral Science." 1980. In *Educational Training Components (ETC)*. Madison, Wis.: The Vocational Study Center.

Ashmore, M. Catherine, and Geannina Guzman. 1988. *Entrepreneurship Program Database*. Columbus: The Ohio State University, National Center for Research in Vocational Education.

Ashmore, M. Catherine, and Sandra Pritz. 1986. *PACE Revised*. Columbus: The Ohio State University, National Center for Research in Vocational Education.

Brockhaus, R. H. 1980. "Psychological and Environment Factors Which Distinguish the Successful from the Unsuccessful Entrepreneur: A Longitudinal Study." *Academy of Management Proceedings*, pp. 368–372.

Cooper, Arnold C. 1980. *Entrepreneurship: Starting a New Business*. San Mateo, Calif.: The National Federation of Independent Business.

———. 1983. *Entrepreneurship: Starting a New Business*. San Mateo, Calif.: The National Federation of Independent Business.

Drucker, Peter F. 1985. *Innovation and Entrepreneurship*. New York: Harper and Row.

Fischer, Lisa Mazzei, M. Catherine Ashmore, Terry W. Southwick, and Laurel A. Zlotnick. 1986. *Risks and Rewards of Entrepreneurship*. Columbus: The Ohio State University, National Center for Research in Vocational Education.

National Commission on Jobs and Small Business. 1987. *Making America Work Again: Jobs, Small Business and the International Challenge*. Washington, D.C.: National Commission on Jobs and Small Business.

Report to the President. 1986. Washington, D.C.: Government Printing Office, U.S. Small Business Administration.

Rosenfeld, Stuart. 1986. *Vocational Education and Economic Growth: Connections and Conundrums*. Columbus: The Ohio State University, National Center for Research in Vocational Education.

Shapero, Albert. 1982. "Taking Control." Commencement Address. Columbus: The Ohio State University, December.

United States Small Business Administration. 1986. *Small Business in the Year 2000*. Washington, D.C.: Small Business Administration.

United States Small Business Administration, Office of Private Sector Initiatives. 1987. *"A Tribute to Small Business" America's Growth Industry*. San Francisco: Pacific Bell Directory.

Vesper, Karl H. 1980. *New Venture Strategies*. Englewood Cliffs, N.J.: Prentice-Hall.

15

Case Studies and Other Student-Based Programs in Entrepreneurship Programs

Judith Staley Brenneke

Tell me, I forget.
Show me, I remember.
Involve me, I understand.
—*Ancient Chinese Proverb*

How do we introduce our students to the world of the entrepreneur? That world is full of risk—both split-second and long-considered—offering success or failure for the adventurer. In the world of the entrepreneur, things depend on *you.*

"TELL ME, I FORGET"

We can tell students what being an entrepreneur means. We can tell them what entrepreneurs do, and what they need to study in order to do this themselves. We can tell them that entrepreneurship and small business are essential to the growth and development of the U.S. economy. We can even have real, live entrepreneurs come into the classrooms and tell our students why and how they started their businesses. Personal stories of hardship or determination can be the highlight of the class. Students may even remember some stories of how one entrepreneur obtained his start-up capital through the insurance payment on his supposedly totaled

Jaguar coupe, or how another was the first Native American to be admitted to Harvard.

More likely, however, students will thoroughly enjoy hearing these stories and remember that a successful chocolate distributor brought some great chocolate candies to devour; that the "Diamond Man" distributed fake diamond rings to everyone; or that the teenage magician showed some "neat" magic tricks (ignoring the fact that his grammar was atrocious enough to affect his sales).

Unfortunately, these memories are seldom the foundation for any long-lasting understanding of entrepreneurship. They will not provide the knowledge of how to compare interest rates or even a source of where to find the information needed. Most of the essential information taught during the class, such as explanations of how supply and demand interact in the market to determine price or descriptions of financial intermediaries, will be forgotten once the test is completed.

"SHOW ME, I REMEMBER"

Provide students with a chart showing what $100,000 will cost them if they obtain it from different sources, and the types of financial intermediaries will become much more understandable. Determine the amount of start-up capital needed for a business and then brainstorm with them how that capital can be raised—and they will remember the role of financial intermediaries.

Show some of the excellent films on supply and demand or the market system and debrief from these films using charts and graphs, and students will remember the interaction. Expand this to include price ceilings and floors, shortages and surpluses, or changes in supply or demand, and you will have provided information that may be useful someday in the future when that student's product is not selling well.

Have you really involved your students in entrepreneurship? Granted, they may be more absorbed by entrepreneurship than they are by eighteenth-century Western Europe, but have you engaged the emotions, the interests, or commitment of your students? Do they really understand what it means to be an entrepreneur? Have they examined whether this is a road they want to travel some time in the future, and do they understand the consequences of that decision?

"INVOLVE ME, I UNDERSTAND"

Only by involving your students in the entrepreneurial process can you insure understanding. Only thus can you promote the carryover knowledge from your high school course to their future real-world needs.

By participation in simulations, gaming, or role playing, your students will have the opportunity to formulate responses to issues in a situation with less risk, where they can make mistakes that will not affect their futures. Through analyzing case studies and proposing alternatives or solutions, your students will be able to foresee problems and opportunities and will develop the thought processes to deal with both.

Understanding takes place when the students are involved. This skill in dealing with entrepreneurship and familiarity with a subject that lies completely outside your students' realm of experience should be the goal of the class. This type of understanding seldom takes place through traditional dialectic teaching. As early as 1949, Ralph Tyler stated that "for a given objective to be obtained, a student must have experiences that give him an opportunity to practice the kind of behavior implied by the objective" (p. 64). Experienced-based programs permit this type of involvement in the subject area. In examining the results of an elementary simulation of the economy, Marilyn Kourilsky pointed out that learning is enhanced when children participate in

- real as opposed to vicarious experience;
- active rather than passive roles in the learning situation; and
- actual decision-making activity whose consequences they will bear. Through the development and use of a case study dealing with start-up capital, students can actually analyze situations and make decisions on ways to obtain those capital funds. Like the entrepreneur mentioned earlier, they may also decide that insurance money from the destruction of a prized car could be the answer to their problem. (Kourilsky, 1974)

A simulation on retail locations may lead them to conclusions similar to those that the Diamond Man must make. This process enhances the visit of entrepreneurs from the community and takes the students beyond the interesting stories they have heard. Activities such as these enable the students to practice their decision-making skills in advance of their actual need.

EXPERIENCE-BASED TEACHING

Once it has been determined that students will benefit from experience-based teaching, the next question is how to prepare for those experiences that students have yet to personally encounter. For a high school student, studying entrepreneurship can be somewhat akin to seeing *Star Wars*. Both are events that take place outside the student's realm of experience and concern activities in which he or she may or may not participate sometime in the distant future. Therefore, the objective is to find ways to supplement the standard textbook and lecture with experience-based activities to encourage students in the use of both inductive and deductive thinking. Students need to be placed in the middle of a real-world situation and provided with the opportunity to reason their way to a solution.

In their everyday lives, students have many opportunities to talk and listen to people who are looking at events and situations in a variety of ways. Their parents and their peers often see situations differently from themselves. Students are often frustrated by their inability to come to terms with these conflicts and dilemmas (Paul, 1984).

By allowing students the opportunity to practice their decision making in such situations, without the risk that is attached to failure, educators will provide them with understandings that will last a lifetime. There are a variety of methods that will allow for this experience-based learning. The common thread between the following activities is that reinforcement is provided. Experience-based activities allow students to participate in an experience and then get reinforcement in class regarding what was decided and what learning took place. Reinforcement also allows the teacher to highlight faulty processes or analyses. Without it, students are in danger of misunderstanding the situation and continuing the use of faulty processes in the future. Experimental learning does not utilize this reinforcement process. If students spend the summer working without any follow-up analysis of their activities, their primary learning from the summer probably will be the fact that they earned money in return for reporting to a job. This is a much more limited form of learning. For this reason, the methodologies discussed in this chapter are termed *experience-based*—that is, they allow the student to participate in the experience, but then follow this activity with a formal classroom analysis.

CASE STUDIES

Experience-based learning is accomplished through case studies because, "in analyzing a case situation by casting himself or herself in the role of protagonist, developing criteria for alternative decisions, and generalizing to other situations," students are led into participating in the situation (Shapiro 1967, p. 5). They have the opportunity to analyze the situation and to introduce and advance ideas of their own as well as listen to other students' ideas. Then they can debate and discuss all these possible alternatives. In addition, opportunities arise for the teacher to highlight appropriate theory to be used in this analysis. Instead of economics remaining a series of definitions, it can become the key to analyzing opposing ideas.

Cases can be simple or detailed. Likewise, they can require the use of a few basic economic tools (for example, scarcity or opportunity cost) or they can require the use of more sophisticated concepts (such as comparative advantage or price theory). The case's level of sophistication should be determined by the abilities of the students with which it will be used (Brenneke, 1985).

However, cases *must* contain adequate information for the analysis to take place. The case should provide enough background information, facts about the situation, and details to allow the reader to reach a conclusion. Many times newspaper or magazine articles provide the appropriate information in an easily read format.

As an example, in the chapter's appendix, the case study, "Contact Lens, Dilemma," introduces some of the problems of beginning a new venture. Traditionally, contact lenses were sold by the optometrists who prescribed them. However, one entrepreneur, Dr. J. William Kren, hypothesized that consumers would be willing to go to an optometrist and obtain a prescription for their lenses and then take that prescription to a separate retail facility to have the lenses made if the price of the new contact lenses was low enough. However, as with many new ventures, Dr. Kren was faced with the effects of tradition. How should he convince consumers that the new lenses were medically safe and effective, and that they should investigate his product? This case was developed by Ms. Liela Gay and Ms. Cecilia Sexton for use with their 7th-to-9th-grade students (Brenneke, 1985, pp. 24–30). It provided these students with an opportunity to investigate the problem themselves and arrive at alternative solutions to the dilemma.

If we are attempting to teach our students a reasoned approach to economic decision making, cases will provide an ideal tool with which they can practice. Using the decision-making process recommended in the JCEE (Joint Council on Economic Education) *Master Curriculum Guide in Economics* (Saunders et al., 1984, p. 6), an orderly analysis of any case should follow these steps:

1. State the problem or issue. Important facts of the case should be identified.

2. Determine the personal, business, or broad social goals to be attained. It may also be necessary to prioritize the goals.

3. Consider the principal alternative means of achieving these goals. Considering the limited resources available and any other restrictions on action, an attempt should be made to identify as many alternatives as possible (include doing nothing).

4. Select the economic concepts needed to understand the problem and use them to appraise the merits of each alternative.

5. Decide which alternative best leads to the attainment of the most goals or the most important goals.

Economics is an analytical science. Once learned, economic concepts and theory can be used to analyze specific situations and human reactions. Case studies can provide the raw information that allows students to examine the economics of entrepreneurship.

GAMES AND SIMULATIONS

A powerful means of duplicating reality is through games and simulations. Although these are similar, gaming generally employs competition with one side winning. Simulations are working models of the real world with the students taking the parts of the participants. This enables students to encounter situations, make their own analysis and decisions, and attempt to reach certain objectives under rules set up by the simulation. These rules tell the students under what options they will be working— usually simulating choices available in real life. Students then have the opportunity to choose among these options. While some distortion may exist, simulations and games usually simplify the real world while maintaining its major features.

An example of a highly successful simulation is the Mini-Society (and the related Kinder-Economy), developed by Marilyn Kourilsky. Mini-Society allows elementary students to develop an economy in their classroom. The economy develops as needs are determined and students adopt the roles in which they feel comfortable. Soon the banker discovers that paying a higher rate of interest to savers than is collected from borrowers means financial disaster. This understanding is much better arrived at under educational conditions than after becoming an entrepreneur as an adult (Kourilsky, 1983).

Similarly, The Stock Market Game sponsored by the Securities Industry Association, allows students to learn difficult lessons about the stock market without risking their worldly funds. This computer-driven simulation allows students to risk $100,000 of "funny money" while learning about selling short, buying on margin, and *puts and calls.* The market crash of 1987 (occurring a week or two after the students first bought their stocks) taught some serious lessons to high school students. These duplicated the difficult lessons being learned by adults at the same time—but with much less risk.

It is essential that the classroom be used to debrief from these experiences. Allow students to discuss their concerns or decisions and point out any additional alternatives or consequences. Relate these games and simulations to the real world and show how similar options really exist.

ROLE PLAYING

By vicariously living an experience, the student can practice decision making with low risk. Role playing does not provide a script for the students. Instead it describes a situation and allows a student to react spontaneously. Ronald Banaszak and Dennis Brennan suggest the following steps in introducing role playing:

1. Introduce the problem and begin a discussion of how to deal with it.

2. Select students for the roles. These students should have an understanding of the problem and identify with the role they are to assume.

3. Allow the students an opportunity to organize and plan what they are going to do.

4. Prepare the nonparticipants to observe actively. They should watch for alternate ways of dealing with the issues as role play commences.

5. Conduct the role play without teacher intrusion. Unless the players' conduct goes beyond classroom rules, the teacher should allow the role play to continue until its resolution.

6. Finally, reinforce through discussion and evaluation the learning that took place. It is essential that the class and the role players participate in a discussion of what occurred and what additional alternatives were available. Consequences of the actions taken should be emphasized and the learning generalized to other experiences. (Banaszak and Brennan, 1983)

FIELD TRIPS

One of the more common experience-based activities is the field trip. However, because of legal, financial, or time constraints, field trips are becoming increasingly impractical. Therefore, it is essential that the field trip, when allowed, contain a successful learning experience. Preplanning for learning experiences and reinforcement of these experiences after returning to the classroom are necessary. Both students and representatives of the field trip should be briefed on what is to take place. What operations are you seeking to illustrate? What concepts or learning are you attempting to draw out of this experience? Why is this location a good example of the particular activities?

Field trips provide opportunities that cannot be found in the textbook and are difficult to describe through a lecture. They allow students to feel the size, hear the noise, and experience the actual production process. However, planning must be thorough and debriefing likewise for this experience to be successful.

SUMMARY

Why should we utilize experience-based activities? How will they help students learn about entrepreneurship? Barry Keating and Delores Martin provided an answer when they stated,

Only reading sound advice or simply listening to economic statements does little for anyone. The key to grasping and understanding the tools of economic analysis is to practice them. A child learns to walk and talk by trying; students can learn about the tools and methods of economic analysis by applying them. (Keating and Martin, 1978, p. ix)

Likewise, students can learn about this new world of entrepreneurship through the use of educational methodologies. Case studies, simulations and games, role playing, and field trips allow the teacher to bring the real world into the classroom. They allow the students to practice their skills of analysis and decision making under conditions that are less risky than those found after graduation.

It is this process that will take entrepreneurship beyond mere classroom teaching, producing students who have important skills and abilities that they will be able to use in their future. They are students who will understand entrepreneurs and the need for these ventures in our economy; students who will, when the opportunity arises, be able to begin their own ventures with less trepidation and fewer disasters than their untrained peers. They are students with more control over their own lives, young people who will be prepared to adapt to situations rather than be manipulated by them.

REFERENCES

Banaszak, Ronald A., and Dennis C. Brennan. 1983. *Teaching Economics: Content and Strategies.* Menlo Park, Calif.: Addison-Wesley.

Brenneke, Judith Staley, ed. 1985. *Cleveland Casebook 1985: Making a Case for Business.* Cleveland, Ohio: Cleveland Center for Economic Education.

Keating, Barry, and Delores Tremewan Martin. 1978. *Cases and Problems in Political Economy.* New York: McGraw-Hill.

Kourilsky, Marilyn. 1974. *Beyond Simulation: The Mini-Society Approach to Instruction in Economics and Other Social Sciences.* Los Angeles: Educational Resource Associates, Inc.

———. 1983. *Mini-Society: Experiencing Real-World Economics in the Elementary School Classroom.* Menlo Park, Calif.: Addison-Wesley.

Paul, Richard W. 1984. "Critical Thinking: Fundamental to Education for a Free Society." *Educational Leadership* 42, no. 1: 4–14.

Saunders, Phillip, G. L. Bach, James D. Calderwood, and W. Lee Hanson. 1984. *Master Curriculum Guide in Economics: A Framework for Teaching the Basic Concepts.* 2d ed. New York: Joint Council on Economic Education, p. 6.

Shapiro, B. P. 1967. *Introduction to the Case Method.* New York: McGraw-Hill.

Tyler, Ralph W. 1949. *Basic Principles of Curriculum and Instruction.* Chicago: The University of Chicago Press.

Appendix: Contact Lens Dilemma (Case Study)

USE OF CASE

Health education

Consumer education

Current events

(This is an actual situation; only the names and places are fictitious.)

SOURCES

Newspaper articles that may be available from your local newspaper

Interviews with Dr. George H. Mack (personal) and Dr. J. William Kren (televised)

OVERVIEW

Consumers are predisposed to purchase soft contact lenses from their examining physician. An entrepreneur, Dr. J. William Kren, a Euclid optometrist, has a new idea—mass filling prescriptions from his own warehouse. This new company, called *Personal Contact Lens, Inc.,* began operations sixteen months ago as a wholesaler of lenses to Value Packed drugstores. Dr. Mack, an optometrist from Willoughby, feels that service and confidence may be more important to the consumer and that in the long run discount lenses may be more costly.

THE PROBLEM: THREE VANTAGE POINTS

Personal Contact Lens, Inc. (Dr. Kren): How do I expand the market by convincing the consumer that my way of selling replacement lenses is safe, cheaper, and more convenient?

Optometric Association (other optometrists): How can we prevent the entrepreneur, Dr. Kren, from capturing the major portion of the replacement lens business?

Consumer: All aspects considered, where should I buy my contact lenses?

GOALS

Kren: profit/self-interest, expand and increase the market, be competitive

Optometric Association: profit/self-interest, maintain a monopoly, expand and increase the market, be competitive

Consumer: cost, choice, safety, and convenience

ALTERNATIVES

Kren	Optometrists	Consumer
1. advertise	1. advertise	1. choice of Kren
2. increase service	2. lower prices	2. choice of examining physician
3. add incentives	3. join the discount market	3. wear glasses
4. do nothing	4. increase service	
	5. add incentives	
	6. encourage state regulation	
	7. do nothing	

ECONOMIC CONCEPTS

supply and demand   economic efficiency

opportunity cost   economic freedom

competition   trade-offs

DECISION MAKING

Which of the alternatives appears to be the most feasible? Which are most desirable? What are the trade-offs among the different goals; in other words, how much of one goal must be given up in order to achieve more of another?

Decision Grid: make a grid from the perspective of each interest group that would help find a solution to their particular situation.

STUDENT READING: CONTACT LENS DILEMMA

J. William Kren, M.D., a Euclid State optometrist who thought of mass filling prescriptions from his own warehouse, launched Personal Contact Lens, Inc., sixteen months ago as a wholesaler of lenses to Value Packed drugstores.

He saw massive opportunities and expects sales to increase 300 to 400 percent in the next 10 years. "By law, the optometrist must provide a copy of the prescription to the patient," said Kren. "This prescription can be used effectively to get replacements for lost or damaged lenses or extra sets from a drugstore at 35 to 70 percent less than by going back to the doctor."

A lens at a drugstore can cost about twenty-two dollars, without insurance. A similar replacement without insurance from a physician can cost fifty to sixty dollars per lens or more, Kren said. The drugstore has no expense and does not have to keep an inventory. "I keep enough lenses to meet 90 percent of the needs and I supply them to the drugstores as their need arises. The patient also saves the doctor's fee," said Kren.

Kren operates out of a small warehouse in Euclid. His runners make daily rounds to more than fifty drugstores in Lake and Cuyahoga counties where prescriptions for replacement lenses are picked up and filled by his company.

Local optometrists are complaining because Kren's operations are taking business away from them. Is there a need to go back to one's eye doctor simply to replace an identical lens? Eliminating this visit saves the consumer money and encourages the purchase of replacement lenses whenever necessary.

Kren contends lens buyers could check out their purchases by wearing them or showing them to a physician and, if they did not meet the consumer's expectations, there would be five days to return them for a replacement or refund.

One of the problems Kren sees is that the contact lens user is conditioned to returning to the examining physician for a replacement lens. Usually the patient has little if any contact with the optometrist at this encounter. The customer returns to the physician out of loyalty or because, prior to this, there was no other way to make the purchase.

Kren commented that it usually took twenty-four to forty-eight hours to provide the lens for the patient in a sealed vial, depending on the delivery service; he has twenty-two thousand lenses in inventory in his warehouse ready for delivery.

The envelope in which the lens is sold bears the comment, "Any questions regarding your eyes or your lenses should be referred to your eye doctor where it is advised that a final evaluation be given. We cannot be responsible for the fitting of contact lenses."

In assessing the quality of his lenses, Kren confided that his suppliers include: Bausch & Lomb, Inc.; American Hydron; Wessen Ltd.; and American Optical Co. The consumer is guaranteed a replacement lens or a refund in the unlikely event of a problem because they do arrive in factory-sealed vials.

Dr. Kren sees great growth for his business as large numbers of people turn to contact lenses. "So far we are just scratching the surface of our business," he said. "So few lens wearers are aware that drugstore lenses are now available."

In response, Dr. Mack, an optometrist at the *Eye Center* in Willoughby, Ohio, does not feel that *Personal Contact Lens, Inc.,* has had much bearing on his contact lens business in the past sixteen months, although there is a Value Packed drugstore very close to his practice. He mentioned that if a patient asked for his or her prescription it would be furnished, but added that few have done so. Dr. Mack went on to say that in the long run it could end up costing the patient more money, especially if fittings and additional office calls were required. The latter service is included as a package with his lenses. Furthermore, Dr. Mack said that his patients seldom even inquire about cost before an examination. He interprets this as stemming from customer confidence and satisfaction.

EVALUATION AND DISCUSSION QUESTIONS (discuss, role play, take a survey, or debate)

1. What motivated Dr. Kren to start his *Personal Contact Lens* company? (increased profits)

2. What possible action could the Optometric Association take? (take away Dr. Kren's license to practice, encourage state regulations to ban wholesale lenses, ignore the situation)

3. What services come from the optometrist? (exams, replacement lenses, aid for eye problems)

4. Do you see a possibility for the future expansion of *Personal Contact Lens?*

5. Divide the class into three groups and role play the positions of consumers, the Optometric Association, and Dr. Kren. Discuss the advantages and disadvantages of each position.

6. How is Dr. Kren attempting to operate independent of the Optometric Association's monopoly? (by selling in a way advantageous to himself and to the disadvantage of other optometrists—by providing an alternative to buying contact lens replacements)

7. How does the U.S. Government intervene in citizens' health and welfare matters? (by requiring members of certain professions to be licensed, and by restricting the health care products available)

8. How does exclusion strengthen a monopoly? How does this relate to cost? (only certain people can meet standards for inclusion. Any limitation on entrance will limit competition and increase costs)

9. How could the advent of tinted soft lenses (prescription or non-prescription) affect the demand for lenses made by Personal Contact Lens? (changes in tastes and preferences increase demand)

10. If you could change your eye color, at what price would you consider doing so?

11. How would buying lenses from Dr. Kren affect the insurance companies that insure soft lenses for twenty-five dollars per year? (if the consumer can buy a replacement lens for $22, the demand for insurance at $25 per year should decrease)

12. What professions are licensed? What affect does this have on supply? (examples include teachers, physicians, pharmacists, cosmetologists, etc. Since this limits entry into the profession, it would reduce supply)

16

Interns and Mentorships in Entrepreneurship Education Programs

Margaret M. Murphy

A brief review of pedagogies will yield many alternative means of instruction. Lecture, discussion, films and filmstrips, role plays, and simulations are all popular choices for the classroom teacher. Using these vehicles, students can read about, see and try to imagine the real world from their own classrooms. However, often "on-the-screen" participation provides the very best means of learning about specific concepts, skills, and values.

This chapter will address one model for such experiential learning to take place within the areas of economics and entrepreneurship education. An internship program brings together students and mentors in an on-the-job learning situation, which provides invaluable opportunities to experience the world of work in a safe environment—one in which students do not stand to lose actual jobs and mentors are not asked to commit to employees, while otherwise both function in an employer/employee situation.

As might be expected, designing and implementing such a learning situation is far from simple. This chapter will suggest some means for accomplishing this end while facilitating the desired learning and skill development. Complete guidelines and support materials for implementing such a program are contained in a specially developed manual, and can be obtained from the author if desired.

PROGRAM OBJECTIVES

The internship program is designed to provide the experiential component in a program with conceptual instructional elements before and after the internship. The classroom component is addressed to teaching basic concepts of both economics and entrepreneurship to students in the spring semester of their junior year and fall semester of their senior year of high school. The target audience initially was comprised of urban students in a densely populated metropolitan area on the East Coast. Internship characteristics may be modified to meet the needs of other target audiences as well.

PARTICIPANTS

Student Interns

Participants in this particular program were chosen by virtue of membership in particular classes in a public school setting. Strong support was given by district administration and building administrators, with external support given from a nationally chosen group of curriculum developers known in either economics education or entrepreneurship education.

Mentors

Mentors were chosen for each individual by the program director and the internship liaison working together. Mentors must exhibit the characteristics of working actively in applied economics/entrepreneurship, having an understanding of the adolescent learner, and be interested in or actively committed to the principles of economic and entrepreneurship education.

PROGRAM DESCRIPTION

This model was originally designed to facilitate the implementation of an internship component for a program under the sponsorship of the Center of Economic Education at Widener University to develop both economics and entrepreneurship concepts in high school students in the Philadelphia schools between the junior and senior years of high school. Instructional programs in both spring of the junior year and fall of the senior year supported the internship program and made links to the theoretical components of the program easy to accomplish. The internship program consisted of two sequential three-week placement periods in two different placement sites, chosen to provide very different perspectives on the world of work. The model is designed to provide the guidance necessary to implement a similar program in another place, given somewhat the same situation.

Students are expected to perform a number of tasks during the internship experience. They are expected to complete the terms of a contract, maintain a log, develop a company profile folder, and participate in regular evaluation sessions with their mentor and internship liaison.

Mentors are expected to facilitate completion of the terms of the contract, orient the student to the firm, and provide regular feedback to the program director. In return, the mentor receives the opportunity to preview potential employees and to serve as a trainer for potential members of his or her industry group, in concert with peer mentors.

This model addresses itself to the questions of how to accomplish this easily described, but not so easily accomplished, task. Time frames and responsible parties are identified for each part of the program.

INTERN PROGRAM STRUCTURE AND INTERN ORIENTATION

Due to the nature of the program, orientation of the interns takes place in two discrete parts. The first part is designed to prepare the students for the initial interview with the mentors, while the second part will address itself to preparation for the placement itself.

Interview Preparation

Students will be most effective for the interview if they have plenty of information about the firm and some practice in skills of interviewing. The company profile folder is a key tool in this particular part of the program. The internship liaison is initially responsible for developing the firm profile library prior to the first placement period, but the quality of this resource will be enhanced by the information provided and augmented by interns as they return from the site.

In preparation for the interview, each student should become thoroughly informed about the firm through a review of the firm profile folder. Students should then prepare answers to the potential mentor questions list, and develop several questions of their own to ask the interviewer based on the information contained in the company folder. Each student should then develop a transportation plan for the interview, and a time schedule designed to get them to the interview ten minutes early, using appropriate transit schedules when necessary. Students should then submit the list of answers, their list of questions, and their transportation plan and schedule to the internship liaison.

The liaison will then arrange a simulated interview designed to closely match the interview situation. (If four department heads will meet the student at once, a group of four strangers should be arranged, and so forth.) Students should arrive for the mock interview dressed in the same clothes they plan to wear to the actual interview. If possible, the liaison should arrange to have the interview videotaped in a nonintrusive manner, such as by a fixed camera that runs continuously without an operator.

Feedback should be provided immediately through oral discussion and later through written communication which the intern may review prior to the actual interview. Positive features of the interview should be presented first with specific suggestions for improvement in areas of need. Areas of review should include

- appropriate dress, hairstyle, makeup, accessories;
- timeliness of arrival;
- listening without interrupting and using information acquired in subsequent responses;
- familiarity with the firm;
- appropriateness of questions;
- use of eye contact with interviewer;
- posture during interview;
- entrance and exit smoothness;
- voice clarity, consistency, confidence;
- language accuracy in standard English;
- appropriate self-confidence; and
- thanks at end of interview (closure).

This process will be enhanced if the mock interviewers also participate in the debriefing of students, as they will help to provide multiple reinforcement of the skills being developed. Repeat simulated interviews are advisable for poor performers in the initial interviews. The internship liaison should also develop some insight through this process about the likely interaction of personalities between potential mentors and interns, thus arranging interviews with a high probability of success.

Students should then be reminded of their obligation to provide feedback after the interview. Again, the simulated interview will be a good practice area for this aspect of the placement period. Students should be sensitive to their role in the interview process, and should feel free to share the instinct that they just could not function well in a particular environment. There should be a distinction made between the general discomfort to be expected in an unfamiliar setting and a real insight into a block that would be hard to overcome. (Examples of the latter would include a recognition that the placement would demand mathematical or computer skills the student lacked, or a recognition that the interviewer had a terrible prejudice against people with characteristics close to the student's own, such as hair length, age, or hobbies. It should be emphasized that such conflicts are unlikely, but may occasionally surface in the initial interview, at which point the student must bring it up immediately. Technical problems, such as unreliable or overly long commutes, should also be brought up immediately following the initial interview.

The internship liaison should develop a schedule of interviews, based on mentor and student preferences, geographical constraints, skill demands, and time frames. Following each interview, the liaison should contact both the student and the mentor to elicit their reactions, and enter the data on a master placement form. Ideally, students and mentors should have multiple opportunities; three is the ideal, being neither too limiting nor too burdensome. The liaison job will be much easier if final decisions are made after all the interviews are completed to fit each intern and mentor into the most ideal situation. Final placements should then be made through a confirming letter to both intern and mentor. Rejection of mentors should also be accomplished via a letter designed to maintain mentor availability for subsequent programs. Samples of all these letters follow in the chapter's appendix. Once placements are finalized, it is appropriate to develop an initial press release about the coming program, using this information to help publicize the program, and also to begin to reward the mentors.

INTERN ORIENTATION FIELD PLACEMENT

The second part of the intern orientation consists of preparing the student interns for the placement site, after the location has been finalized. The objective of this part of the orientation is to provide some basic minimum performance skills that might be required at most of the placement sites. As the range of skills within the intern group may vary considerably, one way to streamline this part of the program might be to enable students to test out of a particular part of the orientation. All students should be expected to be familiar with the regular expectations of all interns, however, which is best accomplished in a training session with the whole group.

Critical to the success of the internship program is the ability of the intern to fit in with the regular employees. This implies that the student approach the internship exactly as though it were the paid position he or she needed to survive. This attitude will answer many questions immediately, by posing the qualification: "How will this affect my job?" In practicality, this means that interns will adhere to placement site standards for hours of work, duration of the workday, number of and duration of breaks, meetings with supervisors, sign-in procedures, and so on. Visually fitting in should be stressed, emphasizing that the organizing criterion that an intern should use is the prevailing standard for employees at their level or in their department location. (This may have a range within the intern group as considerable as the number of placement sites. "When in Rome, do as the Romans do" is a good motto for this issue.) Students should be expected to make a master list of these details the first day on site and keep it in their log.

All interns must be oriented to the log-keeping procedures. The logs serve several functions. First of all, they provide a good reference point for the internship liaison to consult on site visits for strengths and weaknesses in the placement. Second, they provide the basic information students can use in their follow-up analysis and assignments, which may occur months after the placement has finished and their memories have faded about particular details. In the short run, they provide a record of individuals the intern should thank at the end of the program.

The log should hold basic reference information and emergency contact numbers for the interns. Each day's entry should specify the individuals contacted and the nature of activities the student has engaged in, as well as an indication of the amount of time spent on each activity. This will also facilitate early spotting of "intern abusers," who, for instance, are using them as free duplicating help for seven hours a day while working only thirty minutes on the projects specified in the contract.

It is important to emphasize to the interns that all places of work involve some menial, non-exciting types of work, and that some of this should be expected. It should also be explained, however, that one role of the intern liaison is to insure that not all the student's time is to be spent in such tasks.

One sort of thing that might be entered in a log is information about a job of particular interest to the intern. The intern might want to find out the demands for such a position from the individual employed in the job, perhaps through an informal lunchtime interview. These bits of anecdotal information will help the student develop career goals after later reflection.

The inside front cover of the log can serve as a ready reference tool. The students should be encouraged to use the log to remind them of names of people, locations of key places, and procedures for specific needs, to eliminate asking for the same critical information over and over again. For this sort of constant use, a spiral-bound notebook the size of a steno pad is recommended.

Students should also be reminded that they are expected to gather information about their placement site in order to customize the profile of their firm in the internship library. Often interns will identify materials that employees are happy to share for this purpose. Interns will also use the file in the post-placement period to present information on their placement site. This information will enable the entire intern group to compare and contrast the size of firm, the type of industry, the private versus public sectors, and profit versus nonprofit operations. It should be emphasized that it is easier to weed through too much information at a later point in time than to try to remember where to go and who to ask for it later. Interns should be sure about the spelling of people's names as well as their precise titles for use in thank-you notes after the placement period is over.

Basic business skills should be reviewed, as well (this is the part of the orientation some students might well test out of). All interns should be competent in answering multiple-line business phones and taking appropriate messages. They all should be able to screen phone calls professionally.

All the interns should be conversant with basic library research skills, and be able to look up information of a standard nature in common business references if asked. (Normally, university reference librarians are happy to run an introductory session to meet this need.)

All interns should be able to locate and use mass transit schedules, and know the fares, for their own personal use. Each intern should have two plans of how to get to the placement site for work, and a time schedule for each.

Interns should be able to book business travel by rail or air. All interns should also be familiar with running a copier, including recognizing the need for replacing paper and toner, and knowing the operator codes. Of course, performing simple arithmetic procedures on a calculator is also expected.

Finally, it is highly desirable to conduct an intensive orientation to computers for novices, so that they are familiar enough with basic terms and sources of information to proceed to ask questions on-site if needed. (This would basically address the question of available documentation and tutorials, as well as names for parts of the computer and printing systems.) If arrangements can be made for interested interns to have access to a computer lab should they wish to bone up on a program outside of work hours, this will be helpful both for interns and mentors alike.

It will help prepare the mentors for the interns to provide a checklist of skills in which the intern has displayed proficiency, as well as a list of the types of training the interns have received in the areas indicated above. This will, of course, be a function of the time and resources available for this part of the orientation.

Finally, a word about timing for maximum retention: The orientation for students should take place as close as possible to the start of the placement period.

TYPES OF CONTRACTS

The number of variations of contracts is limited only by the number of placement sites to be used. The word *contract* may be intimidating originally, but the purpose is to provide a set of guidelines for both interns and mentors through the presentation of a plan for the placement period activities. Some elements will, no doubt, appear in all contracts. For example, ordinarily a period of time is set aside at the beginning of the placement for touring the firm site and meeting various individuals.

Some potential mentors will have a project in mind when they agree to serve as mentors. They might, for instance, be thinking of replacing their office copier, and need someone to find out what alternatives exist and to compare prices. This task shows great specificity, and is easy to manage both in terms of expected outcomes and in terms of skills the intern will require.

Some mentors will have several tasks "on the back burner," and will be quite willing to be flexible about which one the intern will ultimately spend time working on. This gives more flexibility in terms of intern skills and offers a greater range of potential activity. The liaison will need to work closely with the intern-mentor team to insure that the structure of tasks is accomplished in a timely manner.

A very different sort of situation might exist with a very small business operation with few employees. The mentor might approach the contract by specifying a wide range of areas, usually on a less-than-predictable schedule. The opportunities implicit in such a placement often offset the somewhat global description of tasks in the contract. It should be noted that highly organized interns are not likely to cope well with this sort of arrangement.

Finally, another model is often found in a rather large firm, such as a bank. In this type of contract, the mentor really serves as a coordinator, arranging for the intern to spend a relatively short period of time with several other "sub-mentors" in different departments doing very different sorts of tasks. This is a somewhat Renaissance type of experience for a person who functions well with highly structured, but varied, situations.

Ideally, interns should experience two different types of placements. The differences might often be reflected in the types of contracts specified above. Sometimes, however, the differences might be in the size of the firm, or switching from the public to the private sector, or from a profit to a non-profit operation.

STUDENT ASSIGNMENTS

Contract

If one has not been completed prior to the start of the placement period, a contract must be developed by the end of the second day. It is signed by the mentor, the intern, and the internship liaison. A contract should specify what the intern will be doing over the placement period. It is a plan that states goals and objectives and specifies projects that the student should be able to complete during the placement period. It is not a legally binding document, nor is the objective to limit an evolution of the placement experience beyond that originally envisioned in an initial contract. It is designed to provide guidance for both intern and mentor, and it certainly may be modified in conjunction with a conference with the internship liaison. Should the original contract be completed prior to the end of the placement period, it is expected that the intern will do additional types of tasks to fill in the time appropriately.

Company Profile

Hopefully, each intern will have had the opportunity to review an initial company profile folder prior to interviewing for the position. If not, the intern's task is to develop such a profile. In the case of an existing file, the intern is expected to augment the information in light of his or her own experience and information in such a way as to maximize good decision making on the part of subsequent interns. Two elements will help accomplish this goal. First, the facts of the firm must be developed, using the company profile questions as a guide. Second, the personality of the firm should be described, and the interns are in the unique position of being able to flesh out the facts to present the personality of "their" firms.

Logs

Each intern is expected to develop a log. The log should include all critical contact information about the internship program, and critical maintenance information about the firm, meaning the who, what, when, and where of functioning in the same manner that was expected of employees. Second, daily entries must be made in the log concerning all persons worked for or with, the nature of tasks accomplished, and the approximate time spent on each task. Anecdotal information may also be noted in preparation for liaison meetings. This information may be in the form of questions, or comments about attitudes, problems, and particularly wonderful events.

Communication

The intern is expected to keep the internship liaison informed of any irregularities outside the elements specified in the contract. Interns are expected to call the liaison if they must be late or absent from the placement site, if there are any problems, if an opportunity arises that demands travel from the regular placement site, or if they need help of any kind. Interns are expected to keep track of the regularly scheduled internship liaison visits, and let the liaison know if they must be rescheduled due to mentor scheduling problems. Interns are expected to keep the log current and on hand at all times for liaison review.

After the Placement Ends

Student interns are expected to use their logs to identify individuals who significantly contributed to their placement experience. Each such person should receive a personalized letter of thanks from the intern. The model letter of thanks may be used if desired. Notes may be legibly hand-written on appropriate stationery (perhaps from the university), typed, or word-processed. The comparative advantage of learning to use a word-processing computer program for such a project will become immediately evident to those interns with a relatively long list of individuals to thank, developing yet another skill as a by-product of the internship.

Rewards

Evaluation, both internal and external, will show the results of the program in standard measures. Sample forms are indicated for anecdotal and narrative evaluations from mentors, students, and parents. These forms will yield little in the form of useful publishable data but a great deal in terms of program modification to meet the direct needs of the constituents served.

However, it is useful to note that one can rarely overdo thanking those who have facilitated such a demanding program. A recognition ceremony is strongly suggested, in which certificates or other tokens of appreciation are presented to those most intimately involved with the program. Other programs have found certificates useful for all, paperweights well received by mentors, and t-shirts universally appreciated by interns. Inviting local political figures and academic leaders to join business leaders in the recognition ceremony is highly desirable for all concerned, even more so if a perfectly chosen person addresses the gathering. Food and drink, judiciously chosen, will smooth the event yet further. Finally, the importance of follow-up news releases, hopefully in well-chosen moments, will result in crediting participants in print, thereby cementing their permanent commitment to the program in the future.

Appendix

**SAMPLE TIMETABLE FOR SUMMER
INTERNSHIP PROGRAM**

TASK	TARGET DATE COMPLETION
SECURE PROGRAM FUNDING	DECEMBER 1
DEVELOP PUBLICITY PLAN	JANUARY 1
SELECT MENTORS	FEBRUARY 1
SELECT STUDENT PARTICIPANTS	MARCH 1
ORDER MATERIALS FOR INTERNS	MARCH 1
OBTAIN EXTERNAL EVALUATOR	MARCH 1
ARRANGE STUDENT/MENTOR INTERVIEWS	APRIL 15
FINALIZE PLACEMENTS	MAY 1
CONDUCT MENTOR TRAINING	MAY 15
ORIENTATION FOR INTERNS	JUNE 1
FINALIZE SCHEDULES FOR	
- EXTERNAL EVALUATION	MAY 15
- MENTOR LIAISON VISITS	JUNE 1
ON-SITE EVALUATIONS	LAST PLACEMENT DAY
DE-BRIEF STUDENT SESSIONS	LAST DAY OF PROGRAM
DE-BRIEF MENTOR SESSIONS	SEPTEMBER 15
EVALUATION OF INTERNSHIP PROGRAM	OCTOBER 1

CHECKLIST FOR INTERNSHIP LIAISON

_____ DEVELOP POTENTIAL MENTOR GROUP

_____ ARRANGE INTERVIEWS BETWEEN MENTORS
AND INTERNS

_____ TRAIN INTERNS PRIOR TO INTERVIEWS

_____ MATCH INTERNS AND MENTORS

_____ HIRE EXTERNAL EVALUATOR

_____ DEVELOP PUBLIC RELATIONS PLAN

_____ TRAIN MENTORS FOR INTERNSHIPS

_____ TRAIN INTERNS FOR INTERNSHIPS

_____ CALL EACH STUDENT THE FIRST NIGHT OF
PLACEMENT

_____ CALL EACH MENTOR THE SECOND DAY OF
PLACEMENT

_____ CONDUCT ON-SITE VISITS

_____ GATHER LOGS, EVALUATIONS, COMPANY
PROFILES

_____ CONDUCT MENTOR EVALUATION SESSION

_____ GATHER FEEDBACK FROM PARENTS

_____ CONDUCT EVALUATION OF INTERNSHIPS

_____ DEVELOP PROGRAM REPORT WITH
RECOMMENDATIONS

_____ RE-DESIGN COMPANY PROFILE LIBRARY
FOR FUTURE USE

_____ RE-DESIGN PROGRAM FOR SUBSEQUENT USE

_____ DEVELOP MANUAL FOR PROGRAM
REPLICATION ELSEWHERE

_____ SHARE RESULTS WITH PROFESSIONAL
COLLEAGUES

DEVELOP AND IMPLEMENT PLAN FOR
LONG-TERM FOLLOW-UP OF INTERNS IN
CAREER PATHS

SAMPLE: CONCERNS OF POTENTIAL MENTORS

(These questions should be augmented with concerns that surface through individual interviews.)

How long will the intern be on site? (Needed for schedule—if multiple choices of time frames exist, this will help.)

What will be intern's working hours? (Concern here is for planning and interference with regular hours—priority of program planners should be minimal interference with routine items by intern location on site.)

What will be demanded of the mentor? (A judicious blend of honesty and practicality is called for here. Usually this is a request for specific details about meetings in terms of total hours and travel time, numbers of papers that must be filled in and meetings requested on-site by the internship liaison. These can all be specified, and should be presented precisely in such detail as a two-hour orientation on the campus of X college on Thursday, June 15. Guidelines are also being requested, and detail may be offered specifically in terms of the sorts of supplementary materials offered in various forms such as interview questionnaires, lists of first-day activities, schedules of visits by the liaison, etc. The level of detail will vary considerably with the mentor, and should be carefully selected to meet the mentor's needs.)

What if the mentor is unable to fulfill his or her obligations due to unexpected travel or some other factor? Backup emergency mentors should always be available. Most desirable is to problem solve a schedule conflict on the original site, if possible, so that intern preparation will still be maximized. Backup mentors on site are also helpful in such cases as illness.

What if the intern does not work out? Future involvement of a mentor will be shattered if a difficult or impossible situation is not immediately ameliorated. Telephone numbers should be provided for immediate contact with program personnel in the event of problems, and there must be a commitment of immediate emergency response. In the case of unresolvable conflicts, the intern must be moved. It considerably defuses this likelihood to involve the mentor in the selection process. If the mentor is sure of vetoing undesirable candidates, and sure that students who do not like the site will not be placed there, the odds of problems will be considerably lessened. It helps to remind the mentors of a priority response to problems having the potential of displacing a regularly scheduled liaison visit, and it is also helpful to fill potential mentors in on the orientation and training all interns will have prior to placement.

Will the intern fit in with the other employees? This is a terrific question, because it provides an easy entry into the development of the company profile. The program contact will try to get a considerable body of information about the firm so that interns may elect interviews wisely, and so that those placed may appropriately prepare for their role on site.

PROFILE OF FIRM SAMPLE QUESTIONS

PLEASE NOTE: THESE ARE TO GUIDE COLLECTION OF INFORMATION FOR THE FIRM PROFILE FOLDER IN THE PROGRAM LIBRARY. THIS INFORMATION CAN BE GATHERED THROUGH REVIEW OF COMPANY MATERIALS, OBSERVATION DURING ON-SITE VISITS, OR DIRECT QUESTIONS ASKED OF FIRM EMPLOYEES AT VARIOUS LEVELS—CHOICE OF OPTION IS A FUNCTION OF THE FIRM.

What is the official legal name of your firm?

How long has it been operating?

What kind of work is done in this firm?

What are the prices of the firm's goods or services?

What are the working hours for the firm?

How many people work in this firm? What kinds of skills do they have?

How many locations does the firm have? Where are they?

How is the firm financed?

Who started the business?

Do you have an annual report for our company profile library?

May we have samples of your brochures, advertisements, press releases, or other information for our profile library?

Who are the competitors for this firm?

What makes this company unique?

What are the long-term plans for this company?

How are management decisions made, and by whom?

Who are the officers of the firm?

Who are the members of the Board of Directors?

Are there any Advisory Groups for the firm? If yes, what sort of groups, and who are the members?

Where do you get information about this particular industry?

What do you look for in new employees you seek to hire?

Do people already working for the firm have a competitive advantage in being promoted into newly vacated positions?

Is your business related? If yes, for what, and by whom?

THE FOLLOWING QUESTIONS ARE ORDINARILY ANSWERED THROUGH OBSERVATION ON-SITE AND RESEARCH:

How are most of the employees dressed? Please differentiate by gender, and location within firm, if appropriate.

What are directions for getting to the firm? Use local landmarks and multiple ways of arriving, if possible, including buses, trains, subways and autos. Where is parking available for those driving cars, and what does it cost?

Where are the restrooms? Are keys necessary for access? If yes, where may they be obtained?

What is the location of the various departments? Are there areas of restricted access?

What is the access procedure to the firm? (Does one have to sign in, or have identification? Where is this done?) What entry should the internship personnel use?

Where can lunch be obtained locally? Give directions, and specifics on price range. Is there a cafeteria on site? Can interns use it? How much will it cost, and can they bring their own lunch? Do other employees bring their own lunches?

INTERN PROFILE SHEET

Name:_____

Nickname:_____

Address: _____

_____

Telephone: _____

School name: _____

Current grade: _____

Date of birth: _____

Current age: _____

Have you ever worked for pay? Yes_____ No_____

If yes, please list place of employment and type of work

_____

_____

_____

Have you ever used a telephone with more than one line?_____

Can you type?_____ If yes, how many words per minute?

_____

Can you use a computer? Yes_____ No_____

If yes, what kind of computer?

_____

Check uses: Word processing ___ Spreadsheets___ Data Base___

What hobbies do you have?_____

_____

_____

What   is   your   favorite   subject   in
   school?_____

Can you drive? Yes_____ No_____ If yes, Automatic?_____
   Shift?____

When   did   you   receive   your   license?

_____

What is your favorite book?_____
   Song?_____
   Hero?_____

What would you like to be doing in 10 years?

_____

_____

WAYS OF SOLICITING MENTORS

In the first year of an internship project, the greatest challenge with regard to mentors is to explain in the absence of any experienced mentors exactly what might be reasonable to expect as a result of agreeing to serve in a mentor role. (Ideally, in subsequent years, satisfied previous mentors will serve the function of supporting the request by appealing to peers to participate.)

The first logical source of mentors is the group of individuals who are familiar with the concept of internships, and preferably those who have direct experience with the internship process. Unfortunately, this route is usually precluded because such satisfied mentors are probably still involved with an already existing program. However, program directors of other sorts of internships probably have developed a resource bank of individuals they are not currently using for one reason or another, who might be most appropriate for the newly developing project. (If, for instance, there is a priority on placing interns geographically close to their homes, other directors may have good mentors currently involved in the process.)

Professional groups related to the subject of the internship are another good resource for the internship liaison to contact. In the case of the E^3 (Entrepreneurship/Economics/Education) project for which this volume was developed, both economics and entrepreneurship special interest groups were likely potential contributors in the role of mentors. Chambers of Commerce, Rotaries, Business Roundtables, Service Corps of Retired Executives, Associations of Collegiate Entrepreneurs, local chapters of the National Association of Business Economists and various banking groups are all likely sources of mentors.

When a program is based at a college or university, appropriate local alumni groups and fraternal organizations may also be good leads for mentors or referrals. After an initial contact is made with a potential mentor, a personal interview is most helpful to explain the program and solicit direct involvement on the part of the individual. Key issues are likely to arise, which can be addressed through prepared materials covering the most likely areas of concern. A master list of questions and answers should be initially developed and augmented as the initial interview process continues to evolve. The contact person from the program has a number of objectives from the initial meeting, these being identification of a good potential mentor, identification of further contacts, and the start of a company profile that can be used to inform the students about the workings of the firm.

A sample list of concerns is provided to give the program representative a guideline for the initial contact. Such contact should be made by whichever program staffer is likeliest to be well received by the potential mentor, and not necessarily by the internship liaison.

17

Approaches to Education for the Economically Disadvantaged: Creating Tomorrow's Entrepreneurs and Those Who Will Work for Them

Michael A. MacDowell

American business has traditionally voiced its concern about the poor preparedness of students for the world of work. Today business complaints can no longer be ignored because the country is starting to confront a new problem, which promises to become more threatening as the twentieth century wanes and as the next century begins. The problem is arising because there is a conflict between the changing nature of work and the changing nature of the emerging labor force. The new jobs today as well as those for tomorrow require workers who are more skilled and educated than their predecessors. However, far too many youngsters of school age are dropping out before finishing high school or are being insufficiently trained to hold jobs in an era of increasingly sophisticated technology and growing global competition.

Unless steps are taken to halt the disparity between the prospective needs of employers and the prospectively inadequate skills of a large portion of the labor force, not only business, but the country as a whole, will suffer. As a recent analysis of the subject suggested, American business will lose productivity, competitiveness, and revenue, and will be overshadowed by countries with better products, greater technology, and labor forces that are significantly more productive ("Retooling the Work Force," 1987).

Those remarks are from a report by the National Alliance of Business (NAB), but their thrust also appears in a spate of other reports on shortcomings in American education that have appeared in recent years. During the 1987–1988 academic year alone, the NAB, the Committee for Economic Development or CED (Committee for Economic Development, 1988), and a group of thirty-seven college presidents (Magnet, 1988) issued statements of alarm about the condition of education or about the large numbers of students at risk of not completing school.

An important facet of that problem is the fact that the shortcomings in education today will have a resounding impact on the nations' productivity tomorrow. Traditionally, much of the concern about the lack of preparation has been echoed by large companies, such as those represented by NAB. Today, however, the cry is being heard from small companies as well. The National Commission on Jobs and Small Business spent fifteen months preparing a report delineating the belief that job creation in the twenty-first century will be primarily driven by small companies. These companies (National Commission on Jobs and Small Business, 1987), are looking not only for talented workers, but also for individuals who understand the process of entrepreneurship and are willing to be entrepreneurial in their own work environment. The ability of the country to produce these workers and entrepreneurs is severely limited by the fact that in many of the nation's largest school districts, 50 percent of the students drop out before they are eighteen years old ("Retooling the Work Force," 1987).

AT-RISK STUDENTS AND ENTREPRENEURSHIP

The difficulties in solving the dropout problem are complex, and while they are related to schooling they are not the fault of the schools alone. The problems are also tied up with the frequently inferior social status of minority groups, the precarious family situation of many one-parent households, and the fact that 40 percent of Hispanic and 43 percent of black children live below the poverty line (Duncan and Rodgers, 1985). The cycle of poverty faced by these students and their families is stultifying, shortchanging them and their communities. Youngsters in these groups may have little understanding about the labor market or about the skills and attitudes necessary to hold a job successfully. They have very little understanding of the concepts of self-initiation or self-esteem which are so important in creating the entrepreneurial talent the country needs. Worse yet, these youngsters are the ones most prone to drug and alcohol problems, poor health, and other serious personal and family adversities.

The 1987 CED report *Children in Need: Investment Strategies for the Educationally Disadvantaged* reports that nearly one million students will drop out of high school before graduating. These youngsters are generally a good deal below par in scholastic performance. They are marginally literate, but they are virtually unemployable (Committee for Economic Development, 1988). Still another 700,000 will receive their diplomas but will be as deficient as the dropouts in basic skills—reading, writing, and mathematics—and in work habits (Duncan and Rodgers, 1985). The combined 1.7 million students that the two categories represent equals the average annual addition to the U.S. civilian labor force in recent years.

The one million students at risk of not ever graduating from high school, as well as the 700,000 who will graduate with deficient skills, share many characteristics. Typically, they think they have little choice in getting good jobs, feel a low sense of self-esteem, assume they are powerless in society, believe they face continued failure, and harbor a general sense of frustration and humiliation. This sad litany by no means exhausts all the difficulties that many young people, employers, and society face, according to all the reports of recent years on the state of education and on the future requirements of employers. However, they do give some indication of the immense problems employers and employees have started to encounter.

The problem is particularly acute for smaller firms, especially those that tend to be entrepreneurial. The National Commission on Jobs and Small Business suggests that approximately fifteen million of these small firms produce about half the nation's gross national product and also about half of its private non-farm labor force (National Commission on Jobs and Small Business, 1987).

Conventional wisdom suggests that at-risk students, particularly those who are economically disadvantaged, often make the best entrepreneurs, and many examples of individuals who could not make it in school but could succeed as independent business persons are often cited. These are obviously the exceptions, and statistics tell a very different story. The teenage unemployment rate for minority youth approaches 40 percent in major urban areas ("A Drop in Dropouts," 1988). While small business hires more dropouts per capita than do *Fortune* 500 firms, they tend to be less satisfied with them, and hence turnover is greater (National Commission on Jobs and Small Business, 1987). Large companies have training programs and "career ladders" that help the relatively few dropouts they hire adapt and make the necessary changes.

Small firms, especially those that are entrepreneurial, demand much more from their employees. Employees are expected to perform a variety of functions that are often beyond the capability of the dropout. Few training opportunities exist, and small firms with little profit margin or room for error are less willing to put up with marginal employees.

Finally, those entrepreneurs who have beat the odds—dropped out and begun their own business—are almost always the first to suggest that the skills one obtains in school are essential to the continued successful operation of a new business. Most entrepreneurs are walking billboards for anti-dropout programs and, while they are sometimes willing to hire dropouts, they usually demand high performance standards—which dropouts do not usually meet.

The probability of an at-risk student succeeding in an entrepreneurial-based company is slim, and the probability of such a student buying his or her own business is so small as to be almost nonexistent. For those reasons, the small business sector that will create most of the jobs in the 1990s and beyond has the most to fear from the significant increase in at-risk students.

The owners of small, particularly entrepreneurial, firms are not the ones who need to be made aware of the pending shortage of new employees. Most are already painfully aware of the problems, having been unable to hire even the most rudimentarily prepared workers. The problem is no longer simply one that these employers must face alone, however. With the effective and productive efforts of small business, the CED report entitled *Investing in Our Children* warns that for the first time in recent history our children's standard of living may not equal, much less exceed, our own (Committee for Economic Development, 1985). The entire business community and the public in general must be made aware of the issue. However, the panel suggested that the public has little or no understanding of the job-creating role of business—particularly small business—or the contributions of entrepreneurs.

It is also difficult for the general public to understand the two kinds of inadequacies exhibited by at-risk students. The first is the basic lack of key skills taught as both an implicit and explicit part of the schooling process. The second is a lack of economic knowledge that allows these students to translate inherent interests they have in being economically viable into actions that allow them to be just that.

THE DESIRABLE QUALITIES

What qualities are needed for success in the workplace now and in the future? *Investing in Our Children* summarizes them quite well (Committee for Economic Development, 1985). The most important qualities for such success are good English language skills, positive work habits, the ability to solve problems, and the desire to continue to learn.

These abilities, the report goes on to say, are imparted by both the visible school curriculum and the "invisible" curriculum. The latter consists of the messages a school conveys about what is valued in the adult world and what is important in the world of work. An effective, invisible curriculum stresses good work habits, cooperation, perseverance, honesty, self-reliance, and consideration for others. They are, not coincidentally, the characteristics that most list as prerequisite skills exhibited by entrepreneurs. These elements of character are as important to future success in the workplace as academic skills. The invisible curriculum lays the foundation for employability and success on the job. This foundation should be started long before kindergarten and should be reinforced throughout the educational process.

The lack of economics understanding and sophistication also severely limits at-risk students' ability to enter the labor market. The National Commission on Jobs and Small Business emphasizes that many American high school students "do not understand how the American economy works" (National Commission on Jobs and Small Business, 1987, p. 18). Hence, according to the study, students are unfamiliar with the role of business, government, and labor in the economy. The result is that these students often choose early on not to participate in the economy by dropping out of school. For at-risk students, the situation is exacerbated as most do not have even the passing familiarity with key economic institutions that other students exhibit.

HOW CAN BUSINESS HELP?

What are some of the most important things business and businessmen can do to help improve the schools in order to improve the quality of the emerging labor force? Here are some of the salient points made in the most recent reports of the CED, the NAB, and other groups.

Many businesses have entered into partnerships with schools in order to better the quality of education. The experiences in partnership have already laid a basis for paying special attention to at-risk students, but collaboration will need to be widened to include other groups besides the schools themselves—for example, parents, community agencies, and local governments. However, a simple partnership with one school or support of only one area of the curriculum is not enough. There are more than 16,000 school districts in the country, enrolling an average of about 2,500 students each. If only a quarter of these 40 million students—a conservative estimate—are at-risk, then about 10 million need the kind of extensive support that only community-wide efforts can provide. Therefore, specific efforts directed at all schools and at all parts of the schools' curriculums must be undertaken.

Business can set the pace in many aspects of improving the job the schools do by encouraging their own employees to help teachers and administrators to develop and sharpen new skills, by offering to train teachers in subjects in which employees have special skills, by becoming mentors for internship students, by providing students with career counseling, by establishing tutorial services, and even by furnishing or giving suggestions for obtaining jobs. Some of the most innovative programs involve internships.

Another strategy business uses to assist the educationally disadvantaged student is to reach beyond the traditional confines of education. For example, business and education forged a special compact in Boston. The first so-called Boston Compact committed business to provide summer jobs and to give hiring preference to increasing numbers of Boston high school students each year (Hargroves, 1986). On their part, the schools committed themselves to improve attendance records and achievement scores as well as to guarantee that graduates would be competent in basic skills.

There have now been two additional Boston Compacts. In the second agreement, twenty-five area colleges and universities agreed to annual increases in acceptances and scholarship aid for local students. In the third compact, unions agreed to give qualified high school graduates greater possibilities for apprenticeship.

In 1985 and 1986, it turned out that 94 percent of the graduates who had participated in the compact's program went on to higher education, a job, or the military. This is the highest placement rate in the country.

The Boston Compact, however, is not the answer to all the problems of education and the educationally disadvantaged. There is still a high dropout rate in the Boston schools even though the city's total unemployment rate is approaching a very low 2 percent. Boston's continuing dropout problem is therefore now being combatted with a special two million dollar effort. Clearly even more extensive or effective programs for at-risk students will have to be undertaken in those cities where unemployment rates are much higher than 2 percent (Rothman, 1988).

WHY ENTREPRENEURSHIP AND ECONOMICS EDUCATION?

Many of the hidden curriculum skills identified by the CED and known to educators and employers for years are exactly those skills introduced in a solid entrepreneurship training program. These skills should then be buttressed by an understanding of the economic system and a student's potential role in it. When this occurs, at-risk students, often alienated from the system by their own economic depravity, can become the best advocates and participants for that same system.

The skills that are so much a part of business thinking today, whether for a small or a large firm, are those that can be taught in an entrepreneurial setting. Self-discipline and self-confidence are particularly important, and yet the profile shows that these are parts of the hidden curriculum that most at-risk students never receive.

What psychologists call *inner control* is often obvious by its absence for most economically underprivileged and, therefore, at-risk students. Further, another key lesson that must be part of all entrepreneurs' training—the ability to defer gratification—is difficult to teach to at-risk students. Many do not know where their next meal is coming from nor have ever seen a parent or guardian get up and go to work in the morning.

Self-discipline—the commitment to singleness of purpose toward the completion of a task—is similarly an important attribute for those in small business or in an entrepreneurial setting. These characteristics are often not present among at-risk students.

Finally, at-risk students consistently and almost inevitably show less ability to make viable long-term decisions than do other students. Forced by the immediacy of their own often desperate situations, they tend to make decisions based on immediate returns. They often cannot define a problem or consider alternative solutions, never having been exposed to individuals who exhibit these skills. Alternative scenarios are hardly ever reviewed by at-risk students, and whatever feedback they receive about alternatives is usually offered by peers who themselves share the same inability to make such decisions.

BEYOND PARTNERSHIPS: BUSINESS'S ROLE

Helping students become a vital part of the economic system takes more than a casual partnership between one large institution (the school) and another (business). It takes new efforts directed specifically at the problem of at-risk students and their families. It may involve a variety of activities not traditionally or comfortably handled by big business. For example, there is a demonstrable need to prevent children from falling into the at-risk category in the first place by directing efforts at such children starting from their prenatal period to the age of five. Taking preventive approaches this early requires having parents as well as children participate because the parents are often young, poor, and in need of help themselves.

Another innovative program, one studied by AT&T, shows that worker satisfaction and productivity are related to the employer's ability to provide proper child-care arrangements (Telsch, 1988). When parents know that their young ones are taken care of responsibly, they can concentrate on their work rather than worrying. Reassurance on this score is especially significant for single parents and for families whose children are liable to become at-risk. Further, if a community or a possible employer wishes to encourage parents or guardians of potentially at-risk students to join the labor force, then the provision of adequate child care even by small firms may be essential.

ENTREPRENEURSHIP AND ECONOMICS EDUCATION

Good programs that teach about entrepreneurship must be entrepreneurial themselves. To convey the basic school curriculum, the hidden curriculum, and enough about our economic system to pique a student's interest to participate in it, takes an adequately trained educator.

Above all, programs that train potential entrepreneurs, especially those at risk of leaving school, must not be so structured as to stifle students and teachers alike. Instead, such programs must be flexible and allow the school and the individual teachers the opportunity to amend the materials and training to meet their students' needs.

The Joint Council on Economic Education (JCEE) is now engaged in two major projects to assist at-risk students to eventually and effectively become part of the economic system. Both involve new and innovative materials, both concentrate on teacher education, and both involve active participation from local companies. The first is being field-tested in Detroit, Cincinnati, and Los Angeles. Called Choices and Changes, the effort places economics units in early grade levels, where research shows JCEE-based programs can be instrumental in inducing a student to stay in school.

Choices and Changes introduces at-risk students to basic decision making as early as the third grade. In the fifth grade, they will learn about potential roles and rewards in the workplace if they stay in school. In grades seven and nine, the program is designed to help at-risk adolescents aspire to succeed in the economic system.

The program is based on the premise that economic understanding and entrepreneurial knowledge have a great deal to contribute to at-risk students because their logic provides a framework for critical thinking. As a discipline, economics stresses the need to make choices, a methodology for decision making, and the relationship between productivity and rewards in the economic marketplace. Through this program, at-risk students will acquire skills and knowledge that will help them see clearly the choices that face them, evaluate alternatives, and pursue opportunities that will provide them the greatest benefits in the long run.

As a result of participating in Choices and Changes, at-risk students come to understand that the opening of a business in their community means future opportunities for themselves and their families. They know why entrepreneurs start businesses, and they understand what inhibits business. For instance, they understand what vandalism and shoplifting will cost, not just to the owner of that business, but to the community and those who work or shop at the firm as well.

Built into Choices and Changes is the opportunity for teachers to communicate the positive achievements of students to themselves and to their parents. By emphasizing how the decisions students make about school relate to future career possibilities, students learn how preparation in school is linked to the world of work. Teaching goal setting, study skills, and planning techniques shows students that they have some control over their destinies. The program's activities are also designed to let students at each grade level see themselves as participants in the economy right now—that is, as consumers whose choices have outcomes that are significant to themselves.

Because the project changes the way at-risk children and their parents or guardians look at their community, these families come to see the community as a place that has opportunities. Through Choices and Changes, students come to see the businesses as making a difference—as adding to the community. They no longer feel that it is "us" and "them" when they go to the store.

Economics/Entrepreneurship/Education (E^3) is a high school–level program directed at economically disadvantaged students. Its goal is to help at-risk students become part of the local economy and perhaps help begin new businesses that will create jobs in their community. Many economically disadvantaged students do not feel they have a viable role in the economic system. All too often economically disadvantaged students assume they are powerless. They face continual failure and harbor a sense of frustration and humiliation. Paramount to the success of E^3 is the assumption that, by enhancing students' human dignity and self-respect and by generating knowledge and positive attitudes about the risks and rewards of owning a business, students will be motivated to succeed as entrepreneurs. Graduates of the program will be eligible for scholarships in order to pursue their studies further.

The most innovative facet of E^3 is the role of the individual local entrepreneur. As part of the program, students serve an internship during the summer of their junior year of high school. The entrepreneur mentor is carefully selected. Mostly minorities themselves, the mentors' job is to demonstrate how the attributes of the hidden curriculum combine with traditional learning and economic understanding to make a business work. The student's summer experience is bolstered by in-class programs, including a full-semester entrepreneurship/economics/education introductory course in the eleventh grade and a capstone economics course stressing entrepreneurship in the twelfth grade.

Through E^3, students are exposed to success in their own communities by people who, in most instances, share the same backgrounds, desires, and aspirations. Further, unlike other entrepreneurship training programs, E^3 emphasizes the academic side of economic understanding and then combines it with a real-life experience. Students are taught not just to mouth economic and business terms, but to use newly created thinking and decision-making skills in the economic world.

There is hardly any question that businesses must become more involved with the schools and the problems of at-risk students. Furthermore, the nation faces no more pressing question than that of preparing the next generation of wealth-creating entrepreneurs and those who will work for them.

In "Choices and Changes" and E^3, businesses—both large and small—have an integral role to play. Involvement is the key to solving the problem of at-risk students. In fact, business must help in the process. Efforts cannot be limited to casual partnerships which William Woodside, former chairman of Primerica, points out are often no more than well-meaning public relations efforts (Woodside, 1988). Rather, concerted efforts must be directed at solving the long-run issues. Business must help because it is in its own interest to secure enough new employees to cope with increasingly sophisticated production-line technology and increasingly more complex white-collar jobs. Business must help if the country is to continue its tradition of creating new jobs through entrepreneurship. There are already too many young people unable to meet the requirements of the jobs that employers offer today. Should this situation persist year after year, the accumulated number of positions business is likely to find itself unable to fill may become devastatingly large. Thus, a failure to stop and reverse the number of at-risk children in our schools can have far-reaching consequences—some of them foreseeable, and others we may perhaps be unable to predict or imagine.

Business can join hands with parents, educators, all levels of government, and other citizens and groups to see that the dire outcomes that may lie ahead are identified and then stopped. Pilot programs such as "Choices and Changes" and E^3 must be emulated all around the country. Businesses' participation will be vital; not just that of big business, but of small business as well, for small enterprises will be doing most of the hiring in the next decade. Investments in people—investments in tomorrow's entrepreneurs and those who will work for them—will enable American business to compete effectively in an increasingly complex global economy and could well prove to be the best investment business can make.

REFERENCES

"A Drop in Dropouts." 1988. *U.S. News and World Report,* May 23, p. 13.

Committee for Economic Development, 1988. *Children In Need: Investment Strategies for the Educationally Disadvantaged.* New York: Committee for Economic Development, May.

————. 1985. *Investing in Our Children: Business and the Public Schools.* New York: Committee for Economic Development, pp. 5, 6–7.

Duncan, Greg J., and William L. Rodgers. 1985. "The Prevalence of Childhood Poverty Survey" Research Center, University of Michigan. Cited in Committee for Economic Development, 1988, pp. 3, 9.

Hargroves, Jeanette S. 1986. "The Boston Compact: A Community Response to School Dropouts." *The Urban Review,* 18, no. 3: 207–217.

Magnet, Myron. 1988. "How To Smarten Up the Schools." *Fortune,* February, p. 89.

National Commission on Jobs and Small Business. 1987. *Making America Work Again.* Washington, D.C.: Government Printing Office, pp. 7, 16, 18.

"Retooling the Work Force" [The National Alliance of Business.] 1987. *The New York Times,* September 20, pp. 73, 79.

Rothman, Robert. 1988. "Business Refuses to Sign Boston Compact II." *Education Week* (November 9): 5.

Telsch, Kathleen. 1988. "Business Sees Aid to Schools as a Net Gain." *The New York Times,* December 4, p. 50.

Woodside, William. 1988. "The Committee for Economic Development and Education, National Impact and Next Steps," Transcription from the Committee for Economic Development, Annual Board meeting. New York, May 19.

18

Entrepreneurship/Economics/ Education in the Urban Environment: The E^3 Project

Calvin A. Kent

This chapter deals with the implementation of entrepreneurship education in the urban schools. Over the past twenty-five years, much has been published concerning the failures of the American high school in general and the urban school in particular. The best known of the early studies was James B. Conant's *The American High School Today* (1959). This was quickly followed by a report from the Rockefeller Foundation (Gardner, 1961). During the 1970s, several more reports were published (National Panel on High School and Adolescent Education, 1976; California Commission on Reform of Intermediate and Secondary Education, 1975; and Passow, 1976). The early 1980s saw even further studies, the most widely publicized of which was the report of the National Commission on Excellence in Education entitled *A Nation at Risk* (1983). Other works included those by Adler (1982), Goodlad (1983), Boyer (1983), and Sizer (1984). Added to these were reports from education panels (New York State Education Department, 1983; Twentieth Century Fund Task Force, 1983; College Board Education Equality Project, 1983; Education Commission of the States, 1983; and National Science Board, 1983).

These reports have been extensively reviewed in the literature by Howe (1983), Grey (1982), Finn (1983), and Passow (1984). While differing in scope, methodology, and conclusions, these reports and their reviewers all reached a central conclusion: American education is no longer delivering the quality product that the nation needs. As a result, the country is vulnerable to its industrial, commercial, and military competitors. While not all the reports separate out the urban school, the review of the literature makes it clear that Passow's conclusion is correct: "If there is a real crisis in education, it is in the urban schools" (Passow, 1984, p. 680).

There is no use in regaling the reader with a recitation of the problems of the nation's core cities. Suffice it to say, our urban areas are decaying and there is no evidence to indicate that they are getting anything other than worse. There is abundant evidence attesting to the crime-drug nexus that characterizes the urban school setting. As E. I. Boyer stated, "Troubled high schools are typically in inner cities where problems of population, dislocation, poverty, unemployment and crime take priority over education" (Boyer, 1983, p. 16).

The lack of job opportunities in the central city core results in low incomes, which in turn produces a culture of poverty that now perpetuates itself from generation to generation (Murray, 1984). The result is the presence of despair for most urban residents, including school children. This is compounded by the climate of dependency created by government programs designed to alleviate the most cruel manifestations of poverty. The residents of the core city have become virtually dependent for their very existence on government handouts in various forms.

In the last couple of years an idea that is fundamentally wrong has begun to develop. Unfortunately, it may well be on its way to becoming the foundation for a national policy. The idea is simply that the economic problems of the core city, including school dropouts, drugs, crime, and teenage pregnancy could be solved if every ghetto youth could somehow or another be converted into an entrepreneur. Not only would they become independent, self-reliant, and capable of supporting themselves, they would also generate jobs for others, and, as a by-product, become enthusiastic advocates of the free enterprise system. As a result of this idea, a variety of programs from both the federal government and from private groups directed toward developing entrepreneurship in the central city among the hard-core unemployed have become fashionable. These programs are well intended but misguided.

THE ENVIRONMENT FOR ENTREPRENEURSHIP EDUCATION IN THE URBAN SCHOOL

In order to evaluate entrepreneurship/economics/education in the urban areas, we must first understand the environment in which formal education takes place. That environment consists of three elements: the students, the schools, and the teachers. Each one of these is worthy of being examined separately.

Students

The overwhelming majority of students in the urban schools demonstrate the following four characteristics:

1. *First, they are poor academic achievers.* Their scores on standardized math and reading examinations place them among the lowest quartile, usually among the lowest decile, and often within the lowest 2 percent of the nation. In one urban school with which the author worked, the highest SAT score (achieved by the class valedictorian) was 720, which included a 240 on the mathematical portion. In this same school, less than 20 percent of the high school seniors who were preparing to graduate were able to correctly determine the answer to the question, "What is 20 percent of a dollar?" Boyer found that most students in central cities are at least two or more years below grade level in reading and math (Boyer, 1983, p. 17). A. H. Passow found that the levels of literacy and numeracy among students in urban schools tend to fall below those in the nation's schools in general (Passow, 1984, p. 680) and *A Nation at Risk* found that 13 percent "of all 17 year olds in the U.S. are functionally illiterate with the percentage among the minority youth running as high as 40 percent" (National Commission On Excellence in Education, 1983, p. 8). These students simply lack the basic skills either for entrepreneurship or for success in the real world.

2. *The second characteristics of students is that they come from nontraditional families.* The data indicates that in core city families, as likely as not, at least one parent (usually the father) is absent. Many urban students may not even know who their father is. A disproportionately large number of these students are illegitimate, with the psychological baggage that this implies. Finally, the urban schools are characterized by the problem of "babies having babies" (Brown, 1984, p. 132). Teenage pregnancy is rampant, which not only removes the female students from the classroom, but saddles her with the responsibilities associated with child care. The author was told that twenty percent of the females in an urban high school will drop out to have a baby.

The result of these two characteristics is not only a high dropout rate when students turn the legal age to remove themselves from the classroom setting, but also high absenteeism. For example, in one core city high school, the author was informed that the typical student misses fifty-five to sixty days of classroom instruction each year. Even this figure is below the national average of 50 percent for inner city schools (Brown, 1984, p. 6). This level of absenteeism severely limits the ability of any educational program that relies on continuity of instruction to have any impact.

3. *A third characteristic of urban students is that they have had little*

experience with the market economy. A study conducted by Soper and Walstad for the Joint Council on Economic Education has adequately demonstrated that most high school students are woefully ignorant of the American economy and its operation or benefits (Walstad and Soper, 1989).

This is probably more true for the urban students who have most likely spent their lives in government housing, been fed with government food stamps, received medical attention financed by Medicaid, and have been in a family where the principal source of income was the Aid for Dependent Children (AFDC) payment. What has developed is a "rights revolution" in which many of these students reflect the attitudes of their elders—that they have a right to such programs because of their ethnic or social characteristics (Passow, 1984, p. 681). The relationship between effort and reward is not an idea with which these students have familiarity. For many students, their experience with the market may be socially undesirable. The dropout pushing drugs will earn many times more than the student at the entry level in a legitimate job (Mayer, 1989). The result is a cynicism and breakdown of moral values.

4. *The fourth characteristic of the students is that they lack entrepreneurial role models.* The research demonstrates the most effective way to teach entrepreneurship is by "elbow rubbing" (Kent, 1989). The closer an association students have with practicing entrepreneurs, the more likely it is that students will not only appreciate the economic system, but will become entrepreneurs themselves. For the students who live in the ghetto, the only entrepreneurial role models they have are pimps, prostitutes, and pushers.

Schools

If this were not discouraging enough, the schools these students attend do not provide the appropriate environment for entrepreneurship/economics education, or any other education, for that matter. There are three things that characterize the urban schools and that limit their effectiveness.

1. *The first thing these schools lack is resources.* Even though the urban schools tend to spend more per pupil than do schools in suburban and rural areas, there is a pitiful lack of even the basic necessities for effective teaching (Herschinger, 1979, p. 22). Money simply is not available to provide necessary materials, release time for teachers, or alternate experiences for the students that would enrich their lives and enhance their understanding of the world in which they function.

2. *A second characteristic of the schools is that they are bureaucratic.* The euphemism used to describe the administrative structure of the schools is *multitiered decision making.* This simply means that the many layers of bureaucracy stifle any new ideas or innovative programs by subjecting

them to a long harassment of review and delay (Seely, 1985, pp. 21–26). The bureaucratic structure also produces a lack of decision making. No one wants to be responsible for making a decision because of the fear of failure. It is easier to pass on an idea to another higher level of review than it is to implement it.

The result of this bureaucratic structure is a school system that resists change and innovation. Nonetheless, change and innovation are the essence of entrepreneurship. If the schools themselves are neither innovating nor providing the necessary incentives and freedom, then it is unlikely that their programs will be entrepreneurial and innovative. Maintaining a bureaucratic hierarchy diverts scarce resources from the classroom.

3. *The third characteristic of the schools is that they tend to be custodial rather than educational* (National Committee on Excellence in Education, 1983, p. 29). One school principal remarked to this author that he considered his day a success if no teacher or student had been wounded while the school was open. Protecting students and teachers from physical assault and from the entreaties of drug pushers has become a principal objective of the urban school. In one sense this is good. Without their personal safety secured, teachers are unlikely to teach effectively and students certainly will not learn. Boyer's research showed that as many as 35 percent of the nation's teachers felt unsafe at school (Boyer, 1983, p. 21). However, in the urban school today, with rare exceptions, education may proceed very little beyond incarcerating the students for the necessary hours. It is no small wonder that the students use any possible excuse to not attend and drop out altogether as quickly as possible.

Teachers

The third part of the urban environment in which entrepreneurship education takes place is the teacher.

1. *There is strong tendency among teachers in urban schools to be inflexible.* This may be because many of the urban school districts are unionized, and the union rules carefully and explicitly define every detail of the environment (Brown, 1984, p. 41). These rules themselves, because they have been carefully and painfully negotiated, are not likely to be changed even if they should stand in the way of the introduction of new ideas. The inflexibility may also come from the need to keep control over an increasingly chaotic school environment. Whether the desired end of a controlled learning environment is served by inflexible rules is debatable.

2. *Urban teachers also face heavy teaching loads.* It is not uncommon to find teachers saddled with teaching three or four separate courses in areas as diverse as social studies and business. This limits the amount of preparation time that the teachers have. Their teaching loads coupled with generally large classes not only reduce the amount of time that teachers

and students can interact with each other, but also limit the amount of homework that the teacher will assign.

Those engaged in entrepreneurship education are well aware that entrepreneurship can best be taught by creative entrepreneurship teachers. The hallmark of entrepreneurs is their flexibility and ability to adapt to change. Such is not the characteristic of the typical urban teacher. However, this may not be the fault of the teacher. T. R. Sizer feels that teachers become frustrated and demoralized because of the environment in which they work (Sizer, 1984, p. 678).

3. *The third characteristic of teachers in the urban area is that they are poorly trained in either economics or entrepreneurship.* Teachers neither understand nor appreciate the private enterprise system or the key role that the entrepreneur as change maker plays within it. But equally important, teachers lack the technical understanding to teach the foundations of the market system or the skills of business planning and entrepreneurial management (Walstad and Soper, 1989). There is an old saying in education: "You cannot teach what you do not understand." For that reason, entrepreneurship and economics are poorly and rarely taught in the urban classroom.

4. *The fourth characteristic of the teachers is that they tend to have negative attitudes toward and low expectations of their students.* One of the old saws that almost always comes true is "You get what you expect." The attitude of many urban teachers toward their students is that the students cannot achieve and it is unrealistic to expect them to do so (Brown, 1984, p. 11). Teachers do not assign homework because they feel students will not do it, and do not expect them to read much because their reading level is below grade. Entrepreneurship/economics/education should stretch students, yet this does not seem to be encouraged in the urban classroom.

THE ENTREPRENEURSHIP/ECONOMICS/EDUCATION (E^3) PROGRAM

Faced with this urban environment, the Entrepreneurship/Economics/Education (E^3) program has attempted to devise a way of reaching the inner city student. The E^3 program is completing the second year of a three-year developmental process in the Philadelphia school district. If successful, it will be made available for distribution nationwide. Its success will depend on how well it can be fitted into the urban school environment.

Objectives

The objectives of the E^3 program are simple:

First, it is designed to help the students to develop a more positive attitude toward themselves, which will enable them to be more willing to venture forth, to take risks, and to learn how to see opportunity and seize it.

Second, E³ seeks for the students to acquire a more disciplined life style, which is a key element in success, not only in entrepreneurship, but in all aspects of life.

Third, it is anticipated that the students will acquire certain insights about the American economy and how it operates by generating opportunities for those who see them and seize them.

Fourth, the students should learn something about the process of entrepreneurship and the specific skills that entrepreneurs need.

Materials Development

E³ consists of three components. The first of these is Materials Development.

1. First, in order to make students aware of the importance of entrepreneurs, infusion units have been developed for the world history and American history courses. These infusion units are designed to be integrated into the curriculum already being taught in the Philadelphia schools. It is hoped that by seeing the historical contributions of entrepreneurship that students will begin to appreciate the fact that history is more than politicians and generals—that entrepreneurs have propelled humankind to ever greater heights.

2. Second, an eleventh grade introductory course in the area of entrepreneurship/economics/education is under development. While this course includes materials designed to familiarize the students with the basic economics of the market system and some of the survival skills that are needed by entrepreneurs, a principal emphasis of this course is to change the students' attitudes and conceptions about themselves and their abilities to control their own lives. Units are included on subjects such as inner control, decision making, goal setting, self-evaluation, and confidence building. In addition, the students learn how to look for opportunity.

3. Third, materials are also being developed for the twelfth grade final course. This course is taken by the students who have completed the eleventh grade introductory course and the mentorship program described below. The twelfth grade capstone course further develops the students' insights about themselves and their own capabilities. Much of the material is student-directed in which the students experience and innovate on their own. Also included are several economics units, principally in the area of macroeconomics. These are designed to convey to students what entrepreneurs need to know about topics such as the business cycle, inflation, unemployment, interest rates, and international markets. Macroeconomic material which is not directly related to the process of entrepreneurship is not included.

During the final portion of the course, students develop their own venture plans either for a new business or for a social project. These are reviewed by other class members and a team of outsiders (probably mentors) who evaluate the proposals. The last activity is for the class as a whole to develop and implement a plan to deal with a problem or issue facing their school. This activity will allow the students to know that they can make a difference.

The philosophy of all these materials is simply that they are experimental, innovative, and entrepreneurial. They are not mastered by students reading, listening to a lecture, and regurgitating. Instead, these materials are student-based, and require students to do nontraditional things in classrooms that, hopefully, will also be nontraditional.

Mentorships

The second component of the E^3 project is the mentorship program. The mentorships have been developed at Johns Hopkins University and are described in a previous chapter. As has been stated before, the key to successful entrepreneurship education is elbow rubbing. The idea behind the mentorships is to have the students develop a close working relationship with at least two mentors over the summer. This is not to be merely a work-study program, but rather a process whereby the students actually stay with the entrepreneurs, watching how they perform and make decisions while experiencing both their joys and defeats.

A manual has been developed to assist in the selection of students and the training of mentors. The students have a mentorship notebook that they keep during their summer employment. The student notebook focuses the student on the lessons learned in the first course by requiring them to identify entrepreneurial behavior and economic principles when they are observed. The material in the notebook is used throughout the second course to illustrate the lesson contained therein. Good mentorships do not just happen; they require preparation of the students and the mentors. The result of this program is two six-weeks summer internships in which the students are paid to experience entrepreneurship firsthand.

Teacher Training

The third and final component is teacher training. Previous chapters have pointed to the lack of teacher training and the essentiality of well-trained teachers. Teacher training should involve the use of the materials developed for the Entrepreneurship/Economics/Education sequence. The more specific the training, the more familiar the teachers will be with the E^3 content and the more likely they are to effectively implement in the classroom. Teacher training is done by graduate-level course work during both the school year and in the summer. In-service programs are also offered as supplemental training activities.

CONCLUSION

What then would be realistic expectations for entrepreneurship education in urban areas? There are five limited but important goals that can be achieved.

1. The students should be allowed to realize that lifestyles other than the one they are currently experiencing are possible. They should be able to see that they can take control of their own lives, that they are not powerless, and that they can bring about change. There are opportunities out there for them to seize.

2. The second goal is to develop the attitudes of inner control, self-confidence, goal setting, and decision making among the students. These attributes are not uniquely needed by entrepreneurs, but are required by all successful people. Urban students generally are not fortunate enough to possess them. Conveying these insights to them may be the most important content for an entrepreneurship/economics/education program.

3. A third goal is to inspire them to take school more seriously. No one should claim that entrepreneurship education will eliminate school dropouts or absenteeism. Nonetheless, by involving students in innovative, creative, and, hopefully, exciting activities, it makes it more likely that students will remain in school and pay attention. Developing this fundamental discipline, which can carry over to any jobs students hold in later life, is the third principal objective.

4. The fourth expectation is to provide urban students with enough understanding of the basic skills necessary to be a successful entrepreneur so that they will know what to do when the urge to entrepreneur comes upon them. The traditional entrepreneurship curriculums too heavily emphasize the technical skills such as marketing, location, product selection, accounting, inventory control, and the like. These should be only a fraction of an entrepreneurship education program. If the students do not possess the insights about themselves and an understanding of the economy, teaching these managerial talents to them may be a waste of effort. However, students do need to know what they do not know and what they will need to know should they ever strike out on their own to be an entrepreneur. More important, they need to know where they can go for help. There are a wealth of training programs available to them. Entrepreneurship education should not seek to duplicate these, but rather make the students aware of their availability and the need to participate.

5. The final goal is that students acquire a working knowledge of economic principles. The economic environment for the urban student requires them to function as producers, consumers, and citizens. They must

make economic decisions almost constantly. The greater their insight into the operation of the economic system, the more rational those decisions are likely to be.

If an entrepreneurship education program can achieve these objectives, then it will be a success, and in a small way it may be one factor that will bring some hope to those students who now live and labor in the urban environment.

REFERENCES

Adler, M. J. 1982. *The Paideia Proposal: An Educational Manifesto.* New York: Macmillan.

Boyer, E. I. 1983. *The High School.* New York: Harper and Row.

Brown, B. Frank. 1973. *The Reform of Secondary Education.* New York: McGraw-Hill.

————. 1984. *Crisis in Secondary Education.* Englewood Cliffs, N.J.: Prentice-Hall.

California Commission on Reform of Intermediate and Secondary Education. 1975. *The RISE Report.* Sacramento, Calif.: Superintendent of Schools.

College Board Education Equality Project. 1983. *Academic Preparation for College: What Students Need to Know and Be Able to Do.* New York: College Board.

Conant, J. B. 1959. *The American High School Today.* New York: McGraw-Hill.

Education Commission of the States, Task Force on Education for Economic Growth. 1983. *Action for Excellence.* Denver, Colo.: Denver Education Commission of the States.

Finn, C. E., Jr. 1983. "The Drive for Educational Excellence." *Change,* pp. 21–24.

Gardner, J. 1961. *The Pursuit of Excellence: Education and the Future of America, Prospects for America. The Rockefeller Panel Reports.* Garden City, N.Y.: Doubleday.

Goodlad, J. I. 1983. *A Place Called School: Prospects for the Future.* New York: McGraw-Hill.

Grey, D. 1982. "1980s: Season for High School Reform." *Educational Leadership,* 39, no. 8: 564–568.

Herschinger, F. M. 1979. "Schoolyard Blues: The Decline of Public Education." *Saturday Review,* January 20, pp. 20–22.

Howe, H., II. 1983. "Education Moves to Center Stage: An Overview of Recent Studies." *Pi Delta Kappan* (November): 168–170.

Kent, C. A. 1989. "Awareness: Cornerstone of Entrepreneurship Education." *Business Education Forum* 44, no. 7, pp. 35–37.

Martin, J. H. 1976. *The Education of Adolescents.* National Panel on High School and Adolescent Education. Washington, D.C.: Government Printing Office.

Mayer, J. 1989. "In the War on Drugs the Toughest Foe May Be the Alienated Youth." *The Wall Street Journal* 74, no. 48, September 8, p. 1.

Murray, C. 1984. *Losing Ground: American Social Policy 1950–1980.* New York: Basic Books.

National Commission on Excellence in Education. 1983. *A Nation at Risk.* Washington, D.C.: Government Printing Office.

National Panel on High School and Adolescent Education. 1976. *The Education of Adolescents.* Washington, D.C.: Government Printing Office.

National Science Board Commission on Pre-College Education of Mathematics, Science and Technology. 1983. *Educating Americans for the 21st Century.* Washington, D.C.: Government Printing Office.

New York State Education Department. 1983. *Proposed Action Plan to Improve Elementary and Secondary Education Results in New York.* Albany, N.Y.: State Education Department.

Passow, A. H. 1976. *Secondary Education Reform: Retrospect and Prospect.* New York: Columbia University, New York Teachers' College.

———. 1984. "Tracking the Reform Reports of the 1980s." *Pi Delta Kappan* (June): 674–683.

Seeley, David S. 1984. *Education Through Partnership.* Washington, D.C.: American Enterprise Institute.

Sizer, T. R. 1984. *Horace's Compromise: The Dilemma of the American High School.* Boston: Houghton-Mifflin.

Twentieth Century Fund Task Force on Federal Elementary and Secondary Education Policy. 1983. *Making the Grade.* New York: The Twentieth Century Fund.

Walstad, W. B. and J. C. Soper. 1989. "What is High School Economics? Factors Contributing to Student Achievement and Attitudes." *Journal of Economic Education* 20, no. 1, 23–28.

———. 1988. "What is High School Economics? Post-Test Knowledge, Attitudes, and Course Content." *Journal of Economic Education* 19 (Winter): 37–51.

Conclusion

Perusing the chapters in this volume will lead the reader to reach some definite conclusions, all of which are fully supported by the research and experiences documented therein.

1. *We do not fully understand the process of entrepreneurship.* Entrepreneurship is a creative event that can take place in a variety of settings. It is the capacity to see what others have overlooked and to act on the insight. It requires incredible knowledge which is focused on exploiting a particular niche that had previously gone unnoticed.

2. *Entrepreneurship is more than just starting a small business.* Despite the traditional focus on small business start-up, entrepreneurship is vastly more than that. While often the entrepreneurial urge results in the formation of a new business venture, to limit entrepreneurship in that way misses its true character. Entrepreneurship can take place within corporations, nonprofit organizations, and even government bureaucracies. The essence of entrepreneurship is bringing about change that is beneficial in its result. Those who bring about these changes are the entrepreneurs.

3. *Entrepreneurship involves innovation. Innovation is more than just having a good idea.* It means perfecting and developing the idea and then implementing it in an organization or bringing it to the market. Innovation is then the final step in the creative process, which sees the idea from its inception through its incubation into its adoption.

4. *There is tremendous entrepreneurial talent available.* Although only

a relatively small number of people become entrepreneurs, there is a significantly larger number who could be the creative change makers the nation needs. It is at least in part the responsibility of the education system to cultivate and develop the entrepreneurial potential that exists.

5. *Entrepreneurship education is in a period of rapid development.* Entrepreneurship education at the college level has evolved from courses in small business management to full-scale curriculums at many schools. While these programs are struggling to shed their traditional orientations, progress has been made in creating courses that are more relevant and designed to appeal to students who may not be in traditional business school programs. At the precollegiate level, entrepreneurship education began in the vocational schools and is now beginning to take hold throughout the school curriculum. Much more needs to be done to recognize that entrepreneurship can and should be an integral part of courses in government, business, sociology, and history. At the elementary level, entrepreneurship education can be a way of freeing the creative instincts of young students.

6. *Entrepreneurship education must be entrepreneurial.* These pages shout that message. The traditional structure of elementary, secondary, and postsecondary courses simply will not suffice. Entrepreneurs, both potential and practicing, are different from other people. Courses designed to nurture and inspire them will be radically different from those now offered in most educational settings. These courses will recognize entrepreneurs' need for achievement, desire for autonomy, craving for independence, and latent hostility about structure.

7. *Entrepreneurship educators must be entrepreneurial themselves.* The key in the process of entrepreneurship education is the teacher. It goes without saying that the teacher must be well-informed and highly motivated. More important, however, the teacher must be flexible. He or she must be willing to try new methods and institute less structure in course content and delivery. This means that entrepreneurship educators must be entrepreneurs themselves. Particularly at the collegiate level, this will require that they have had some first-hand knowledge and experience with entrepreneuring.

8. *Entrepreneurship education must be more than teaching technical and managerial skills.* While the traditional focus in entrepreneurship courses in both the secondary and collegiate levels has been on communicating certain management skills to students, this approach is too limited. Although there is a place for skills training, the first part of an entrepreneurship curriculum must be awareness; students must become aware of the contributions of entrepreneurs and the fact that they themselves can be entrepreneurs. Without this original awareness as part of an entrepreneurship curriculum, the supply of entrepreneurs produced by the education system will remain meager.

9. *Entrepreneurship education deals with attitudes and values.* There are certain personal attributes and attitudes that entrepreneurs have. They possess a great deal of inner control; they are highly disciplined, self-motivated, and willing to tolerate risks and uncertainty. Entrepreneurship educators reject the idea that people are born with these characteristics. Rather, an education system that is entrepreneurial can and should develop these traits within students. This is particularly true of inner city students who, because of the environment in which they live, will probably lack these characteristics.

10. *Entrepreneurship must be relevant.* It is a waste of time to teach about entrepreneurship. Entrepreneurship needs to be portrayed as a real event in which others have succeeded and in which the student can also participate and succeed. This means that entrepreneurship education involves elbow rubbing, close contact with entrepreneurs who possess the same characteristics and come from the same backgrounds as do the students. While the entrepreneurship curriculum must be more than just having practicing entrepreneurs tell their war stories, creating a relationship between a practicing and a potential entrepreneur should be at the core of any entrepreneurship education program. This means that experience-based programs in entrepreneurship education are the most desirable.

11. *Entrepreneurship education must be multi-disciplinary.* It is unfortunate but true that at the collegiate level entrepreneurship education is becoming increasingly more a subdiscipline within management. This bias is reflected in many secondary programs as well. These programs are usually too narrow in their scope, omitting the important insights that can be supplied by economics, history, psychology, and sociology. Entrepreneurs themselves are able to integrate a vast amount of data and ideas. For that reason, they are successful. Courses designed for them should reflect that same sort of integration.

12. *Entrepreneurship and economics education should be fully integrated.* Economists have had great difficulty in integrating the entrepreneur into economic theory. The activities of the entrepreneur do not fit the static mathematical models of economists. This means that economists must rethink those models and their appropriateness. The entrepreneur is the dynamic force in any economic system. As a result, any explanation of economic phenomena that omits the entrepreneur must be dismissed as inadequate.

13. *More research is needed.* Hardly a surprising conclusion but still correct. Much of what is "known" about entrepreneurship education is not firmly based on research. Particular emphasis should be placed on relating the theory of learning to entrepreneurship instruction. Much valuable information discovered by other disciplines, particulary the social sciences, needs to be transferred and applied.

There is a greater supply of potential entrepreneurs in society than what is now being produced by the education system. Whether this nation or any other will be able to solve its economic and social problems will depend on the availability of a continued and increasing stream of creative talent. Entrepreneurship education can be a major contributor to creating new education structures that are themselves entrepreneurial. If this happens, then the future of the nation will be insured.

Index

About the Contributors

CRAIG E. ARONOFF is founder and Director of the Family Business Forum and holder of the Chair of Private Enterprise at Kennesaw State College, Marietta, Georgia.

M. CATHERINE ASHMORE is Entrepreneurship Program Director at the Center on Education and Training for Employment at The Ohio State University, Columbus, Ohio.

RONALD A. BANASZAK is Vice President for Educational Programs at the Foundation for Teaching Economics in San Francisco, California.

JUDITH STALEY BRENNEKE is a managing partner of Rational Education Associates in Cleveland Heights, Ohio, and was formerly Co-Director of the Cleveland Center for Economic Education at John Carroll University in Cleveland.

MARY B. CAWLEY is an editor for Enterprise Communications in Marietta, Georgia.

JOHN E. CLOW is a professor in the department of business economics, State University of New York at Oneonta.

GERALD GUNDERSON is the Shelby Cullom Davis Professor of American Business and Economic Enterprise at Trinity College in Hartford, Connecticut.

CALVIN A. KENT is Herman W. Lay Professor of Private Enterprise and Director of the Center for Private Enterprise and the National Center for Entrepreneurship in Economics Education at Baylor University in Waco, Texas.

W. F. KIESNER is a professor of entrepreneurship at Loyola Marymount University in Los Angeles, California.

MARILYN KOURILSKY is Dean, Teacher Education, and a professor of education, at the University of California in Los Angeles, California.

MICHAEL A. MACDOWELL is Vice President of External Affairs at Hartwick College, Oneonta, New York, and formerly was President of the Joint Council on Economic Education.

MARGARET M. MURPHY is Director of the Center for Economic Education at Johns Hopkins University in Columbia, Maryland.

GARY RABBIOR is Executive Director of the Canadian Foundation for Economic Education in Toronto, Ontario.

ROBERT RONSTADT is Chief Executive Officer of Lord Publishing, Inc., in Natick, Massachusetts, and was formerly Academic Head of Entrepreneurial Studies at the Center for Entrepreneurship at Babson College in Wellesley, Massachusetts.

FRANCIS W. RUSHING is Associate Dean and Director of the International Center for Entrepreneurship, as well as a professor of economics at Georgia State University in Atlanta, Georgia.